Interdependencies Between Fertility and Women's Labour Supply

European Studies of Population

Volume 17

The book series *European Studies of Population (ESPO)* aims at disseminating population and family research, with special relevance for Europe. It may analyse past, present and/or future trends, as well as their determinants and consequences. The character of the series is multidisciplinary, including formal demographic analyses, as well as social, economic and/or historical population and family studies. The following types of studies are of primary importance: (a) internationally relevant studies, (b) European comparative studies, (c) innovative theoretical and methodological studies, and (d) policy-relevant scientific studies. The series may include monographs, edited volumes and reference works. The book series is published under the auspices of the *European Association for Population Studies (EAPS).*

Editorial secretariat:
Helga de Valk
European Association for Population Studies
PO Box 11676
NL – 2502 AR The Hague, Netherlands
Phone.: +31 70 356 5200
Fax.: +31 70 364 7187
E-mail: valk@nidi.nl

Anna Matysiak

Interdependencies Between Fertility and Women's Labour Supply

Springer

Anna Matysiak
Warsaw School of Economics
Institute of Statistics and Demography
Ul Madalińskiego 6/8
02-513 Warsaw
Poland
amatys@sgh.waw.pl

ISSN 1381-3579
ISBN 978-94-007-1283-6 e-ISBN 978-94-007-1284-3
DOI 10.1007/978-94-007-1284-3
Springer Dordrecht Heidelberg London New York

Library of Congress Control Number: 2011926631

Printed on acid-free paper

Springer is part of Springer Science+Business Media (www.springer.com)

To my Paweł

Acknowledgements

This book is a modified version of my PhD thesis prepared under the supervision of Prof. Irena E. Kotowska and defended in Mai 2009 at the Warsaw School of Economics. I would like to express my gratitude to Prof. Irena E. Kotowska for her scientific advice and emotional support throughout the project. I appreciate highly her openness to discussions and as well as the freedom she offered to me for developing my own ideas. I am also grateful to the three reviewers of my thesis, Prof. Elżbieta Gołata, Dr. Gerda Neyer, and Prof. Urszula Sztanderska, for their comments and suggestions that allowed me to improve my work.

The study was largely conducted during my work contract at the Institute of Statistics and Demography (Warsaw School of Economics) and my scholarship at the Max Planck Institute for Demographic Research where I participated first in the European Doctoral School for Demography and later in the International Max Planck Research School of Demography. Both institutions offered me very stimulating environments for conducting this research and I would like to thank all my colleagues for their support, fruitful discussions, comments and suggestions I received at various stages of my work. I particularly acknowledge Dr. Monika Mynarska and Dr. Daniele Vignoli with whom I spent endless hours discussing demographic concepts and exchanging research ideas. I am also grateful to my mentor at the MPIDR, Dr. Gerda Neyer as well as Prof Gunnar Andersson who were always ready to discuss problems I encountered during my work me and provided me with valuable advice. Finally, I highly acknowledge the support I received from Anna Baranowska and Marta Styrc in the data collection I used in Chapter 6 of this book.

At the Max Planck Institute for Demographic Research, I took part in a variety of courses that broadened my knowledge in demography. I wish to thank all the teachers who invested their time in my education, including the Dean of the IMPRSD, Dr. Heiner Maier. My special thanks go to Professor Jan M. Hoem, Prof. Michaela Kreyenfeld, and Dr. Hill Kulu for providing me with a solid knowledge of event history analysis as well as to Dr. Bart de Bruijn who significantly widened my horizons during his fantastic courses on fertility theories.

During the time I was preparing the thesis I was financially supported by the Foundation for Polish Science, as a beneficiary of the Start Programme directed at young researchers (2007–2008), as well as by the Polish Ministry of Higher Education and Science, from which I received a research grant for the years 2008–2009.

Some pieces of this study constitute parts of the research reports and research articles I prepared in the meantime. Most importantly, Chapter 2 was prepared within the LoWER network. This gave me the opportunity to use the European Labour Force Survey, which was made accessible to LoWER members by Eurostat. Chapter 5 includes the meta-analysis, which in the initial version was conducted with Dr. Daniele Vignoli and was published as an article in the *European Journal of Population*. Chapter 6 in a modified version was submitted to *Population Studies*. I am grateful to the anonymous reviewers of the two journals for their useful comments and suggestions that helped me to improve my work. The editorial process of this book was overseen by Evelien Bakker and Bernadette Deelen-Mans at Springer who provided me with motivation to complete the manuscript. The English was edited by Dr. David Harrison to whom I am grateful for his precision and flexibility.

Finally, I would like to thank all friends without whose emotional support the completion of this study would not be possible. I am also deeply grateful to my parents for their love, patience, and understanding. Last but definitely not least, I thank my husband, Paweł Książyk. He is one of those persons who have always understood my choices, believed in my abilities and supported me in reaching my goals.

Contents

List of Figures

List of Tables

Chapter 1
Introduction

1.1 Background and Impetus for the Study

In the last decades of the twentieth century, Period Total Fertility Rates (TFRs) decreased in almost all industrialised countries, reaching values well below the replacement level. Particularly severe declines were observed in countries of Southern Europe and Central and Eastern Europe (CEE), i.e., that part of Europe[1] where the transition to low fertility occurred relatively late. Whereas by the end of the 1970s the average TFR in Continental and Northern Europe was around 1.66, in Southern and CEE state-socialist countries it was still at a level slightly above 2.1.[2] Less than a decade later, the average TFR in Mediterranean countries was already below 1.4, a level the majority of the Northern and Continental European countries had never reached. At that time, fertility in CEE was still relatively high, with the TFR exceeding 1.8 in all of them apart from Slovenia and East Germany. This was, however, one of the very last times in which fertility in this region was the highest in Europe. Just after the economic transformation had begun, the post-socialist countries experienced an abrupt fall in childbearing, with the TFR reaching the lowest-low level of below 1.35 around the turn of the century. Since the early 2000s nearly all European Union (EU) countries have been experiencing improvements in fertility. Despite this fact, in the post-socialist countries (except for Estonia) as

[1]The term 'Europe' is used wherever we refer to the European Union (EU or EU-27) plus Norway and Switzerland. Europe is divided into two main regions: (1) 'Central and Eastern European' (CEE), encompassing the new EU-12 member states (NMS-12), except for Cyprus and Malta; the terms 'post-socialist countries' or 'former socialist countries' also refer to this region; (2) 'Western Europe', covering all EU-15 member states plus Norway and Switzerland.

Additionally, within the Western European countries we distinguish three groups: (1) 'Southern' or 'Mediterranean' countries (Greece, Italy, Portugal, and Spain); (2) 'Northern countries' (the Nordic states of Denmark, Finland, Norway, and Sweden, plus Ireland, and the United Kingdom), and (3) 'Continental Europe' (Austria, Belgium, France, Germany, Luxembourg, the Netherlands, and Switzerland, and not, as in common usage, all the countries on the geographical continent of Europe) . See also Section 1.6.

[2]The average Total Fertility Rate was calculated by Sobotka (2004: 1–2) by weighting the country-specific Total Fertility Rate by the country's population size.

A. Matysiak, *Interdependencies Between Fertility and Women's Labour Supply*, European Studies of Population 17, DOI 10.1007/978-94-007-1284-3_1,

well as in Southern European countries, Austria, Germany, and Switzerland fertility remains exceptionally low (with TFR most often below 1.5). By contrast, in the majority of other EU countries TFR exceeded the value of 1.75 and in some it even reached the level of around 2.0 (Norway, France and Ireland).

Certainly, low fertility in the Southern European and CEE countries is partly an effect of a massive postponement of childbearing that at least in post-socialist countries has not come to an end yet. The recent slight improvement in fertility observed in all low-fertility countries is likely to result from recuperation in childbearing at higher ages. Nevertheless, even after eliminating the tempo effects, a fall in fertility quantum was estimated to be substantial as well (Sobotka, 2004: 196–201; Sobotka et al. 2005). It is thus very likely that under current cultural, institutional, and economic conditions, cohort fertility will decline below the replacement levels, as has been observed in those European countries where the transition to the below-replacement fertility began first. Together with the decline in mortality, these developments led to a profound change in the age structure of the EU population. This effect will be additionally intensified by the ageing of the post-war baby boomers. According to the baseline scenario of the latest Eurostat demographic projection (EUROPOP2008), by 2061 there will be only 187 working-age persons (aged 15–64) per 100 citizens aged 65+ in the whole EU, whereas in 2008 this ratio was 393:100. Furthermore, an important feature of the described demographic change is not only an increase in the percentage of persons aged 65+ and a decline in the proportion aged 15–64, but also an increment in the share of the oldest-old (aged 80+), which is supposed to triple.

The changing age structure of the population poses a serious threat to the economic potential of Europe. On the one hand, an increase in the elderly population will boost the demand for financial support as well as for health care and long-term care provision. On the other hand, along with the declining working-age population, the potential supply of those who provide resources for the elderly will shrink. Thus, the demographic change Europe is undergoing constitutes a major challenge for economic growth, the sustainability of the social security systems, social cohesion, and intergenerational relations. There is no doubt that special strategies need to be developed and implemented if the EU is to remain a competitive and growing economy with relatively low social disparities at the same time. This challenge was recognised by the European Commission (e.g., European Commission, 2005, 2006, 2007). In its Communication 'The demographic future of Europe – from challenge to opportunity' (2006a) EC outlined five major policy directions. These were: (1) demographic renewal, (2) higher employment and longer working lives, (3) higher productivity, (4) receiving and integrating immigrants, and (5) increasing sustainability of public finance. Undoubtedly, all five policy directions are of great importance and should receive sufficient attention among researchers and policy makers. The motivation to conduct this study was driven by the first two.

The underlying idea of demographic renewal is that an increase in fertility is possible only if obstacles to childbearing are eliminated. This belief stems from the fact that demographic surveys consistently show discrepancies between actual and desired number of children (e.g., Goldstein et al. 2003; Fokkema & Esveldt,

2006: 39; Testa 2006a, 2006b; Van Peer & Rabušic 2008). This discrepancy opens an opportunity window for policies to create more appropriate conditions for parenthood. This is not an easy task, however. Various empirical studies show that policy impacts are highly dependent on the context, bringing satisfying effects in some countries, social groups, or periods and no effects or some unexpected effects in the other (Neyer, 2006; Neyer & Andersson 2008). Although in general the average effect seems to be positive, it is weak, tending to facilitate timing of births rather than the completed family size, whereas the policies are rather expensive (Gauthier, 2007). Nevertheless, even if Europe succeeds in reaching higher fertility, which is highly desirable from the long-term perspective, it is evident that this is not sufficient to counteract the negative consequences of the changing age structure of the population in the short term. The underlying reason is that higher fertility will affect the balance between the active and inactive population – at least after two decades. This is already quite late, taking into account that the cohorts born during the post-war baby boom are already entering the post-productive age.

Raising employment rates would come as a solution to this problem. Although the number of the elderly relative to the working-age population will increase, it is in fact not the ratio between these two groups but the ratio between the economically active and inactive (the labour market support ratio) that matters for economic growth, social cohesion, and sustainability of the social security systems. In that respect, the simulations conducted by Bijak et al. (2007) show that an increase in labour force participation rates in countries with low economic activity to the levels observed in European countries characterised by high economic activity will have a much larger impact on the labour market support ratio than an increase in TFR by 0.5. Thus, there is no doubt that a rise in labour force participation is highly desirable from this perspective. A potential for an increase in economic activity lies in attracting those groups to the labour market that are currently most underrepresented in employment, i.e., the elderly, the low-skilled, and women. In this study we focus on the last group. Our choice is motivated by two reasons. On the one hand, increased women's integration in the labour market has several advantages. We discuss them in the next paragraph. On the other hand, this integration constitutes a major challenge for policy makers due to its interaction with fertility.

A gradual increase in female labour force participation has been observed in all European countries since the Second World War. Although the pace of this process has been highly differentiated, there is no doubt that the gender employment gap has declined remarkably everywhere in Europe. The increase in female labour force participation has been driven by several factors, among which a change in the structure of labour demand, growing educational attainment of women, and cultural changes seem to be most crucial. Hence, there is no doubt that the strong increase in the labour market integration of women is deeply embedded in a much wider process of social change; in that respect, it is irreversible (Kotowska, 2005: 230).

For several reasons, this increase is also desired from the economic and social point of view. First, as the education level of women is comparable with that of men in all European countries (Pissarides et al. 2005: 19), keeping women out of the labour market would be a serious waste of human capital. Second, although the gender wage gap is still noticeable, women's earnings have been making up an even larger share of the household budget. Hence, for many households, women's work may be necessary for affording the desired, not to mention the minimum, living standard. This argument gains additional importance after taking into account the growing employment instability in European labour markets. Since it affects not only women but more and more often also men, women's work serves to secure the household income. Finally, empirical studies provide evidence that the rising earning power of women has a positive influence on children's outcomes as well and may even compensate for the emotional losses that are inevitable consequences of both parents' decision to work (Aaberge et al., 2005: 154–293). These benefits stemming from the increased involvement of women in the labour force have been recognised by the European Commission and consequently the necessity to raise women's employment has become one of the strategic goals of the EU. Nevertheless, apart from these positive aspects of women's work, it is clear that women's involvement in the labour market lowers the amount of time and energy women can devote to childbearing and childrearing. Therefore, a question emerges whether and under what conditions it is possible to increase the labour force participation of women without negative repercussions on fertility. This issue constitutes the main research problem of this study.

In fact, until the mid-1980s it seemed that female labour force participation did reduce fertility, at least in the market economies. Among the Western OECD countries, those with a high percentage of economically active women had the lowest fertility (e.g., Denmark, Finland, Norway, Sweden), while those where it was not so common for women to participate in employment were characterised by relatively high fertility (e.g., Greece, Ireland, Italy, Spain). Furthermore, the decline in childbearing was indeed accompanied by an increase in the economic activity of females. This downward trend in fertility was most pronounced in countries characterised by the lowest levels of women's labour supply, however. As a result, around 1985 the cross-country correlation between the TFR and female labour force participation rate (LFPR) changed sign from negative to positive thereafter (Ahn & Mira, 2002; Brewster & Rindfuss, 2000; Rindfuss et al. 2003; Engelhardt & Prskawetz, 2004; Engelhardt et al. 2004; Kögel, 2004). Countries that now have the lowest fertility levels are those with the lowest female labour force participation whereas those with highest fertility tend to be characterised by highest women's economic activity. This finding has been explained by the cross-country differences in the incompatibilities between childrearing and female employment, resulting from variation in the cultural and institutional settings such as attitudes towards working mothers and family policies (Castles, 2003; Rindfuss et al., 2003; Brewster & Rindfuss, 2000). Furthermore, Ahn and Mira (2002) and Adserà (2004, 2005) underline the role of labour market characteristics, such as unemployment levels and income effects of women's wages as well as labour market rigidities.

A reversal in the cross-country correlation has challenged the existing knowledge on the association between the TFR and LFPR. If women's employment were indeed to facilitate childbearing, the prospects for counteracting the negative consequences of the changing age structure of the European populations would be very optimistic.

The relationship, however, may not be as simple as it might have seemed, and some issues still require clarification. First, the studies by Kögel (2004) and Engelhardt et al. (2004) provide evidence that time-series association between the two variables has remained negative. Second, the findings described so far refer explicitly to Western countries. The relationship between fertility and female labour force participation in the new EU member states remains largely unexplored. Yet, the macro-level trends for these two variables diverge strongly from those observed for the EU-15. This implies that we do not fully understand the mechanism underlying fertility and employment behaviours. This in turn prevents policy makers from shaping appropriate policies. Finally, it is notable that so far there has been not much research testing the overall impact of the policies, gender norms and labour market characteristics on the relationship between fertility and women's labour supply. The majority of studies investigates the impact of single policies on one of the two variables or discuss the cross-country variation in fertility and women's labour supply across welfare regimes or family policy models. Admittedly, the studies enumerated in the previous paragraph explain the cross-country variation in this relationship by differences in the cultural and institutional settings, but do not provide any empirical support for this hypothesis. A notable exception is the recent study by Engelhardt (2009) in which the author investigates the role of changes in family policies and labour market characteristics for the weakening of the negative time-series correlation between TFR and LFPR. The author did not find, however, any support for the hypothesis that changes in labour market rigidities or development of public support for working parents had any substantial influence on this process, except for the increase in the enrolment rates in pre-primary education programmes and part-time employment.

1.2 Objectives of the Study

Given the state of current knowledge and the demand for further investigation in the field, this study provides new insights into the interdependencies between fertility and female labour force participation. Its main research objective it to answer the question *whether and under what conditions it is possible to increase women's involvement in paid employment without negative repercussions on childbearing*. In order to address this question, we look into the role of the country context for mediating the relationship between the two variables, taking into account family policies, labour market structures, gender norms as well as the living standards. In our discussion we focus not only on the Western economies, as is commonly done, but also introduce the new EU member states into the comparative framework, with the aim of explaining the distinctness of the developments in post-socialist countries from what is observed in the West. Additionally, the study assesses the extent to which the empirical research on the interdependencies between fertility and women's labour supply conducted by the mid 2000s explains the mechanism underlying women's fertility and labour market decisions. Following our critical review of theories and empirical studies, we propose a theoretical framework and an empirical approach that should bring us closer to the understanding of the complex interdependencies between childbearing and women's economic activity.

The study is concentrated on the specific regions at the particular point in time. More specifically, we mainly focus on the EU-27 member states, plus Norway and Switzerland, and discuss developments in women's labour supply and fertility in these regions in the period from the early 1970s till 2009. As for the CEE countries, we are mainly interested in the developments following the collapse of state socialism. However, we also provide some background information on the pre-1989 period. We limit our discussion mainly to women. However, we recognise the key role that men play in many aspects of women's decisions on fertility and economic activity and share the view that this aspect should be incorporated in future research on the topic.

1.3 Major Theoretical Concepts

Our study is organised around three major theoretical concepts: methodological individualism, rational choice approach, and life-course perspective. They underlie the theoretical foundations of the work and hence provide the basis for our empirical investigations and discussions.

1.3.1 Methodological Individualism

Although our main research question refers to the macro-level, we view individuals as the primary subject of our investigation. It is the actions and interactions of individuals that create the social phenomena we observe at the macro-level. This assertion is inherent in the concept of *methodological individualism*, which is adopted as the first major conceptual scheme underlying this study.

Methodological individualism is a doctrine that was already established in social sciences in the nineteenth century. Over time and across disciplines, various versions of methodological individualism have been developed. The overall tendency has been from versions presupposing that social phenomena are fully to partly explained by individual behaviours (Udehn, 2002). For the purpose of this study we apply the approach proposed by Coleman (1990) and adopted in demography (de Bruijn, 1999: 19–22). It is classified as a less extreme version of the concept for the recognition of the social structure and its impact on individual behaviour.

The concept of methodological individualism implies that understanding of individual behaviour is crucial for explaining the social phenomena observed at the macro-level. This is because causality operates through the micro-level. However, individuals do not live in a vacuum but in a social environment, a macro-context. The context is a multi-level and multi-dimensional 'structure of institutions that embody information about opportunities and restrictions, consequences and expectations, rights and duties, incentives and sanctions, models, guidelines, and definitions of the world' (de Bruijn, 1999: 21). This information is continuously transmitted to the individuals who acquire, process, interpret, and evaluate it. In this way, the context influences people's life choices, which are subsequently transformed into a social outcome observed at the macro-level.

1.3.2 The Concept of Rational Choice

Following the concept of methodological individualism in our study, we focus on individuals and their fertility and labour market behaviours rather than on analysing the relationship between the two variables at the macro-level. We assume women to be *rational actors* who have *preferences* as regards number of children as well as participation in the labour force, but who also face certain constraints that restrain them from choosing the most preferred option. In the process of decision-making, women predict the consequences of childbearing on their labour force participation, and vice versa. These consequences depend on the *context* in which women operate. The context defines to what extent employment can be combined with childrearing and to what extent the two activities exclude each other. The contextual opportunities and restrictions range from the institutional (family policies) through structural (barriers to the labour market, flexibility of work arrangements) and economic (living standards) to the cultural (gender norms prevailing in a society). Once the consequences of childbearing on labour force participation or vice versa are predicted, they are evaluated from the perspective of women's life goals and life values. The perceived contribution of these consequences to the fulfilment of women's needs is crucial for the *final choice* we observe. In that respect, if childbearing is expected to have a negative impact on females' work career, then women who set a high value on labour force participation will tend to have fewer children than women who attach greater importance to family. Likewise, provided that employment is assessed to affect childrearing unfavourably, women who are more family-oriented will opt for longer child-related career breaks than will work-oriented women.

1.3.3 Life-Course Perspective

In this study fertility and women's employment are not perceived as time static constructs but as *careers* which develop continuously over individual's life-course, interacting with each other as well as with the context an individual operates in (Willekens, 1991, 1999). The characteristic feature of these two careers is that they are at critical stages at about the same time – after a woman graduates from education but well before she reaches the end of the reproductive age. Thus, they compete for a woman's time and energy, which leads to *incompatibility* problems, using the terminology of Willekens (1991). The incompatibilities can be resolved by resignation from one career, lower involvement in a career, or by shifts in timing of events pertaining to one career – postponement. The choice of a strategy depends on the woman's preferences towards family and work, while the necessity to make use of these strategies depends on the intensity of the conflict or, in other words, on the opportunities and restrictions to work and family reconciliation imposed by the macro-context.

1.4 Relevance and Outline of the Study

Interdependencies between childbearing and female labour force participation have received a prominent position in the economic, demographic, and sociological research as a response to declining fertility, transformations in the labour markets, and a growing threat of an increment in the old-age dependency ratio all over Europe. Analyses were conducted at both the macro- and the micro-levels. The macro-level analyses have a largely descriptive character. They portray the developments in fertility and women's labour supply from the time-series and cross-country perspective, providing first insights into the problem and a basis for formulating further research questions. Since each individual is different and does not exhibit characteristics of the whole nation, however, the macro-level studies do not allow for explaining the mechanism underlying fertility and women's labour supply under the risk of ecological fallacy. Given this limitation, researchers have turned their attention to the micro-level approach. Improving access to individual-level longitudinal data and development of the techniques of event history analysis raised the hope of understanding women's choices with respect to fertility and labour force participation. Unfortunately, evidence at the micro-level, although abundant, is fragmented and often provides contradictory results. The reason is that the micro-level studies focus on a specific context, constituting only a piece in the overall puzzle of understanding the relationship between fertility and women's work. The need to draw general conclusions on the size and direction of the effect under investigation calls for a systematic overview of the existing evidence. Furthermore, the majority of the micro-level research fails to account for women's unobserved characteristics, such as their material aspirations and other career orientations. This leads to endogeneity bias on the estimate of the relationship between fertility and women's labour supply. Finally, most studies concentrate on the Western economies while the evidence for the new EU member states is scarce and often fragmented.

In this work we try to fill these gaps. In order to explain the macro-level developments in fertility and women's labour supply, we follow the three major theoretical concepts underlying the study. This approach implies that we focus on individual choices, view individuals as rational actors embedded in the macro-context, and observe them throughout the life-course. Consequently, individual decisions are seen as a product of two components: individual preferences, needs, and life goals (orientations) on the one hand and contextual opportunities and restrictions people face on the other. In the study we discuss the role of *both components of decision-making*. Since, in common with other researchers, we face severe data limitations regarding women's material aspirations as well as regarding their orientation towards family and work, we pay proportionally more attention to contextual opportunities and restrictions. We do not ignore the role of women's preferences, however. Instead, we discuss the consequences of omitting them from the analysis and propose to model fertility and women's employment jointly to account for the endogeneity bias on the estimate of the relationship between the two careers, using such analytical methods as multi-process hazard models. Furthermore, we *systematise the existing micro-level evidence* on the interdependencies between fertility and women's labour supply in order to get a better understanding of the micro-level relationship. Instead of conducting a narrative literature review, we make use of meta-analytic techniques. This methodology, relatively new in the social sciences, has been developed in order to synthesise, combine, and interpret the abundance of empirical evidence on a certain topic. It offers a clear and systematic way to compare results of different studies, standardised for the country investigated, the method applied, the control variables employed, the sample selected, etc. It also allows for testing the impact of certain study characteristics on the obtained estimates. In this way we *explore the role of the macro-context for fertility and labour market choices of women.* We propose to *look at the context from a multi-dimensional perspective*, while many researchers take a single-dimension perspective and focus solely on the impacts of policies or gender norms. In this study, we consider four dimensions of the context to be relevant for fertility and labour market behaviours: institutional (family policies), structural (labour market structures), cultural (gender norms), and economic (living standards). Finally, a unique aspect of this study is that we *extend the discussion to the new EU member states.*

The book is organised into seven chapters. In Chapter 2 we present the main developments in fertility and female labour force participation at the macro-level in the European Union, Norway, and Switzerland in recent decades. We refer to the existing studies on the topic, but also extend these analyses by including post-socialist countries in the comparative framework. Furthermore, in contrast to the available research, we focus on women in the reproductive ages rather than on all women aged 15–64 and extend the analysis to most recent periods. Our discussion is divided into two parts. First, we portray the macro-level developments in child-bearing and women's labour supply in the EU, Norway, and Switzerland, paying special attention to the relationship between these two variables from the time-series and cross-country perspectives. Second, we explore the cross-country and temporal variation in fertility and women's economic activity by analysing the variation in women's labour supply and employment indicators by child status. Hence, Chapter 2 serves as point of departure for our further investigation. It demonstrates the complexity of the interrelationship between fertility and women's labour supply at the macro-level and shows that they are largely mediated by some common exogenous third variables. It concludes with a statement that these factors need to be further explored if the interdependencies between the two variables are to be understood.

Nevertheless, the macro-level analyses do not provide sufficient information to meet this goal. Therefore in subsequent chapters we move from the macro- to the micro-level in order to explore the mechanism underlying fertility and labour market behaviours of individuals. Chapter 3 constitutes a theoretical basis for the further micro-level analyses. Here, the central position is occupied by the economic theory of fertility and women's labour supply as proposed within the New Home Economics. It represents an economic approach to modelling rational choice. Within this theoretical framework, we discuss the role of macro-contextual opportunities and restrictions as well as individual preferences. The chapter closes with a list of conditions, derived from the theory, which should be met if the interdependencies between fertility and women's labour supply are to be understood.

Chapters 4 and 5 are devoted to the first component of decision making, i.e. the contextual opportunities and restrictions. In Chapter 4 we discuss the cross-country variation in family policies, labour market structures, gender norms, and economic conditions. These four dimensions of the macro-context are considered to be highly relevant for fertility and employment decisions. The major contribution of this Chapter to the discussion on the interdependencies between fertility and women's labour supply is that it develops quantitative indicators of the intensity of the incompatibilities between paid work and care imposed by the macro-context. These indices are further used for assessing the cross-country differences in these incompatibilities and for building a country ranking. Attempts to construct such indices have been already undertaken in the literature, but in reference to one context dimension only, such as family policies (e.g. Gornick et al. 1997; Gornick and Meyers, 2003) or gender roles (Muszyńska, 2007). In this study all three context dimensions that generate or ease incompatibilities between women's employment and childbearing are taken into account (i.e. family policies, labour market structures and social norms for gender roles).

In Chapter 5 we examine the association between the macro-level incompatibilities between women's employment and fertility and the micro-level relationship between the two variables. This Chapter contributes thus to the discussion on the influence of the macro-context on women's fertility and employment choices, supplementing the macro-level studies conducted by Brewster and Rindfuss (2000), Ahn and Mira (2002), Castles (2003), Engelhardt and Prskawetz (2004), Engelhardt et al. (2004), Kögel (2004) and Rindfuss et al. (2003). For our analyses we make use of the existing empirical studies exploring the micro-level relationship between fertility and women's economic activity in various countries and hence various institutional, structural, cultural, and economic settings. Our units of observation are estimates of this relationship, standardised for the across-study differences. This approach is commonly known as meta-analysis. Finally, the empirical studies are not only used as data sources but are also critically assessed against the theoretical framework presented in Chapter 3.

The majority of studies collected for conducting the meta-analysis fail to account for women's unobserved characteristics such as material aspirations as well as their orientation towards family and work among others. Thus, the estimated relationship between childbearing and women's employment cannot be interpreted as a measure of a conflict between the two activities. The data required for assessing the intensity of the micro-level incompatibilities between paid work and care in a proper way are often unavailable, however. Therefore, in Chapter 6 we suggest modelling fertility and women's employment jointly in a common maximum-likelihood framework by using a multi-process hazard model. The proposed method allows for taking the unobserved determinants of the two variables into account and consequently eliminates the potential endogeneity bias. We test it in the context of a post-socialist country, providing additional evidence on the interrelationship between women's employment and fertility for the part of Europe which lacks empirical investigations on this topic and where economic constraints may create important motives for women's employment (in contrast to Western Europe). Among the CEE countries we select Poland as we find it to score the worst in terms of the institutional support to working parents and display most traditional views on gender roles across the EU member states as well as to be characterised by labour market structures that are exceptionally rigid and unfavourable to women's employment. Hence, not only does Chapter 6 demonstrate the benefits from accounting for unobserved characteristics of women, but it also provides new insights into women's employment and fertility choices in a country context where pronounced work-family tensions interact with strong economic constraints.

The concluding Chapter 7 summarises the major findings and provides an answer to our main research question. It states the implications for family and labour market policies with respect to fertility and female labour force participation and critically assesses the theoretical and methodological contributions of the study. Finally, it concludes with suggestions for data collection and future research in the field.

1.5 Limitations of the Study

A proper understanding of the interdependencies between fertility and women's labour supply is an ambitious goal and requires certain data. The perfect solution would be to have access to longitudinal data for all EU member states, comprising information not only on women's fertility and labour market behaviours, but also on their preferences, intentions, values, and life goals (including material aspirations) as well as perceptions of the available options and consequences of certain actions. Furthermore, this information should be linked with contextual data describing opportunities and restrictions at the household, local, regional, and country level. Such an 'ideal' dataset is currently not available even for single countries. Furthermore, despite the recent improvements in data quality and availability as well as the efforts undertaken by the authors of the Generations and Gender Programme,[3] it may not become available in the immediate future. Collection of data on personality traits constitutes the major difficulty here.

These data problems impose certain limitations on an exploration of the interdependencies between childbearing and women's labour supply. The approach we propose aims to overcome these difficulties, but it is far from a perfect one. First, it partly relies on existing empirical studies, with all their methodological drawbacks. Since these studies do not control for woman's orientation towards family and work or her other personality traits and often fail to control for woman's financial situation or her material aspirations, the estimates of the micro-level relationship between fertility and women's employment that they yield do not reflect the conflict between the two activities. This deficiency hampers our interpretation of the cross-country differences in this relationship. Second, the method applied for comparing the studies allows for a standardisation for the across-study differences, but the comparability we reach is not ideal. Third, the statistical methods we use in Chapter 6

[3] For more detailed information on the Generations and Gender Programme, see Vikat et al. (2007).

for modelling fertility and women's labour supply in order to cope with data limitations rely on an assumption that the person-specific unobserved heterogeneity term describing women's unmeasured propensity to have children and to work is constant over the life-course. This is certainly a simplification of the reality in which women's plans and preferences as well as conditions she operates in are subject to constant changes, although it is anyway a step forward from what had been published on the topic by 2006. Further, with our data we are not able to recognise the nature of woman's needs. It is thus not clear to us, whether the strong determination of women to have a job which we find for Poland is merely driven by financial necessities or whether some other higher order needs come into play as well. Finally, although our variable of interest is labour supply, which – contrary to employment – is an outcome of conscious choice, the available data enable us only to analyse employment in the empirical parts of the study.

Despite these shortcomings, the study critically reviews the scientific achievements in the field, proposes some new solutions and marks directions for future research. For these reasons, we believe it constitutes an important contribution to the understanding of the interdependencies between fertility and women's labour supply.

1.6 Methodological Notes

Before we proceed to the next chapter we would like to provide the reader with a few methodological notes.

Most importantly, the labour market and fertility terms require clarification. The terms 'labour force', 'labour supply', 'economic activity', and the more colloquial 'involvement in the labour market' are used interchangeably and cover the population of the employed and the unemployed. The 'employed' are persons who do any work for pay or profit, whereas the 'unemployed' are those who do not do any work for pay or profit and do not have a job, but are available to take up employment within the following two weeks and are actively searching for a job. The rest of the population is 'economically inactive'.

Among the employed, one can differentiate between persons who work full-time and part-time. The national definitions of 'part-time employment' differ largely across countries, depending on the applied working hours threshold. In this study we use the international definition of part-time employment, which is based on the self-classification of a respondent during the Labour Force Survey.[4]

As regards fertility, the only term that in our opinion requires clarification is the Period Total Fertility Rate (TFR). It is the average number of children that would be born alive to a woman during her lifetime if the age-specific fertility rates of a given

[4]During the interview, respondents are asked to assess whether they work full-time or part-time. The assessment should be made based on the employment contract they have. If and only if this information is not available, the respondents are asked to refer to the number of hours they usually work.

year remained unchanged over the woman's reproductive life. TFR refers thus to a fictitious female cohort and is computed by summing the age-specific fertility rates in year *t*. The TFR at the level of 2.1 marks the replacement level.

Wherever we use the term 'Europe' we mean the EU-27 member states, Norway, and Switzerland. The expressions 'Western Europe', 'Western countries' or 'the West' refer to the EU-15 member states, Norway, and Switzerland. They belong to a broader group of 'developed' or 'advanced' countries. These are the OECD countries, excluding Mexico, Turkey and the former socialist countries. The terms 'Central and Eastern European (CEE) countries', 'post-socialist countries' or 'former socialist countries' refer to the new EU-12 member states, except for Cyprus and Malta.

Sometimes, we also divide the Western European countries into geographical areas. Hence, the term 'Northern Europe' covers the Nordic countries (Denmark, Finland, Norway, and Sweden), the United Kingdom, and Ireland. 'Continental Europe' encompasses Austria, Belgium, France, Germany, Luxembourg, the Netherlands, and Switzerland, while 'Southern Europe' or 'Mediterranean Europe' cover Greece, Italy, Portugal, and Spain. Wherever we use the term 'West Germany' we refer to the former Federal Republic of Germany (FRG) while the term 'East Germany' describes the former German Democratic Republic (GDR). Under 'Germany' we mean unified Germany unless we analyse the period prior to 1989 – when it refers only to West Germany.

Each time we write about 'incompatibilities between fertility and women's work' we refer to the theoretical concept of incompatible careers as proposed by Willekens (1991), i.e., careers that develop in parallel, reach critical stages at about the same time, and compete for women's time and energy. This does not mean, however, that under certain conditions childbearing and women's work cannot be combined in practice.

Throughout the study, we refer to the results of several social surveys. Instead of characterising the survey each time it is mentioned, we provide its description in the Appendix (Table A.1).

Chapter 2
Developments in Fertility and Women's Labour Supply in Europe

2.1 Introduction

The decline in fertility experienced by the industrialised economies over recent decades was for a long time attributed to the rising labour force participation of women. For instance, the authors of the concept of the second demographic transition ascribe the fall in the propensity to have children to the rising economic autonomy of women and their desire for self-fulfilment, among other things (Van de Kaa, 1988: 17; Lesthaeghe, 1992). The delegates at the UN Population Conference in Sofia in 1983 came to a similar conclusion (UN 1983 after Willekens, 1991).

The fall in the Period Total Fertility Rate (TFR) experienced by Western economies between the mid 1970s to the early 2000s was indeed accompanied by an increase in female labour force participation (LFP). This negative time-series association between the two variables in some countries has, however, weakened over time (Engelhardt et al. 2004; Kögel, 2004). As a result, the cross-country correlation between TFR and LFP changed its sign from the negative to the positive around the mid-1980s (Ahn & Mira, 2002; Engelhardt & Prskawetz, 2004). Since then until the early 2000s countries with low economic activity of women were characterised by the lowest fertility while those with high women's labour supply displayed higher birth rates.

The macro-level developments in fertility and women's labour supply in the Central and Eastern European (CEE) countries differ substantially from those observed in the Western economies. Under state socialism, the CEE countries were characterised by relatively high female labour force participation and high birth rates. Although some decline in fertility in this part of Europe had started already in the 1970s, being visible particularly in Hungary and Slovenia, it accelerated substantially after the onset of the economic transformation. At the same time, changes in the political and economic systems brought a considerable decline in the labour force participation (and employment) of both women and men.

In this chapter we discuss interdependencies between fertility and women's labour force participation at the macro-level. This issue has been already widely explored (e.g., Brewster & Rindfuss, 2000; Ahn & Mira, 2002; Castles, 2003; Rindfuss et al., 2003; Kögel, 2004, 2006; Engelhardt & Prskawetz, 2004; Engelhardt

A. Matysiak, *Interdependencies Between Fertility and Women's Labour Supply*, European Studies of Population 17, DOI 10.1007/978-94-007-1284-3_2,

et al., 2004; D'Addio & D'Ercole, 2005). The existing studies are, however, predominantly limited to the Western economies. Yet, the macro-level data for the CEE countries suggest that the quantitative relations between the two variables diverge strongly from those observed for EU-15. Hence, excluding them from the analysis precludes a full understanding of the interrelationship between fertility and employment behaviours. Moreover, the available empirical findings on the macro-level relationship between fertility and women's labour supply might be biased by the cross-country differences in the economic activity of women in pre-retirement ages. Therefore, by including the new EU member states into the comparative framework and focusing on the labour force participation of women in reproductive ages, we offer certain extensions to the common approach. Furthermore, we widen the period of analysis to the late 2000s, i.e., the years of gradual improvements in fertility across many European countries.

Our discussion is divided into two parts. First, we portray the macro-level developments in childbearing and women's labour supply in EU, Norway, and Switzerland paying special attention to the relationship between these two variables in the time-series and cross-country perspectives. Second, we explore the cross-country and temporal variation in fertility and women's labour supply by comparing labour force and part-time participation rates of mothers and women with no children.

The chapter is organised as follows. We start with a description of the data sources we use for our analyses (Section 2.2). We then present the macro-level trends in fertility and women's labour supply (Section 2.3). In the following Section 2.4 we explore the cross-country and temporal differences in women's labour supply rates by the number and age of children. Section 2.5 summarises and concludes the chapter.

2.2 Data

The data used in this chapter are merely the aggregate fertility and labour market measures for EU-27, Norway and Switzerland. Two main criteria guided the choice of our indicators. First, we tried to cover the largest number of countries and encompass the longest time period possible. Due to the data limitations, particularly as regards the economic activity in CEE, this objective was not always reached. Second, we were highly concerned about the cross-country comparability. The fertility indicators are generally comparable and are calculated based on vital statistics. The sources of the labour market data, however, are much more diverse (registers, labour force surveys, population censuses). Given the comparability criteria, we limited ourselves to the indicators extracted from the national Labour Force Surveys (LFS). The only exceptions were the CEE countries during the socialist period. Since the LFS were not conducted in this part of Europe at that time, we used data from the national population censuses.

Our basic fertility and labour market indicators were mainly extracted from the international databases. For fertility we used the Eurostat Statistics Database. This database includes the TFRs since 1960 for all EU-27 member states, Norway, and Switzerland. Additionally, the TFRs adjusted for the tempo effect were retrieved from Sobotka (2004: 162). The data sources for the labour market indicators are more diverse. The Eurostat Statistics Database failed to be a sufficient source of labour market information, because the time series it covers range only from 1986 for the EU-15, Norway, and Switzerland and from around 1997 for the NMS-12. Instead, we used the OECD Employment Database. It provides longer time series, starting in 1980 for the majority of the Western economies and for some countries even in 1970. Similarly, for the NMS-12 it includes data starting in the year when the LFS was conducted there for the first time. Unfortunately, only four NMS-12 are covered by the OECD database. We filled this gap by using the ILO Laborstat Database and additionally supplemented the information from the Eurostat Statistics Database, wherever it contained more data than the former. All these databases provide LFS measures, but the ILO data source offers additionally indicators for the CEE under state socialism based on the national population censuses. These three data sources, OECD Employment Database, Eurostat Statistics Database, and ILO Laborstat Database, provided us with labour force participation rates (LFPR), employment rates (EMPR), unemployment rates (UNPR), and proportions of part-timers among the employed (%PT) for women aged 20–44.

Apart from these basic statistics, our analysis required the labour market measures to be disaggregated by the child status (age of the youngest child and number of children). In none of the international online statistical databases or in the publications of the national statistical offices were such comparative indicators available, however. Hence, we computed them using individual data from the European Labour Force Survey 1985–2004 (ELFS).[1] The ELFS contains relatively comparable LFS data for the majority of the EU member states and Norway since 1985. Unfortunately, the survey has also some limitations. The main problem of the ELFS is the lack of data on the number of children a woman has. We only had information on household composition. Hence, it was possible to count children who lived with a mother on the day of the interview, but we missed those who had already left the parental home. Further, the dataset did not allow for identifying kinship relations among the household members for the years before 2000. In order to minimise the risk that the children are women's brothers and sisters or that some of the children have already moved out, we restricted the analysed sample to women aged 25–40. The upper age limit for children was set at 20 and the minimum age difference between mothers and children at 15. In order to check the validity of our assumptions, we compared the distribution of women aged 25–40, by the number of children obtained for 2004, to the distribution computed for the same year, using the information on kinship relations. This information was already available for 2004. In all countries, over 95% of children were correctly ascribed to mothers,

[1]This study was partly conducted under the Low Wage Employment Research Network (LoWER3), funded under the EU Sixth Framework Programme. The ELFS micro-data were available to the members of LoWER3 for the research conducted within the Network.

which provided evidence that the data can be used for analysing patterns of mothers' labour supply without large risk of error. Unfortunately, for Sweden and Norway no information on household composition was included in the ELFS.[2] Therefore it was not possible to disaggregate the labour market indicators by child status in these countries. Statistics Sweden provided us with labour force participation rates of women aged 25–44 by the age of the youngest child (based on the Swedish LFS) for Sweden on request. No such data were available to us for Norway. Another drawback of the ELFS 1985–2004 was its incomplete country coverage. The United Kingdom, Bulgaria, and Romania were not present in this database at all, while the data for Austria and Finland were available only since 1995, for Germany since 2002, and for the CEE countries since around 1997. Finally, the information on the age of the household members was anonymised in the ELFS and hence available in 5-year age groups only. This restricted our choice of children's age categories.

2.3 Macro-level Developments in Fertility and Women's Labour Supply

In this section we portray macro-level developments in fertility and women's labour supply in EU-27, Norway, and Switzerland. In our analyses, we largely focus on women in reproductive ages. The age interval we used is 20–44. Currently, women give birth most often when they are 25–34 years of age. We decided to include younger women (20–24) as well because women in this age group frequently became mothers in the past, and they still do in countries where the changes in fertility patterns started relatively late, namely in the post-socialist countries. Furthermore, we also covered older women, aged 35–44, whose labour force participation is still very likely to be influenced by the presence of young children at home.

Throughout this section, the patterns in fertility and labour force participation are presented separately for the Western and CEE countries. We decided on this distinction since the developments in fertility and women's labour supply in these two parts of Europe have been entirely different.

2.3.1 Classification of Countries

Following Ahn and Mira (2002) and Engelhardt and Prskawetz (2004), we built country groups homogenous with respect to the development of their LFP. The Western European countries were assigned to three groups based on their average LFP over the 10-year time periods starting with 1970. The classification limits of

[2] While in all other countries the sampling units are households, in the Nordic countries the units are individuals. Denmark and Finland provide information on household composition additionally; no such information is available for Sweden and Norway.

LFP were raised in each time period. A similar classification procedure, together with the limits set for Western Europe, was applied to CEE. However, as the labour market indicators for the socialist period were available for certain years only (usually once per 10-year period), the countries were grouped based on these single time points. Furthermore, for the years following 1989 the classification was conducted upon the average LFP over the whole post-socialist period and the average threshold for the 1990s and 2000s was used. The reason underlying this decision was that the LFS data for the majority of these countries are available from the mid-1990s and for Bulgaria from 2000. Detailed classification of the countries is presented in Table 2.1.

The high-LFP cluster was initially composed of Denmark, Finland, and Sweden as well as of all CEE countries under state socialism for which the data were available. Norway entered it in the 1980s, Switzerland in the 1990s and the Netherlands in the 2000s. By contrast, the low-LFP group was originally formed by Greece, Ireland, Italy, Luxembourg, the Netherlands, and Spain. The only country that left it was the Netherlands. It happened in the 1990s when the Netherlands moved to the medium-LFP cluster composed initially of Austria, France, Germany, Norway, Portugal, and the United Kingdom. In the 1990s, this cluster was further extended

Table 2.1 Country groups homogenous with respect to the developments in LFP

	Low-LFP (<45%)	*Medium-LFP (45–65%)*	*High-LFP (>65%)*
Western economies 1970–1979	Greece	Austria	Denmark
	Ireland	France	Finland
	Italy	Germany	Sweden
	Luxembourg	Norway	
	Spain	Portugal	
		United Kingdom	
Central and Eastern Europe around 1970			Czechoslovakia (1970)
			Hungary (1970)
			Poland (1970)
			Romania (1970)
	Low-LFP (<55%)	*Medium-LFP (55–70%)*	*High-LFP (>70%)*
Western economies 1980–1989	Greece	Austria	Denmark
	Ireland	Belgium	Finland
	Italy	France	Norway
	Luxembourg	Germany	Sweden
	Netherlands	Portugal	
	Spain	United Kingdom	
Central and Eastern Europe around 1980			Czechoslovakia (1980)
			Hungary (1980)
			Poland (1978)
			Bulgaria (1975)
			Romania (1977)

Table 2.1 (continued)

	Low-LFP (<65%)	*Medium-LFP (65–75%)*	*High-LFP (>75%)*
Western economies 1990–1999	Greece Ireland Italy Luxembourg Spain	Austria Belgium France Germany Netherlands Portugal United Kingdom	Denmark Finland Norway Sweden Switzerland
Central and Eastern Europe around 1990			Czech Republic (1991) Slovakia (1991) Hungary (1990) Poland (1988) Estonia (1989) Latvia (1989) Lithuania (1989) Slovenia (1991)
	Low-LFP (<75%)	*Medium-LFP (75–80%)*	*High-LFP (>80%)*
Western economies 2000–2009	Greece Ireland Italy Luxembourg Spain	Austria Belgium France Germany Portugal United Kingdom	Denmark Finland Netherlands Norway Sweden Switzerland
	Low-LFP (<70%)	*Medium-LFP (70–80%)*	*High-LFP (>80%)*
Central and Eastern Europe 1990–2009	Hungary (1992–2009)	Bulgaria (2000–2009) Czech Republic (1993–2009) Estonia (1995–2009) Latvia (1996–2009) Poland (1992–2009) Romania (1996–2009) Slovakia (1994–2009)	Slovenia (1994–2009) Lithuania (1996–2009)

Source: author's own elaboration inspired by Engelhardt and Prskawetz (2004)

with the post-socialist countries, where the economic transformation led to noticeable declines in LFP. The only exceptions were Slovenia and Lithuania, which remained classified as high-LFP countries, and Hungary, which moved to the low-LFP cluster. This country classification was adopted throughout this section for describing trends in fertility and female labour force participation.

2.3.2 Developments in Female Labour Force Participation

In all three country groups of Western Europe the general pattern was a gradual increase in LFP and EMP of women aged 20–44 (Figs. 2.1a and 2.2a). The only exceptions were the first half of the 1990s when a sharp decline in the Nordic countries was recorded and the years 2008–2009 where a reverse in the upward trend in EMP was observed across all LFP groups. Both declines were related to temporary economic slowdowns. It is notable also that, compared to other clusters, the low-LFP group experienced a weaker increase in EMP in the 1970s and the first

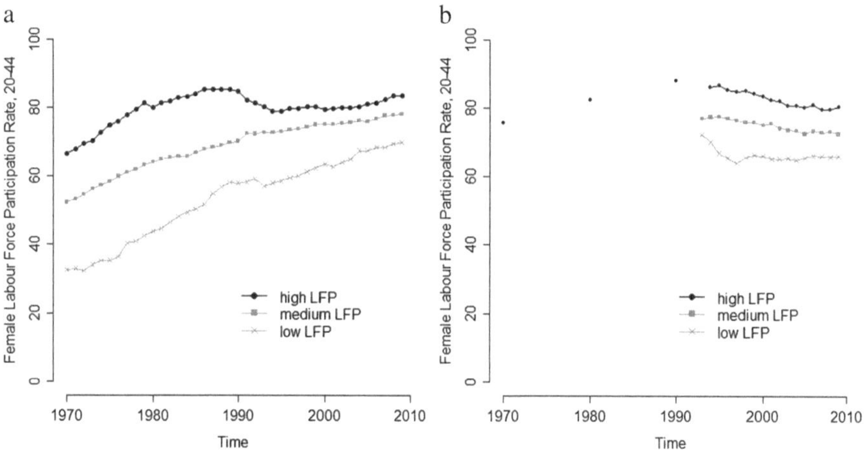

Fig. 2.1 Labour force participation of women aged 20–44, 1970–2009. (**a**) Western Europe; (**b**) Central and Eastern Europe

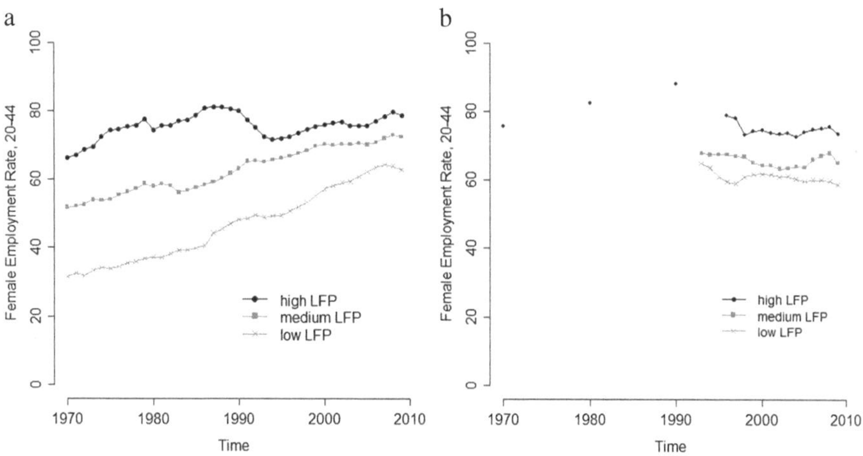

Fig. 2.2 Employment of women aged 20–44, 1970–2006. (**a**) Western Europe; (**b**) Central and Eastern Europe

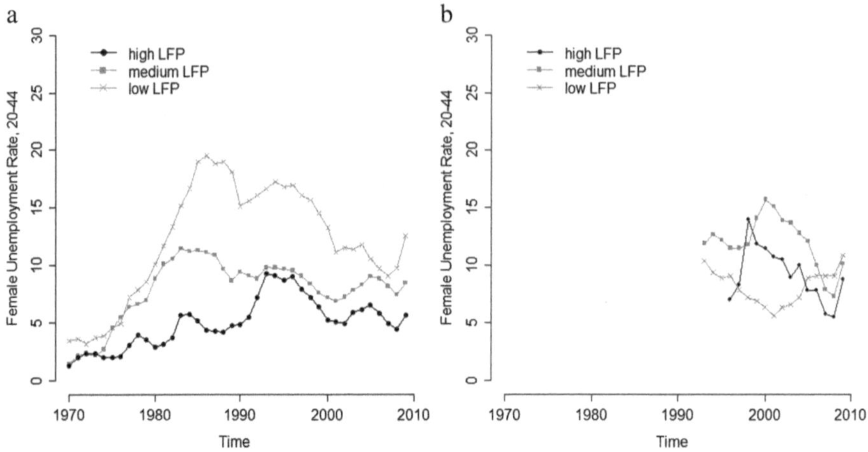

Fig. 2.3 Unemployment of women aged 20–44, 1970–2006. (**a**) Western Europe; (**b**) Central and Eastern Europe

Note: the average LFPR, EMPR, and UNPR are not weighted by population size. Otherwise they would represent mainly the situation in the most populated countries. The data for CEE under state socialism refer to years around 1970, 1980, 1990 (see Table 2.1 for exact years).

Source: author's calculations inspired by Ahn and Mira (2002) and Engelhardt and Prskawetz (2004) based on LFS data from the OECD Employment Database (Western Europe, Poland 1992–2009, Hungary 1992–2009, Czech Republic 1992–2009, and Slovakia 1992–2009), Eurostat Statistics Database (remaining CEE countries 1992–2009) and population censuses from ILO Laborsta Database (CEE countries before 1992).

half of the 1980s, due to an increase in UNP, but following years brought a substantial improvement in that respect and EMP started to increase there more steeply than in the rest of Western European countries. As a result of these developments, the LFP and EMP gaps between the distinguished country groups were narrowing since the mid-1990s. Nevertheless, LFPR and EMPR in the low-LFP cluster in 2009 were still remarkably lower than in the high-LFP group (by 11 and 16% points respectively).

Part-time employment played an important role in the increase in female labour force participation in the majority of Western countries (see Fig. 2.4). This was particularly the case in the Netherlands and Ireland, i.e., countries that experienced strong increments in women's labour supply. In the Netherlands, the percentage of part-timers among employed women increased from already high level of 45% in 1983 to 60% in 2008. In Ireland, this indicator was rather low at the beginning of the 1980s but it doubled over the next 20 years, reaching the level of 36%. Expansion of part-time contracts accompanied an increase in women's employment also in some of the medium-LFP countries: Austria, Belgium, Germany, and the United Kingdom. In the high-LFP group, except for Finland, the proportion of women employed part-time is also quite high, but it did not change over the period analysed (remained at the level of 27% on average). Not everywhere is this employment

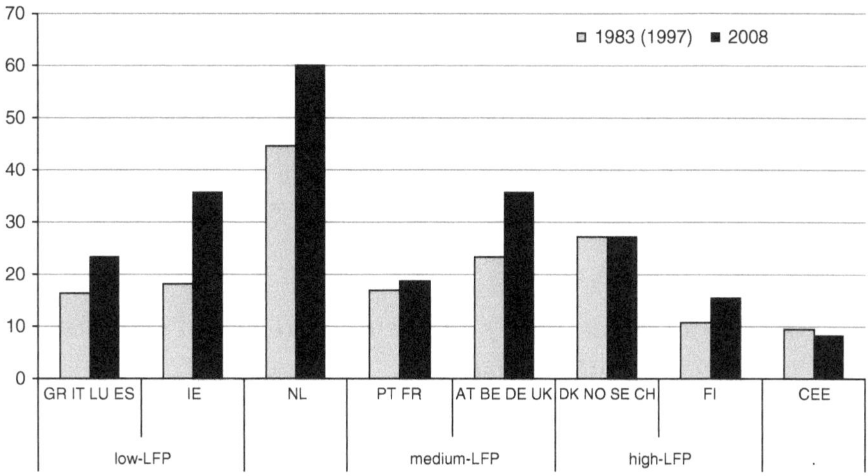

Fig. 2.4 Proportion of part-timers among employed women, Western Europe (1983 and 2008) and CEE (1997 and 2008)
Note: data for Western Europe refer to the years 1983 and 2008, while for CEE countries they refer to 1997 and 2008.
Source: author's calculations based on LFS data from the OECD Employment Database and the Eurostat Statistics Database.

form so important, however. In Finland, Portugal, and France, part-time employment accounted in 2008 for less than 20% of total women's employment.

Completely different developments in LFP and EMP were observed in CEE (Figs. 2.1b, 2.2b, and 2.3b). During state socialism, the majority of women participated in the labour force. As a result, already in the 1980s the average LFPR exceeded 80% there. Only in Hungary and Poland was LFPR slightly lower, at around 75%. In Western Europe, such a high involvement in the labour force was observed only in the high-LFP group. After the breakdown of state socialism, LFP in the majority of the CEE countries fell suddenly in the first years of the economic transformation. Even stronger declines were recorded in EMP. As a result of these changes, only Lithuania and Slovenia remained in the high-LFP cluster. The other countries moved to the medium-LFP; Hungary even moved to the low-LFP group. A downward trend in LFP and EMP in these two groups continued over the 1990s and the beginning of the 2000s. Furthermore, many of the medium-LFP countries (Bulgaria, Poland, Slovakia, Estonia and Latvia) as well as Lithuania experienced very high unemployment in the late 1990s and early 2000s, with unemployment rates exceeding 15%, which led to strong declines in EMP. Only after the EU entry did the EMP started to improve there.

Contrary to the situation in Western Europe, women in CEE are largely employed full-time. The data on part-time labour force participation under state socialism are not available. However, according to Drobnič (1997), this form of employment served a function in the socialist market economies that was different from its role in the developed market economies. Namely, it was mainly used as a means of increasing labour input by retaining in the labour force those persons who otherwise would have probably been excluded from it. The first available data on part-time employment in CEE come from the 1990s. They indicate that the percentage of part-timers among the employed has been stable since that time, at the level of 8–9% on average (Fig. 2.4), with the lowest values of below 3% recorded in Bulgaria. A characteristic feature of CEE is that the proportion of part-timers among female workers is only slightly higher than among male workers.

2.3.3 Women's Labour Supply and Fertility: Temporal Patterns and Cross-Country Differences

In order to compare the developments in women's labour supply with fertility trends we followed Ahn and Mira (2002) and Engelhardt and Prskawetz (2004) and calculated an average TFR for each of the three LFP-groups, separately for the Western economies and the CEE countries. With some exceptions, the clusters are relatively homogenous as regards the childbearing patterns. The outstanding countries were Germany and Austria, with notably lower fertility rates than the medium-LFP countries, and Switzerland, with TFR falling well below the average for the high-LFP group. These three countries displayed fairly similar fertility developments. Therefore, we excluded them from the medium- and high-LFP groups and classified them in the fourth, separate cluster.

In Western Europe, the increase in LFP and EMP was originally accompanied by falling TFR in all country groups we distinguished. There were, however, strong differences across the LFP-clusters as regards the pace of the fertility decline and its duration (Fig. 2.5). The downward trend was the steepest and came to a halt at the latest in the low-LFP group, incidentally composed of countries that in the 1970s were still characterised by the highest fertility. As a result, the average TFR in this part of Europe bottomed out at 1.44 in 1996, with Italy and Spain experiencing even lower fertility (slightly below 1.2). The exception in this group was Ireland where TFR did not fall below 1.9. Recently the situation in this country cluster has improved (in 2009 the average TFR amounted to 1.6), but the Mediterranean countries still belong to countries with lowest fertility levels in Europe. Such strong declines in fertility as in the low-LFP cluster has never been reached by the medium-LFP countries (excluding Austria, Germany and Switzerland). The TFR fell there to the minimum level of 1.58 in 1996. Since then it has been increasing and in 2009 reached 1.78. Finally, the high-LFP group (excluding Switzerland), which displayed the lowest fertility at the beginning of the 1970s, experienced the earliest reversal in the downward trend. An increase in childbearing was already observed there in the mid-1980s. Since that time, the average TFR in the high-LFP cluster has been the highest among all country groups, although it suffered from some fluctuations during the periods of economic slowdown and recovery. In 2009 it reached 1.88. Against this background, Austria, Germany and Switzerland clearly diverge from the remaining countries. Although they were classified as medium-LFP and

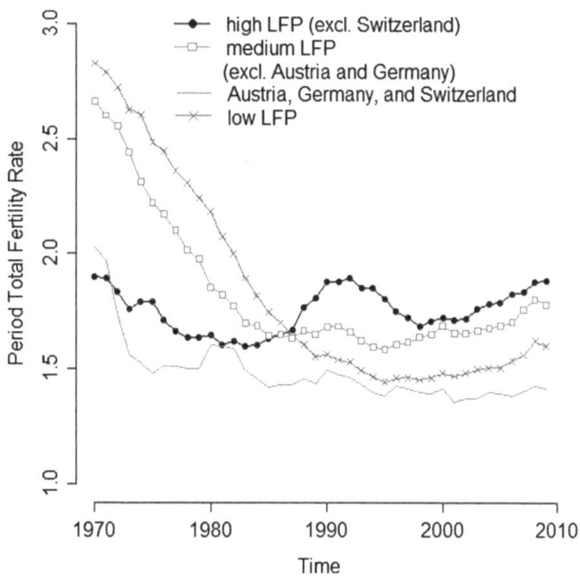

Fig. 2.5 Period total fertility rate, Western Europe, 1970–2009
Note: the average TFRs are not weighted by population size. Otherwise they would represent mainly the situation in the most populated countries.
Source: author's calculations inspired by Ahn and Mira (2002) and Engelhardt and Prskawetz (2004) based on data from the Eurostat Statistics Database (fertility indicators) and the OECD Employment Database (labour market indicators); Data retrieved 3 January 2011.

Switzerland even as high-LFP countries, they have been characterised by the lowest fertility among all LFP groups since the mid-1970s. In 2009, the average TFR in German-speaking countries amounted to 1.42.

The differences in the magnitude of fertility decline across the LFP-groups, as described above, led to a reversal in the cross-country correlation between the TFR and LFP from negative to positive around the mid-1980s (Figs. 2.6 and 2.7a–d).

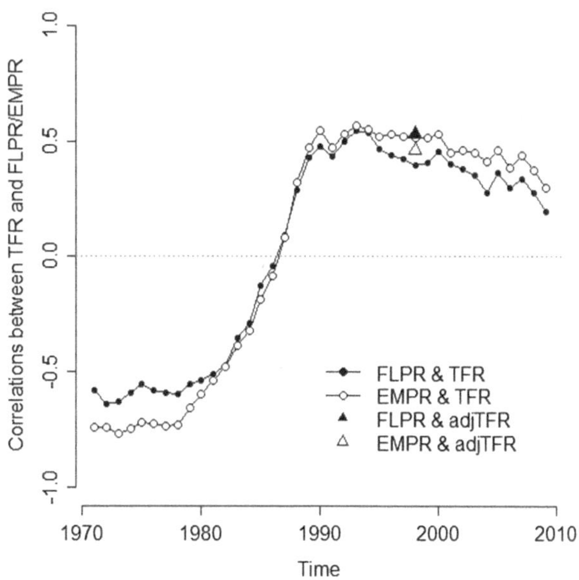

Fig. 2.6 Cross-country correlation between TFR and FLPR/EMPR, Western Europe, 1970–2009

Source: author's calculations based on data from the Eurostat Statistics Database (fertility indicators) and the OECD Employment Database (labour market indicators); data retrieved 3 January 2011. The data on adj-TFR come from Sobotka (2004: 162) and refer to the period 1995–2000.

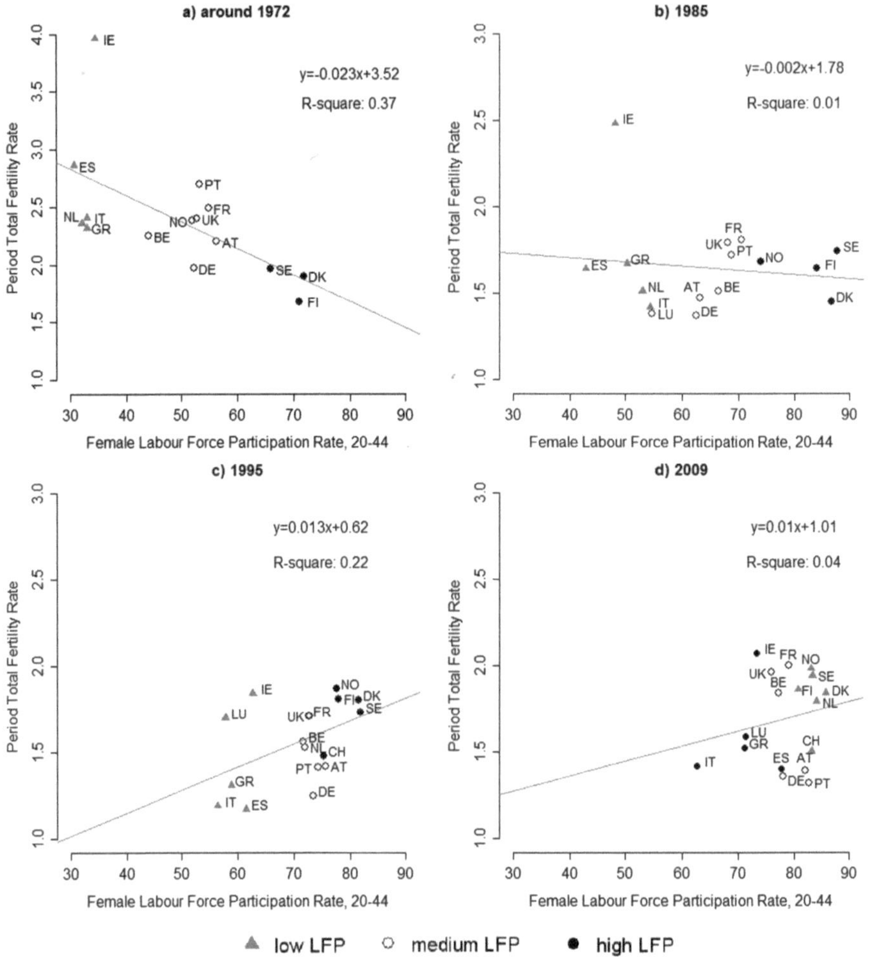

Fig. 2.7 Female labour force participation and the total fertility, Western Europe
Source: author's calculations based on data from the OECD Employment Database (labour market indicators) and the Eurostat Statistics Database (fertility indicators); data retrieved 3 January 2011.

The correlation between TFR and EMP changed its sign as well. This finding was well documented in the literature (Brewster & Rindfuss, 2000; Ahn & Mira, 2002; Kögel, 2004; Engelhardt & Prskawetz, 2004; Engelhardt et al., 2004; Rindfuss et al., 2003; d'Addio & d'Ercole, 2005) and it seemed to be robust to the tempo effects: the correlations between the adjusted-TFR and FLPR / EMPR in the period 1995–2000 closely resemble the correlations between the TFR and FLPR / EMPR (see also Kögel, 2006). The positive association had peaked in the first half of the 1990s. In the following years it was declining, however, and by the late 2000s it was close to zero again. Two developments led to the recent weakening in the positive correlation: a narrowing gap in LFP, particularly between the medium- and high-LFP countries, and an increasing diversity in fertility levels in the medium-LFP group. More specifically, an increase in women's labour supply that was observed in all low- and medium-LFP countries was not evenly accompanied by an increase in fertility. While TFR rose sharply in Belgium, France and the United Kingdom, it remained at invariably low levels of around 1.35–1.4 in Austria and Germany.

In contrast to Western economies, CEE was characterised by both high fertility and high female labour force participation in the 1970s and the 1980s. Note, however, that from the time series perspective a slight decline in childbearing was observed in the socialist countries in parallel to a continuous increase in the economic activity of women at that time. This process of decline in fertility accelerated unexpectedly after the onset of the economic transformation, i.e., at the time when an upward trend in women's labour supply reversed. As a result, the CEE countries experienced a severe plunge in childbearing, with TFRs reaching the lowest-low levels by the late 1990s. It is notable that fertility declined to similarly low levels in all CEE countries, irrespectively of the LFP (Figs. 2.8 and 2.10a). Only since around the year 2002 has some improvement in fertility been observed, probably due to recuperation in childbearing at older reproductive ages. This improvement in fertility was the strongest in countries belonging to high LFP group (Lithuania and Slovenia) and in some of the countries from the medium-LFP group (Bulgaria and Estonia) displaying highest LFP within the cluster. These developments led to an emergence of a positive cross-country correlation between TFR and LFP in CEE by the end of the 2000s (Figs. 2.9 and 2.10b). They clearly resemble the developments in fertility and women's labour supply in Western Europe of the 1980s and 1990s where an increase in fertility was most pronounced in countries characterised by highest LFP.

Despite recent improvements in fertility in CEE countries and the emergence of the positive cross-country correlation between TFR and LFP Total Fertility still remains at low levels there as compared to Western Europe (Fig. 2.11). The TFR does not exceed the level of 1.6 even in those CEE countries that display as high LFP as the Nordic countries (Slovenia) or France, Belgium or the United Kingdom (Bulgaria Estonia, Latvia, and Lithuania).

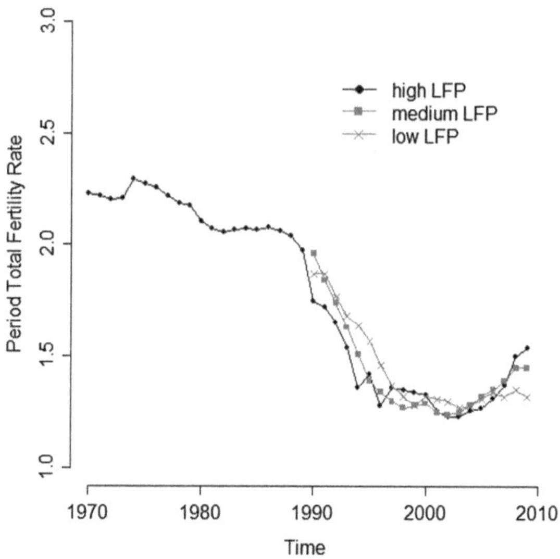

Fig. 2.8 Period Total Fertility Rate, Central and Eastern Europe 1970–2009
Note: the average TFRs are not weighted by population size.
Source: author's calculations inspired by Ahn and Mira (2002) and Engelhardt and Prskawetz (2004); data sources: fertility indicators from the Eurostat Statistics Database, labour market indicators from population censuses (prior to 1990) extracted from ILO Laborsta Database and LFS (after 1990) extracted from the OECD Employment Database and Eurostat Statistics Database, retrieved 3 January 2011. The data on adj-TFR come from Sobotka (2004: 162) and refer to the period 1995–2000.

Fig. 2.9 Cross-country correlation between TFR and FLPR/EMPR, Central and Eastern Europe, 1990–2009
Source: author's calculations; data sources: fertility indicators from the Eurostat Statistics Database, labour market indicators from population censuses (prior to 1990) extracted from ILO Laborsta Database and LFS (after 1990) extracted from the OECD Employment Database and Eurostat Statistics Database, retrieved 3 January 2011. The data on adj-TFR come from Sobotka (2004: 162) and refer to the period 1995–2000.

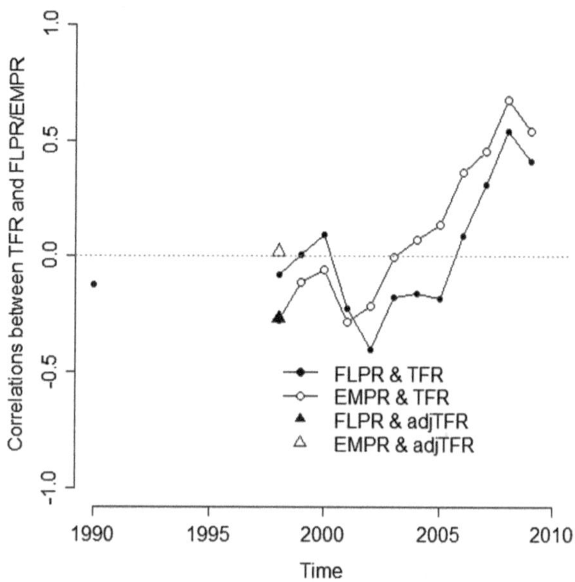

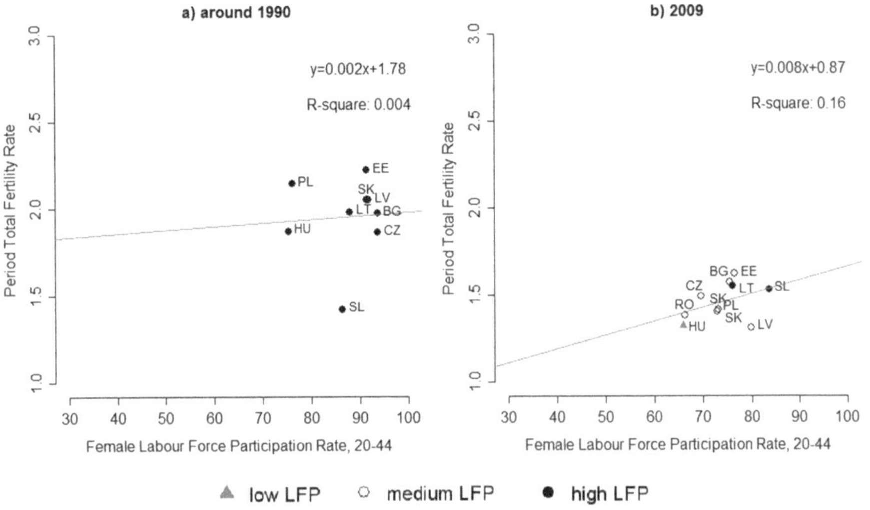

Fig. 2.10 Female labour force participation and total fertility, CEE
Source: author's calculations based on 'around-1990' data from the population censuses and the 2009 data from the Labour Force Surveys extracted from the ILO Laborstat Database, fertility data from the Eurostat Statistics Database, retrieved 3 January 2011.

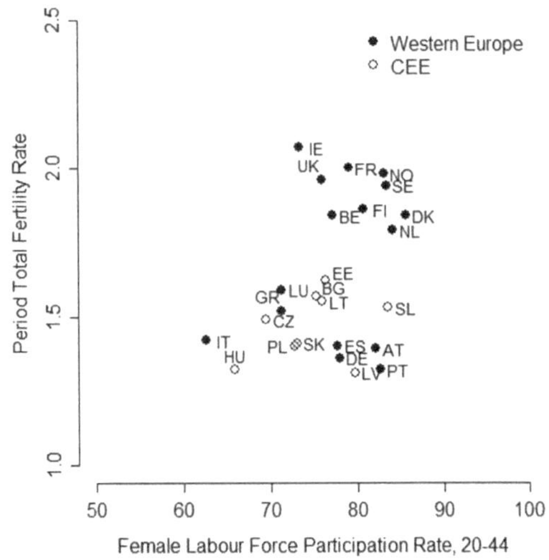

Fig. 2.11 Female labour force participation and total fertility, comparison of Western and CEE countries 2009
Source: author's calculations based on the 2009 data from the Labour Force Surveys extracted from the ILO Laborstat Database, fertility data from the Eurostat Statistics Database, retrieved 3 January 2011.

The developments in fertility and women's labour supply, as presented in this section, point out the large complexity of the interrelationship between the two variables. They illustrate that high labour force participation of females can co-exist with low as well as high fertility, depending on the country and time period. Similarly, a rise or a decline in women's economic activity can be equally accompanied by a decrease as well as an increase in childbearing. For instance, in the past, high fertility was more likely to be observed in low- rather than high-LFP countries in Western Europe, but it was also recorded in CEE, which was characterised by high LFP. The decline in fertility occurred in parallel to an increase in the economic activity of women in Western economies and a decrease in the post-socialist countries. Taken together, these developments suggest that the macro-level relationship between the two variables was largely spurious, i.e., mediated by a set of exogenous country-specific factors. According to the literature, one of them is the intensity of the incompatibilities between fertility and women's labour supply prevailing in a certain country at a certain point in time (e.g., Lehrer & Nerlove, 1986; Brewster & Rindfuss, 2000; Castles, 2003; Engelhardt et al., 2004; Rindfuss et al., 2003; Muszyńska, 2007). This factor was often used to explain the emergence of the positive cross-country correlation between TFR and LFP in Western Europe. Do the cross-country differences in work-family incompatibilities explain also the phenomenon of stronger increases in fertility in those CEE countries that display higher LFP and weaker in those that exhibit lower LFP? Are there any other exogenous factors that mediate the relationship between fertility and women's labour supply in Western and CEE countries? This book attempts to address these questions by investigating the role of work-family incompatibilities for fertility and women's labour supply as well as seeking other country-specific factors.

2.4 Effects of Children on Women's Labour Supply

2.4.1 Labour Force Participation of Mothers

In order to better understand the macro-level developments in fertility and women's labour supply in connection with work-family incompatibilities we look first into the cross-country and temporal variation in the labour force participation of mothers and women with no children. We are most interested in comparing the labour supply rates of mothers with three children or with a child aged 0–5 and non-mothers. While discussing this gap, for convenience we use the expression 'impact of children on women's labour supply rates/part-time employment of women' although it is clearly not a causal effect but simply a difference between two rates.

Among the Western economies for which the data were available, the weakest effects of children on women's labour supply rates were on average found in the high-LFP group (see upper panels in Tables 2.2 and 2.3). Having one or two children did not reduce LFPR by more than 9% points on average. It was already more difficult to combine labour force participation with caring of three children, but still the difference between the LFPR of mothers with three children and non-mothers in the high-LFP cluster was far lower than in the remaining LFP-groups. By contrast, the most negative impact of children on women's labour supply was found in the low-LFP cluster. A characteristic feature of that country group was that women not only reduced their labour supply when their children were young, aged 0–5, but they remained largely inactive even after children reached school age.

Table 2.2 Effects of motherhood on women's labour supply rates, LFPRs of women aged 25–40 by the number of children

Country	No children below age 15	One child	Two children	Three children	Effect of one child	Effect of two children	Effect of three children
	(1)	(2)	(3)	(4)	(1)–(2)	(1)–(3)	(1)–(4)
2004							
CEE							
low-LFP	**85.4**	**65.4**	**65.3**	**32.1**	**20.0**	**20.1**	**53.3**
Hungary	85.4	65.4	65.3	32.1	20.0	20.1	53.3
medium-LFP	**88.0**	**79.1**	**74.9**	**63.5**	**8.9**	**13.0**	**24.5**
Czech Republic	90.3	67.6	70.6	57.1	22.7	19.8	33.2
Estonia	84.8	85.8	66.0	67.7	−1.0	18.7	17.0
Latvia	84.9	82.8	80.9	58.9	2.1	4.0	26.0
Poland	86.9	80.8	77.1	67.9	6.1	9.8	19.0
Slovakia	93.0	78.3	80.1	65.7	14.7	12.9	27.3
high-LFP	**85.0**	**89.8**	**90.4**	**80.2**	**−4.8**	**−5.4**	**4.9**
Lithuania	82.4	86.3	87.6	73.9	−3.9	−5.2	8.5
Slovenia	87.6	93.3	93.1	86.5	−5.7	−5.5	1.2
Western Europe							
low-LFP	**85.6**	**70.4**	**59.8**	**49.1**	**15.2**	**25.8**	**36.5**
Greece	86.1	69.4	64.6	59.9	16.7	21.5	26.1
Ireland	91.2	73.9	59.7	44.5	17.3	31.5	46.7
Italy	78.6	67.0	53.5	38.8	11.6	25.0	39.7
Spain	86.5	71.1	61.2	53.1	15.3	25.2	33.3
medium-LFP	**88.3**	**83.4**	**76.9**	**58.3**	**4.9**	**11.4**	**30.0**
Belgium	88.5	81.7	83.8	57.1	6.8	4.7	31.4
France	88.5	85.9	76.4	56.7	2.6	12.1	31.8
Portugal	87.4	87.6	81.0	69.2	−0.3	6.4	18.2
Austria	88.4	84.1	75.1	59.3	4.3	13.2	29.1
Germany	88.5	77.7	68.0	49.0	10.9	20.5	39.5
high-LFP	**89.8**	**80.9**	**81.1**	**68.3**	**8.9**	**8.7**	**21.5**
Denmark	87.2	84.2	88.9	73.5	3.0	−1.7	13.7
Finland	90.8	76.7	79.0	71.1	14.2	11.8	19.8
Netherlands	91.3	81.7	75.4	60.2	9.6	15.9	31.1
Sweden	na	na	na	na	na	na	na
1985							
CEE	**na**	**na**	**na**	**na**	**na**	**na**	**na**
Western Europe							
low-LFP	**77.9**	**54.7**	**38.1**	**30.3**	**23.3**	**39.8**	**47.6**
Greece	73.3	53.1	44.4	42.0	20.3	28.9	31.3
Ireland	85.2	49.5	28.8	19.4	35.8	56.4	65.8
Italy	75.6	59.5	42.5	31.1	16.1	33.0	44.5
Spain	77.6	56.5	36.8	28.8	21.1	40.9	48.9
medium-LFP	**84.0**	**68.6**	**60.6**	**42.0**	**15.4**	**23.4**	**42.0**
Belgium	83.5	76.4	69.3	45.0	7.1	14.2	38.5
France	88.3	82.6	70.0	41.4	5.7	18.3	46.8
Portugal	80.2	75.9	67.9	55.8	4.3	12.3	24.5

Table 2.2 (continued)

Country	No children below age 15	One child	Two children	Three children	Effect of one child	Effect of two children	Effect of three children
	(1)	(2)	(3)	(4)	(1)–(2)	(1)–(3)	(1)–(4)
Austria	na	na	na	na	na	na	na
Germany	na	na	na	na	na	na	na
Netherlands	84.0	39.5	35.2	25.8	44.6	48.8	58.2
high-LFP	**88.6**	**88.6**	**89.8**	**80.9**	**0.0**	**−1.2**	**7.7**
Denmark	88.6	88.6	89.8	80.9	0.0	−1.2	7.7
Finland	na	na	na	na	na	na	na
Sweden	na	na	na	na	na	na	na

Source: author's calculations based on the European Labour Force Survey

Table 2.3 Effects of motherhood on women's labour supply, LFPRs of women aged 25–40 by age of the youngest child

	No children	Youngest child 0–5	Youngest child 5–10	Impact of children aged 0–5	Impact of children aged 5–10
	(1)	(2)	(3)	(1)–(2)	(1)–(3)
2004					
CEE					
low-LFP	**85.4**	**31.8**	**76.4**	**53.5**	**9.0**
Hungary	85.4	31.8	76.4	53.5	9.0
medium-LFP	**88.8**	**51.2**	**89.5**	**37.7**	**−0.7**
Czech	91.4	31.8	92.9	59.6	−1.5
Estonia	85.7	50.7	90.6	35.0	−4.8
Latvia	86.2	62.7	86.7	23.6	−0.4
Poland	87.2	62.2	83.1	25.0	4.2
Slovakia	93.6	48.4	94.3	45.2	−0.8
high-LFP	**86.9**	**84.0**	**90.6**	**3.0**	**−3.7**
Lithuania	85.9	77.0	87.2	8.9	−1.3
Slovenia	87.9	91.0	94.0	−3.0	−6.0
Western Europe					
low-LFP	**85.0**	**59.6**	**64.6**	**25.4**	**20.4**
Greece	84.9	61.6	69.3	23.3	15.6
Ireland	90.9	56.3	63.7	34.6	27.2
Italy	78.1	58.0	58.2	20.1	19.9
Spain	85.9	62.3	67.1	23.6	18.9
medium-LFP	**87.9**	**70.9**	**81.4**	**17.0**	**6.5**
Belgium	86.5	74.2	82.0	12.3	4.6
France	88.6	69.2	86.6	19.4	1.9
Portugal	87.3	84.1	83.2	3.3	4.1

Table 2.3 (continued)

	No children	Youngest child 0–5	Youngest child 5–10	Impact of children aged 0–5	Impact of children aged 5–10
	(1)	(2)	(3)	(1)–(2)	(1)–(3)
Austria	88.6	68.3	80.9	20.3	7.6
Germany	88.7	58.8	74.4	29.9	14.2
high-LFP	**87.9**	**75.9**	**na**	**12.1**	**na**
Denmark	87.2	81.1	87.6	6.1	−0.4
Finland	91.2	66.2	90.4	24.9	0.7
Netherlands	90.8	74.4	76.5	16.5	14.4
Sweden	82.5	81.8	na	0.7	na
1985					
CEE	na	na	na	na	na
Western Europe					
low-LFP	**75.8**	**39.2**	**39.3**	**36.7**	**36.5**
Greece	69.9	44.0	45.2	25.9	24.7
Ireland	83.6	26.5	26.9	57.1	56.6
Italy	73.9	46.6	45.6	27.2	28.2
Spain	75.9	39.5	39.5	36.4	36.4
medium-LFP	**81.6**	**56.0**	**60.5**	**25.5**	**21.1**
Belgium	79.3	69.9	64.9	9.4	14.4
France	87.5	60.4	70.5	27.0	17.0
Portugal	77.6	66.8	70.7	10.8	6.9
Austria	na	na	na	na	na
Germany	na	na	na	na	na
Netherlands	81.8	27.0	35.7	54.8	46.0
high-LFP	**89.0**	**85.8**	**na**	**3.2**	**na**
Denmark	88.8	86.5	88.2	2.2	0.5
Finland	na	na	na	na	na
Sweden	91.2	85.1	na	6.1	na

Note: for Sweden the age categories of children are different: 0–6 years and no child younger than 16, the data refer to women aged 25–44
Source: author's calculations based on the European Labour Force Survey and for Sweden on the LFS aggregate data obtained from Statistics Sweden

Despite this general pattern, however, the LFP-clusters were characterised by strong within-group variation with some countries clearly diverging from the group average. One such exceptional country in the high-LFP group was Finland, where childran in pre-school age had much more negative impact on women's labour supply rates than in the remaining high-LFP countries. In fact, this country displayed slightly lower female labour force participation in general. In the medium-LFP cluster, the impact of children exceeded the group average substantially in Germany, which was characterised by relatively low fertility compared to the rest of the medium-LFP countries. In this context it was striking that in contrast to Germany the effect of children on women's labour supply rates in Austria was close to the cluster average. Another exceptional country was Portugal, where, for a change, children had a relatively weak impact on women's economic activity rates.

Similarly to Western Europe, in CEE we also found larger gaps in labour supply of mothers and non-mothers when looking at the low-LFP than at the high-LFP cluster. Children, even in pre-school age, reduced labour force participation rates of women only slightly in Lithuania and Slovenia, the high-LFP countries. By contrast, the gap in economic activity rates of non-mothers and women with three children (or mothers of children aged 0–5) was the largest in Hungary, a low-LFP country. It exceeded 50% points there. In medium-LFP cluster the differences were lower, although a high cross-country variation was observed there, with Czech Republic exhibiting the strongest impacts of children on women's labour supply rates. Even though the pattern in the effects of children on women's labour supply rates across LFP-groups was similar in Western Europe and CEE the two European regions exhibit also two important differences. On the one hand, the effects of young children (aged 0–5) on women's economic activity rates were on average stronger in CEE than in the West. Except for Slovenia and Lithuania the gap in LFPR of mothers with young children and non-mothers amounted to 40% points in CEE. While in the low-LFP cluster of Western Europe this difference equalled to 25% points. On the other hand, however, in CEE the LFPRs of mothers with children in school age were almost equal to LFPRs of non-mothers. This was not the case in Ireland, Greece, Italy or Spain. This observation suggests that women in CEE return to the labour market to a much larger extent than their Western counterparts after a child reached school age.

Apart from the fact that the magnitude of children's impact on women's labour supply varied across countries, it was also changing over time. The available data allowed us to assess the temporal changes only in Western Europe.[3] Comparing the lower with the upper panels in Tables 2.2 and 2.3, one can see that the labour force participation of mothers increased in low- and medium-LFP groups. This increase was observed for all categories of mothers – those with one, two, three, or more children as well as with the young children (aged 0–5). What is even more important, however, is that the increase in the labour force participation of mothers with young children was more pronounced than the increase in the labour force participation of women with no children, leading to a decline in the gaps in the economic activity of these two groups (Fig. 2.12). This was particularly the case in the Netherlands, i.e. the country that experienced a rapid growth in women's labour supply over recent decades, and over 30 years advanced from the low-LFP cluster to the high-LFP cluster. It was also substantial among some of the low-LFP countries, particularly in Ireland and Spain. The pronounced increase in the economic activity of mothers with any number or age of children is an important finding. It provides evidence

[3]Individual LFS data for CEE countries are included in the European Labour Force Survey Database since 1998. This was the earliest year for which we would be able to compute women's labour force rates by child status.

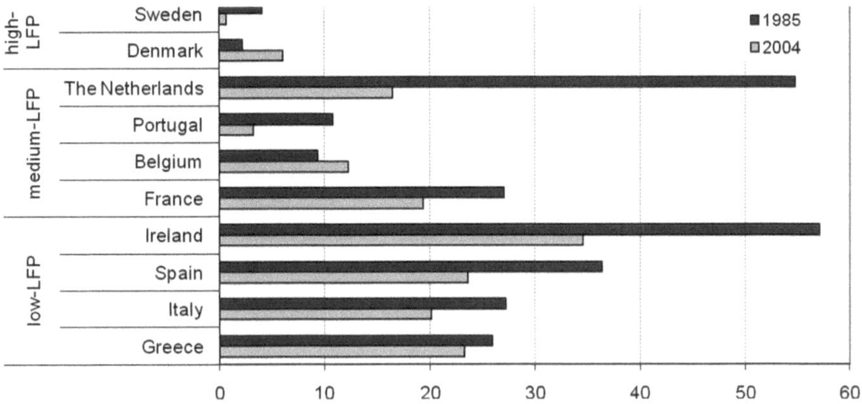

Fig. 2.12 Effects of motherhood on women's labour supply in 1985 and 2004 (absolute difference between the LFPRs of non-mothers and mothers with children aged 0–5)
Source: author's calculations on European Labour Force Survey.

that the rise in women's labour supply observed since the mid 1980s was not caused solely by the increase in the proportion of childless women or women with lower numbers of children, but also by an increase in the economic activity of mothers.

2.4.2 Part-Time Employment of Mothers

As the effects of children on women's employment are similar to those we observed for labour force participation both in direction and magnitude (see Tables A.2 and A.3. in the Appendix), they are not discussed here. Instead, we explored the impact of children on mothers' involvement in the labour market by taking a closer look at the time women devote to work. Our discussion for Western Europe is limited to low- and medium-LFP groups only since the data on part-time employment in high-LFP cluster were available merely for Finland and the Netherlands, two countries that are not representative of the high-LFP group in that respect (see Section 2.3.2).

Mothers in Western Europe are not only more likely to be out of employment, but they are also more prone to reduce the number of working hours compared to women without children (Tables 2.4 and 2.5). The incidence of part-time employment among mothers is largest in the Netherlands (where as many as 90% of mothers work part-time), Ireland as well as in the medium-LFP countries. The only exception in this group is Portugal, where women rarely switch into this employment form after they become mothers. In that respect, Portugal is similar to the low-LFP countries, especially to Greece and Spain, which are characterised by relatively low incidence of part-time employment among mothers. A comparison of data for 1985 and 2004 indicates an increase in the proportion of mothers employed part-time in the medium-LFP countries as well as in Italy. Only in Greece did the incidence of part-time employment shrink during this period.

Table 2.4 Proportion of part-timers among the employed, women aged 25–40 by the number of children

	No children below age 15	One child	Two children	Three children	Effect of one child	Effect of two children	Effect of three children
	(1)	(2)	(3)	(4)	(1)–(2)	(1)–(3)	(1)–(4)
2004							
CEE							
low-LFP	**2.6**	**3.8**	**7.2**	**12.7**	**−1.2**	**−4.6**	**−10.1**
Hungary	2.6	3.8	7.2	12.7	−1.2	−4.6	−10.1
medium-LFP	**5.4**	**8.3**	**9.7**	**14.0**	**−2.9**	**−4.3**	**−8.6**
Czech Republic	4.5	10.5	10.8	13.7	−6.0	−6.3	−9.2
Estonia	3.7	9.0	9.5	10.5	−5.2	−5.8	−6.8
Latvia	7.7	11.2	14.4	21.4	−3.5	−6.7	−13.7
Poland	9.1	8.5	10.1	17.1	0.5	−1.0	−8.0
Slovakia	2.2	2.4	3.7	7.5	−0.2	−1.5	−5.3
high-LFP	**7.3**	**7.8**	**6.2**	**13.9**	**−0.6**	**1.0**	**−6.7**
Lithuania	7.2	10.2	8.9	19.7	−3.0	−1.7	−12.5
Slovenia	7.3	5.3	3.5	8.1	1.9	3.7	−0.8
Western Europe							
low-LFP	**11.2**	**23.4**	**29.6**	**32.8**	**−12.3**	**−18.5**	**−21.6**
Greece	6.8	7.5	10.4	9.4	−0.7	−3.7	−2.6
Ireland	6.5	32.4	44.2	55.3	−25.9	−37.7	−48.8
Italy	18.2	33.2	40.2	42.5	−15.0	−22.1	−24.3
Spain	13.3	20.6	23.6	24.1	−7.4	−10.4	−10.8
medium-LFP	**14.8**	**33.8**	**46.0**	**50.3**	**−19.0**	**−31.2**	**−35.5**
Belgium	20.4	39.0	48.2	54.0	−18.6	−27.9	−33.6
France	14.3	23.3	42.5	49.0	−9.0	−28.2	−34.7
Portugal	6.0	7.7	10.0	19.9	−1.7	−4.0	−13.9
Austria	17.2	47.3	62.6	58.0	−30.1	−45.4	−40.9
Germany	16.2	51.7	66.8	70.7	−35.6	−50.6	−54.5
high-LFP	**27.7**	**48.3**	**51.6**	**53.9**	**−20.7**	**−24.0**	**−26.3**
Denmark	na	na	na	na	na	na	na
Finland	12.1	12.1	11.4	16.3	0.0	0.7	−4.2
Netherlands	43.2	84.5	91.8	91.5	−41.3	−48.6	−48.3
Sweden	na	na	na	na	na	na	na
1985							
CEE	**na**	**na**	**na**	**na**	**na**	**na**	**na**
Western Europe							
low-LFP	**5.2**	**11.0**	**15.8**	**22.3**	**−5.8**	**−10.6**	**−17.2**
Greece	4.2	12.1	12.6	12.1	−7.9	−8.5	−7.9
Ireland	4.0	13.2	26.7	38.8	−9.3	−22.7	−34.9
Italy	5.7	8.1	10.8	16.6	−2.4	−5.1	−11.0
Spain	6.8	10.6	12.9	21.7	−3.7	−6.0	−14.9
medium-LFP	**14.4**	**29.5**	**36.1**	**42.8**	**−15.0**	**−21.7**	**−28.4**
Belgium	9.2	18.7	28.3	39.1	−9.5	−19.1	−30.0
France	10.4	16.0	26.3	39.2	−5.6	−15.9	−28.9

Table 2.4 (continued)

	No children below age 15	One child	Two children	Three children	Effect of one child	Effect of two children	Effect of three children
	(1)	(2)	(3)	(4)	(1)–(2)	(1)–(3)	(1)–(4)
Portugal	4.9	6.3	7.1	13.2	−1.3	−2.1	−8.3
Austria	na	na	na	na	na	na	na
Germany	na	na	na	na	na	na	na
Netherlands	33.2	76.9	82.7	79.6	−43.7	−49.5	−46.4
high-LFP	**na**	**na**	**na**	**na**	**na**	**na**	**na**
Denmark	na	na	na	na	na	na	na
Finland	na	na	na	na	na	na	na
Sweden	na	na	na	na	na	na	na

Source: author's calculations based on the European Labour Force Survey

Table 2.5 Proportion of part-timers among the employed, women aged 25–40 by age of the youngest child

	No children	Youngest child 0–5	Youngest child 5–10	Impact of children aged 0–5	Impact of children aged 5–10
	(1)	(2)	(3)	(1)–(2)	(1)–(3)
2004					
CEE					
low-LFP	**2.7**	**9.3**	**7.3**	**−6.6**	**−4.6**
Hungary	2.7	9.3	7.3	−6.6	−4.6
medium-LFP	**5.3**	**13.8**	**8.6**	**−8.5**	**−3.3**
Czech Republic	5.1	17.3	10.9	−12.1	−5.7
Estonia	3.0	12.9	11.2	−9.9	−8.2
Latvia	6.6	23.7	7.5	−17.0	−0.8
Poland	8.7	12.7	10.6	−4.0	−1.9
Slovakia	2.9	2.6	2.9	0.3	0.0
high-LFP	**6.5**	**9.2**	**6.7**	**−2.8**	**−0.2**
Lithuania	6.3	11.9	11.6	−5.6	−5.3
Slovenia	6.6	6.5	1.7	0.1	5.0
Western Europe					
low-LFP	**11.5**	**27.1**	**29.2**	**−15.6**	**−17.7**
Greece	6.7	9.2	9.3	−2.5	−2.6
Ireland	7.1	40.5	47.9	−33.4	−40.8
Italy	18.5	36.1	38.2	−17.6	−19.7
Spain	13.5	22.5	21.4	−9.0	−7.8
medium-LFP	**16.5**	**39.5**	**46.3**	**−23.0**	**−29.8**
Belgium	25.0	43.8	49.1	−18.8	−24.1
France	15.3	35.0	37.0	−19.6	−21.7

Table 2.5 (continued)

	No children	Youngest child 0–5	Youngest child 5–10	Impact of children aged 0–5	Impact of children aged 5–10
	(1)	(2)	(3)	(1)–(2)	(1)–(3)
Portugal	6.3	8.0	11.0	−1.7	−4.7
Austria	18.5	54.1	63.0	−35.6	−44.5
Germany	17.4	56.7	71.4	−39.2	−54.0
high-LFP	**27.9**	**53.1**	**50.1**	**−25.2**	**−22.2**
Denmark	na	na	na	na	na
Finland	12.1	15.5	10.5	−3.4	1.5
Netherlands	43.7	90.6	89.6	−46.9	−45.9
Sweden	na	na	na	na	na
1985					
CEE	na	na	na	na	na
Western Europe					
low-LFP	**5.7**	**13.9**	**11.3**	**−8.2**	**−5.6**
Greece	4.3	19.1	7.8	−14.8	−3.5
Ireland	4.2	22.6	38.3	−18.4	−34.1
Italy	5.8	10.1	10.5	−4.3	−4.7
Spain	7.0	12.5	15.6	−5.5	−8.6
medium-LFP	**14.3**	**33.3**	**34.0**	**−19.1**	**−19.8**
Belgium	10.6	26.4	27.4	−15.8	−16.8
France	11.3	24.6	25.2	−13.4	−13.9
Portugal	5.1	7.7	8.1	−2.6	−3.0
Austria	na	na	na	na	na
Germany	na	na	na	na	na
Netherlands	35.1	82.3	83.5	−47.2	−48.4
high-LFP	**na**	**na**	**na**	**na**	**na**
Denmark	na	na	na	na	na
Finland	na	na	na	na	na
Sweden	na	na	na	na	na

Source: author's calculations based on the European Labour Force Survey

In contrast to Western Europe, in CEE it is rather unlikely for women to reduce the number of working hours after they become mothers. The only exceptions are Estonia and Latvia, where the proportion of part-timers among mothers with young children is relatively high compared to other women (without children or with older children). Still, this difference is much lower than in the majority of the Western European countries. Overall, this means that part-time employment in post-socialist countries is merely used for combining childrearing with market work. Mothers either choose to remain in full-time employment or withdraw from the labour market for the period of care.

2.5 Discussion

'Given the separation of home and gainful employment that is present in industrialised societies such as our own and the relatively inflexible hours connected with most forms of employment, an incompatibility between the roles of a mother and worker may be said to exist [. . .]. If the woman perceives the roles as incompatible, then she can engage in one activity only by devoting less time to the other' (Weller, 1977: 44). This hypothesis on the role incompatibilities, which became very influential in the literature on fertility and women's labour supply, presupposes that fertility decline is required for an increase in women's economic activity. Such a view has been indeed shared in the literature (Huber, 1980; Westoff, 1978) as well as among policy makers (UN 1983 after Willekens, 1991). If this view were true, fertility would have declined most strongly in countries with the strongest increases in women's labour supply. Furthermore, it would have increased in the post-socialist countries where a fall in women's economic activity was observed after the collapse of state socialism. None of these have happened, however.

In this Chapter it was demonstrated that an increase in women's labour supply in the Western economies did not occur solely as a result of a decline in fertility. This assertion is based on the observation that it was not only an increase in the proportion of childless women or women at lower parity levels that contributed to the rise in the economic activity of women, but also a substantial growth in the labour force participation of mothers, irrespective of the number of children. This finding clearly contradicts the simplistic view that an increase in women's labour supply requires a decline in fertility. Instead, the relationship between the two variables is much more complex.

At the time the incompatibility hypothesis was formulated, fertility in the Western economies was in fact highest where the labour force participation of women was the lowest. Moreover, the decline in childbearing that occurred in successive years in this part of Europe was accompanied by an increase in women's labour supply. Yet, the pace of the downward trend in fertility was often higher in countries where women's labour supply was substantially lower. As a result, the cross-country correlation between TFR and LFP changed its sign from negative to positive around the mid-1980s. This positive cross-country correlation is a well known fact. It persisted in Western Europe over the 1990s and its emergence was widely interpreted in the literature a result of the cross-country differences in the incompatibilities between motherhood and paid employment (Brewster & Rindfuss, 2000; Ahn & Mira, 2002; Castles, 2003; Engelhardt et al., 2004; Engelhardt & Prskawetz, 2004; Kögel, 2004, Rindfuss et al., 2003; Muszyńska, 2007). Our analysis of women's labour force participation rates by the number of children and age of the youngest child seems to confirm this view. Where the gap between the economic activity rates of mothers and women with no children is larger the overall labour supply of women and total fertility are usually lower. A new development, which has not been described so far, is a weakening of the positive cross-country correlation between TFR and LFP. This phenomenon was caused by a continuing increase in women's labour force participation in the low- and medium-LFP countries accompanied by improvements in fertility which were substantial in some of these countries (Belgium, France, the United Kingdom) and very modest in the others (Austria, Germany, Spain). The data for the latter countries point out persistence of strong incompatibilities between work and family. As woman's participation in paid employment became a common behaviour across the Western European economies women no longer give up economic activity for the sake of family and children. Instead, they lower their family size in order to participate in the labour force if the two activities cannot be combined.

The developments in fertility and women's labour supply in CEE also strongly contradict the view that the two activities are irreconcilable. In fact, after the onset of the economic transformation, when combining work and care became more difficult and women's employment rates were falling, total fertility did not remain high, but plunged to the lowest-low levels across all post-socialist countries. Interestingly the very recent improvements in fertility observed in that part of Europe turned out to be the strongest in those CEE countries that display higher labour force participation of women. These developments led to an emergence of the positive cross-country correlation between TFR and LFP this time in CEE. A closer look into the labour market data by child status demonstrates that in the post-socialist countries characterised by highest women's labour supply and highest fertility, the labour force participation rates of mothers do not differ strongly from labour force participation of women with no children. This may indicate again that the work-family incompatibilities are responsible for fertility and labour force participation rates not only in Western Europe, but also in CEE.

The existence of the cross-country differences in the incompatibilities between fertility and women's labour supply is an important finding from the policy perspective. It suggests that easing the conflict between the two activities could lead to increases in at least one of the variables of interest without negative repercussions on the other. Therefore, in the following chapters of this work we explore the country-specific factors that may potentially influence the level of the incompatibilities between childbearing and paid employment and test the impact of the context on the micro-level relationship between the two variables.

Nevertheless, the work-family incompatibilities do not seem to be the only factor mediating the relationship between fertility and women's labour supply. The evidence gathered in this Chapter for CEE suggests that there are clearly some other country-specific factors that influence both variables. One indication in support of this hypothesis is that labour force participation of women in post-socialist countries is similarly high as in the medium- and high-LFP countries of Western Europe whereas total fertility is far lower. This phenomenon can be partly explained by differences in tempo effects between the East and the West but there might be also other reasons that underlie it. It is notable that the gap in economic activity rates of women with no children and mothers of children in preschool age is much larger in CEE than in Western Europe, even in its low-LFP cluster. This observation suggests that the conflict between labour force participation of women and care of a young child in post-socialist countries is exceptionally high. Nevertheless, in CEE countries mothers of older children are nearly as likely to be in the labour force as women without children, irrespectively of the LFP group. Such behaviours are not common among mothers in Western countries where the work-family incompatibilities are strong. These observations suggest that, apart from the country-specific incompatibilities between fertility and women's work, there are some other factors that govern the relationship between the two variables, encouraging mothers entry to employment as children grow older.

Chapter 3
Fertility and Women's Labour Supply: Theoretical Considerations

3.1 Introduction

In Chapter 2 we demonstrated the complexity of the interdependencies between fertility and women's labour supply at the macro-level. The data presented suggest that the interrelationship may depend on the incompatibilities between fertility and women's work which varies across countries, but also on some other country-specific factors. If the mechanism underlying fertility and labour market behaviours is to be understood, the variables governing their relationship, including the intensity of the conflict between the two activities, need to be better explored.

For that purpose, we follow the recommendation of methodological individualism and we move our considerations from the macro- to the micro-level. This does not mean, however, that we ignore the macro-level perspective. On the contrary, we see individuals as rational actors embedded in the macro-context that continuously influences people's life choices. Furthermore, we look at the decisions they make from the life-course perspective, taking into account not only the fact of the occurrence of the events, but also their sequence and timing. Using this general framework, in this Chapter we provide a theoretical background to fertility and employment choices. In Section 3.2, we introduce a micro-economic model of decision-making. Although its application to explaining fertility behaviours has been widely criticised, it is probably one of the most advanced models of rational choice. In the following sections of the chapter, we introduce certain modifications to the model to make up for its shortcomings. Within this theoretical framework, in Section 3.3 we discuss the impact of the context on fertility and women's labour supply decisions. Contextual opportunities and restrictions comprise only one determinant of human choice, however, and the other one is preferences. The role of this factor is considered in Section 3.4 while Section 3.5 discusses some of the problems related to measurement and selection effects, which occur due to the inability of researchers to control for women's plans and preferences. Finally, Section 3.6 summarises the theoretical framework we adopt in this volume and lists certain conditions that should be met if the interdependencies between fertility and women's labour supply are to be understood.

A. Matysiak, *Interdependencies Between Fertility and Women's Labour Supply*, European Studies of Population 17, DOI 10.1007/978-94-007-1284-3_3,

3.2 Micro-Economic Approach to Fertility and Women's Labour Supply: A Price-of-Time Model

The foundations for the micro-economic analysis of the fertility–employment nexus were laid by Mincer's (1963) theory of labour supply and Becker's (1965) theory of time allocation. Willis (1973) built upon their works and integrated them into a theoretical model of fertility and women's labour supply (Ermisch, 2003: 114), known also under the label 'price-of-time' model. It refers mainly to women in union whose fertility outcomes are likely to be outcomes of conscious decisions and assumes that it is chiefly the mother's time that is used for childbearing and childrearing. In this model, a couple chooses an optimal allocation of woman's time between home production (including care) and paid work by maximising household's utility from a certain combination of parental consumption (parents' standard of living), number of children and their quality, subject to the household's lifetime budget constraints. The latter depend on the amount of time a mother spends in employment, her market wage, the father's lifetime earnings, and other non-labour income.

Due to budget constraint, the demand for children depends inversely on their cost. There are direct costs (financial expenditures) and indirect costs of children (opportunity costs of parent's time). The latter are measured with a value of time a parent invests in childbearing and childrearing, which are the woman's market wage as well as the value of depreciated human capital, foregone promotion prospects, etc. As a result, women's employment has an ambiguous effect on the demand for children. On the one hand, it increases household income, which encourages parents to have more children (*income effect*). On the other hand, however, employed women may have higher opportunity costs than women who do not work (*price effect*).

The time a mother supplies in the labour market is also a choice variable that is jointly determined with the time she devotes to childrearing. A woman will take up a job only if her market wage exceeds the value of her time spent at home (her reservation wage). The reservation wage is expected to be higher for mothers of young children than of women with no children or mothers with older children as the necessity to provide care raises the value of mother's time spent at home (*price effect*). On the other hand, however, having a(nother) child means additional financial expenditures to the household, which, as a result, may lower the reservation wage of the mother (*income effect*). In general, it is expected that the income effect starts to outweigh the price effect with a rise in child's age, making a mother enter the labour market (e.g., Leibowitz et al., 1992; Joesch, 1994; Rønsen & Sundström, 2002).

The price-of-time model illustrates a complexity of the interrelationship between fertility and women's employment. It is evident that these two activities compete with each other due to restricted time and financial resources of a mother. Nevertheless, the theory does not presuppose that childbearing and employment exclude each other. Whether a woman will stay at home with children, work in the market and remain childless, or combine employment with childrearing depends on a complex interplay between the income effect and the price effect. There are two problems with that approach, however. First, the price-of-time model relies on absolute income, presupposing that it is taken into account in fertility and employment decisions. This may not be sufficient since people differ in their preferences as regards living standards – whereas for some the certain income may be fully satisfactory, for the others it may fall well below their material aspirations. This implies that disregarding the material aspirations may lead to biased conclusions on the interrelationship between women's employment and childbearing. Second, neither does the model consider women's preferences as regards the number and timing of children nor as regards her involvement in the labour market. On the contrary, it assumes that these preferences are identically distributed across women. This may not necessarily be true. We will come back to these issues in Section 3.4.

3.3 Macro-Contextual Opportunities and Restrictions

Although the mechanism of decision-making, as described in the previous section, is the same for each individual, its outcomes might be different depending on the macro-context an individual operates in. The macro-context is a multidimensional structure that provides individuals with information on opportunities and restrictions. This information defines the choice options people face. These macro-contextual opportunities and restrictions affect the magnitude of the price and income effects, which results in diverse fertility and employment decisions under different contextual settings.

So far, researchers have concentrated mainly on the variation in the price effect across various macro-contexts, referring to two dimensions of the country-context distinguished by Liefbroer and Corijn (1999): cultural and structural. The former refers to 'broad ideologies, values, and norms concerning the role of women in the society' (Liefbroer & Corijn, 1999: 52) that define who should take care of children and who should work (see also Muszyńska, 2004, 2007). By contrast, the structural dimension relates to 'societal opportunities and restrictions [imposed] on the roles of women' (Liefbroer & Corijn, 1999: 52). It encompasses all institutional and structural arrangements that facilitate or hinder mothers' employment, i.e., family policies and labour market structures. The impact of family policies on fertility and women's employment decisions has been widely discussed in the literature. The role of labour market structures, except for an incidence of part-time contracts, was for a long time less recognised. This situation started to change only recently as it has been noticed that strong barriers to employment entry in Southern Europe may constitute an important impediment to fertility and women's work (Adserá, 2004, 2005; Aaberge et al., 2005: 131–135). In order to turn more attention to labour market structures and disentangle their potential effects from the effects of family policies, we propose to analyse these two dimensions of the macro-context separately. Therefore, for the purpose of this volume we will speak of the structural dimension of the macro-context when referring to labour market structures, while the institutional dimension will relate to family policies.

If the price effect refers to the conflict between fertility and women's paid work, pre-supposing that the two activities exclude each other, the income effect operates in the opposite direction. Hence, even in traditional societies, where mothers' work in the market is socially not accepted, institutionally unsupported, and where work arrangements are rigid, women may participate in the labour force to a large extent; paid work may be perceived as an important condition for family formation for economic reasons. This is likely to happen in countries where the husband's income is not sufficient for maintaining the family or meeting the couple's aspirations regarding living standards, i.e., in the less affluent societies.

Against this background, *four dimensions of the context* are considered to be highly relevant for fertility and employment decisions: *institutional* (family policies), *structural* (labour market structures), *cultural* (values and norms for women's social roles), and *economic* (living standards). The role of each of these dimensions of the macro-context in shaping fertility and employment decisions is briefly discussed below.

3.3.1 Family Policies

In this study, we use the term 'family policies' when referring to policies targeted at parenthood. These policies govern the rules of the absence from the labour market during the childcare period and define the access to social benefits and services related to parenthood. By offering women certain conditions for work and family reconciliation, they define the intensity of the *institutional incompatibilities* between the two activities. We now discuss potential impacts of the three most important components of family policies: childcare services, maternity and parental leave policies, and income transfers. They constitute the core of welfare policies targeted at childbearing and childrearing (Neyer, 2003). Wherever it is possible, we complement our discussion with the empirical findings on the impact of the policies on fertility and women's labour supply (or employment). We mainly quote studies based on micro-level data.

3.3.1.1 Childcare Services

Childcare services can be offered by the state, the market, employers, or non-profit institutions (Neyer, 2003). However, what matters mostly for childbearing and employment decisions are childcare supply (in terms of number of places as well as opening hours), childcare costs, and childcare quality. Generally, using private childcare requires financial expenditures. Nevertheless, in some societies parents can be granted childcare subsidies to cover at least part of the childcare costs. Following the price-of-time model one should expect that widely available low-cost and high-quality care increases fertility and women's labour supply. This is due to two reasons. First, a better access to high quality childcare reduces the opportunity costs of parenting and of women's work. Second, the decline in childcare costs and an improvement in quality of public care lead to a reduction in mother's reservation wage.

Generally, the positive impact of childcare on women's labour supply is widely documented in the literature (e.g., Stolzberg & Waite, 1984; Blau & Robins, 1989; Connelly, 1992; Gustafsson & Stafford, 1992; Leibowitz et al. 1992; Michalopoulos et al. 1992; Ribar, 1992; Kimmel, 1995; Powell, 1998; Del Boca, 2002; Rønsen & Sundström, 2002). The effect of childcare on fertility is, however, more mixed. A positive, albeit weak, impact is found for Italy (Del Boca, 2002), USA (Blau & Robins, 1989) and for Norway (Rindfuss et al., 2010). Similar results were obtained by Aaberge et al. (2005: 150) and Del Boca et al. (2009) on the pooled data for several EU-15 member states. On the other hand, studies for West Germany (Hank & Kreyenfeld, 2003) and Sweden (Andersson et al., 2004) yield insignificant coefficients. Finally, Rønsen (2004) found a negative impact of day care coverage on childbearing in Finland and Norway. Gauthier (2007) explained this diversity in the obtained results by cross-country differences in childcare quality and opening hours, which are hardly accounted for in statistical analyses, the heterogeneity of parents' needs and preferences as regards childcare as well as the complex relationship between public childcare provision and other social and welfare state institutions. Other researchers attributed the inconsistency of empirical findings to the inability to account for endogeneity of local fertility rates and childcare provision. In fact, in the analysis by Rindfuss et al. (2010) for Norway the positive effects of childcare provision on the transition rates to first, second and third births became stronger after endogeneity of fertility and childcare provision had been controlled.

3.3.1.2 Maternity and Parental Leave Policies

In contrast to childcare, which enables mothers to spend more time at work, maternity and parental leaves give parents the opportunity to withdraw temporarily from economic activity without terminating the employment contract. The main aim of maternity leave is to protect the health of pregnant women as well as mothers right after birth. In EU member states the right to 14-week protection of this kind has been statutory since 1992.[1] Additionally, parents who want to take care of a young child after maternity leave may often take advantage of a parental leave.

The impact of maternity and parental leaves on women's employment and fertility depends on the length of the leave, its flexibility, and related benefit entitlements. Generally, well-paid but short leave provisions are considered to increase mothers' attachment to the labour market and consequently positively affect women's labour supply. There are several reasons for this state of affairs. First, women may be more likely to enter employment if they know they can make use of a leave in case of

[1] Based on the Council Directive 92/85/EEC of 19 October 1992 on the introduction of measures to encourage improvements in the safety and health at work of pregnant workers and workers who have recently given birth or are breastfeeding.

birth. Parental leaves may encourage women to take up a job prior to childbirth particularly effectively if parental leave entitlements depend on the work experience gathered before the decision to have a child (Baker & Milligan, 2005). Second, the leaves shield mothers from potential job loss. Third, short career breaks have little negative effect on women's human capital; mothers returning from such a leave may be still attractive for an employer due to the firm-specific work experience they accumulated prior to the birth. Nonetheless, the longer a mother stays out of work, the greater the loss in her human capital and, consequently, the stronger the wage penalty. Therefore, long leave provisions may in fact have negative impacts on women's labour supply and employment. In this context, flexible leave schemes, allowing for dividing the leave into several parts and combining it with part-time employment and vocational training, can be very advantageous for parents who want to take care of their children over a longer time. Empirical evidence generally supports these theoretical considerations. Studies conducted for the US, where maternity leaves were introduced only in the 1990s and where it was up to employers whether to grant the right to maternity leave to woman or not, indicate that mothers who were offered such a possibility were returning to work faster than women whose employment contract was terminated due to birth (Berger & Waldfogel, 2004; Klerman & Leibowitz, 1999; Waldfogel et al. 1999). Nevertheless, a study by Rønsen and Sundström (2002) conducted for three Nordic countries (Finland, Norway and Sweden) demonstrated that extensions of parental leaves led to a delay in the return rate to work among mothers. Extended parental leaves were also shown to have markedly negative implications for mothers' wages (Beblo & Wolf, 2000, 2002). It is notable, however, that empirical studies may be biased by selection effects as women who are not entitled to parental leaves in the US can be more family-oriented than women who are entitled to parental provisions. Likewise, women who take advantage of longer leaves may differ in their family orientation from women who make use of shorter leaves.

Turning to the second variable of our interest, maternity and parental leave provisions are expected to increase fertility. This is because they allow mothers to withdraw temporarily from the labour market but give them the right to return to the same job at the same wage. In that respect, they lower the opportunity costs of parenting. The empirical studies indeed find some positive effects of parental leave mandates on childbearing, albeit these effects are assessed to be relatively weak (Hoem, 1993; Andersson, 1999; Andersson et al. 2006 for Sweden; Rønsen, 2004 for Finland but not for Norway; Lalive and Zweimüller, 2005 for Austria; Adserà, 2004 – cross-country study on aggregate data).

3.3.1.3 Statutory Paternity Leaves

Although parental leaves are usually available for both parents it is mainly women who make use of them. Therefore, with the aim of equalising women and men in the labour market and care some countries introduced paternity leaves or daddy quotas, reserved only for fathers. Nordic countries pioneered in launching such policies, individualising rights to parental leaves already in the 1990s and offering fathers benefits with high replacement rates (80–90% of the remuneration prior to the leave). Other European countries followed only in recent years. Among them a relatively long paternity leave (2 months) was introduced in Slovenia in 2007. In the majority of other countries paternity leaves are granted usually for maximum 2 weeks (O'Brien, 2009; Moss, 2010).

There has been very little empirical evidence on the effects of paternity rights on women's labour supply or fertility so far as such policies are relatively new. The experience of Nordic countries suggests that fathers are highly interested in making use of their paternity rights, however. In Norway, for instance, around 85% of fathers entitled to daddy quotas, took advantage of it (Lappegard, 2008). Similarly high interest in making use of their paternity rights was observed among fathers in Sweden (Sundström & Duvander, 2002). Take-up rates depend on wage compensation during the leave – in countries where paternity benefits account for high proportion of fathers' wages take-up rates are higher than in countries where replacement rates are low (O'Brien, 2009). Fathers in Norway and Sweden were also found to be more likely to make use of their paternity rights if their female partners were employed which might have a positive impact on women's labour supply at the macro level (Sundström & Duvander, 2002; Lappegard, 2008). Duvander et al. (2006) showed additionally that couples in which men made use of a leave decided more quickly for another child. Other researchers found a positive correlation between the use of paternity rights and fathers' involvement in childcare after the leave has ended (Haas & Hwang, 1999; Brandth & Kvande, 2009). The authors of these studies underline, however, that their results may be biased by selection effects as more family-oriented fathers may be more likely to make use of paternity rights, get involved in care and opt for higher number of children.

3.3.1.4 Income Transfers

There are two types of income transfers that may be directed to parents: child benefits and tax reductions. Both reduce the cost of children, so they are expected to boost fertility. This hypothesis is generally supported by empirical evidence (Ermisch, 1988 for UK; Zhang et al. 1994, Duclos et al. 2001, and Milligan, 2002 for Canada). The magnitude of the effect is, however, small. For instance, based on their analysis of 22 industrialised countries over the period 1970–1990, Gauthier and Hatzius (1997) concluded that an increase in family allowances by 25% would raise fertility by about 0.6% in the short run and by about 4% in the long run. This means an effect of 0.07 children per woman.

The impact of income transfers on employment is less straightforward. Tax reductions are targeted only at those who work. Since they positively affect the income earned by parents, one could expect them to raise women's labour supply as well. By contrast, child benefits increase household non-labour income and as a result may reduce women's labour supply. Most negative effects are expected from means-tested benefits. These benefits are withdrawn once family income exceeds a certain threshold. This may happen after a woman takes up a job. In such a situation, the value-added of entering paid employment is her market wage reduced by the amount of the benefit lost. A rate at which benefits are withdrawn and the wage is taxed away as a person takes up a job or increases the number of working hours is called marginal effective tax rate (METR). Apart from means-tested benefits, METRs are higher in countries with joint rather than separate taxation or countries granting special social benefits to the dependent spouse (OECD, 2003, 2004a). A fall in employment probability with a rise in METR is a well-established finding in empirical research (Hoynes & MaCurdy, 1994 for USA; Fortin et al., 2004 for Canada; Gurgand & Margolis, 2005 for France; Schneider & Uhlendorf, 2004 for Germany; Smith et al., 2003).

3.3.2 Labour Market Structures

Labour market structures are another important dimension of the context influencing fertility and labour market behaviours. Given the topic of our study, we are particularly interested in two characteristics of labour markets: the magnitude of the barriers to labour market entry and the flexibility of work arrangements allowing for a relatively smooth adaptation of working hours to family responsibilities. By influencing women's opportunities to enter the labour market, to maintain employment, and to combine employment with family duties, they affect the intensity of the so-called *structural incompatibilities* between fertility and market work.

The barriers to the labour market entry are strongest in countries with highly regulated labour markets, where strict rules on hiring and firing of workers apply. Such labour markets are often characterised by a strong insider–outsider divide (OECD, 2004b, Aaberge et al., 2005: 131–132; Adserá, 2005). This means that the employed insiders are strongly protected from a job loss, while the employment opportunities for the unemployed outsiders are severely restricted. This leads to high unemployment, particularly among the youth. Another disadvantaged group is women, who are more likely to become outsiders than men, due to child-related career breaks.

High unemployment pressure leads to lower market wages, which together with low perceived chances of finding employment may discourage women from searching for a job and hence reduce their labour supply. In fact, some empirical studies showed that female labour force participation is indeed lower in regions characterised by higher unemployment (Light & Ureta, 1992; Jaumotte, 2003; Aaberge et al., 2005: 149). On the other hand, an increase in men's unemployment may increase women's determination to participate in the labour force. A finding consistent with this hypothesis was established by Jaumotte (2003) who found that labour force participation rates of women are higher in regions displaying higher male unemployment rates.

The effect of unemployment on fertility is ambiguous: By lowering market wages, high regional unemployment lowers the opportunity costs of children. Thus, a temporary spell of women's unemployment can be perceived as a favourable occasion to have children. Such a relationship was, indeed, found in some empirical studies (Kravdal, 2002 for Norway; Schmitt, 2005 for Finland). However, high and persistent unemployment pressure reduces the expected welfare and increases uncertainty and pessimism about the future. As a consequence, this situation may lead to fertility postponement and finally even to lower family size. In this context, Kravdal (2002) found that short-term unemployment (up to 6 months) among women in Norway tends to facilitate entry to parenthood, while longer unemployment spells exert an opposite effect. Negative impact of the country-specific long-term unemployment on first, second, and higher birth risks was also established by Adserà (2005) on a pooled dataset for thirteen EU-15 member states. In a similar vein, high regional unemployment was found to reduce childbearing in the United States (King, 2005), Spain (Noguera et al. 2005), as well as in a joint analysis for Denmark, the Netherlands, France, Italy, and Spain (Aaberge et al., 2005: 150). Nevertheless, some studies provide also evidence of a rise in the birth risk with an increase in unemployment duration (Kreyenfeld, 2001 for Germany; Vikat, 2004 for Finland; Schmitt, 2005 for Germany and UK). This finding may be explained by deterioration of women's human capital caused by long-term non-employment, discouragement by the job search, and low assessment of the chances for success in the labour market.

In order to reduce high unemployment, some countries (e.g., Italy, Spain, Poland) liberalised the law on temporary employment with the prospect of encouraging job creation. The underlying idea was that many of these jobs would become permanent as soon as the new labour market entrants gathered the necessary work experience. However, in countries with strong insider–outsider divide, fixed-term contracts were rarely replaced by permanent ones, and the new regulation only resulted in a high rotation of workers (Adserà, 2004). This additionally intensified the uncertainty among the youth and could have further worsened the conditions for family formation. Nevertheless, the empirical studies do not provide consistent evidence on the influence of temporary employment on fertility – whereas some studies yield negative estimates of the effect (e.g., Adserà, 2004; Baizán, 2005 for Italy and Spain; Kurz et al., 2005 for Germany; Liefbroer, 2005 for the Netherlands), some other indicate the effect to be insignificant (e.g., Baizán, 2005 for UK and Denmark; Francesconi & Golsch, 2005 for UK; Róbert & Bukodi, 2005 for Hungary).

Other features of the labour market, apart from barriers to labour market entry, which are in our area of interest are the flexible work arrangements. In recent decades, many European countries experienced a rapid growth in part-time employment. This form of employment is often perceived to facilitate women's integration into the labour market since it allows for combining market work with parenthood. Empirical studies generally show that the availability of part-time jobs tends to increase female labour force participation (Del Boca, 2002; Jaumotte, 2003; Aaberge et al., 2005). Similarly, women working part-time are generally more likely to give birth (Liefbroer & Corijn, 1999 for the Netherlands and Flanders; Corijn,

2001 for Flanders; Baizán, 2005 for Italy, Spain and UK; King, 2005 for USA; Liefbroer, 2005 for the Netherlands). Nevertheless, some studies find no impact of part-time employment on childbearing (Kreyenfeld, 2001, 2005 for Germany; Olah, 2003 for Sweden and Hungary; Baizán, 2005 for Denmark). According to Del Boca et al. (2009) it is not only the availability of part-time jobs that matters but also their quality, assessed on the degree of job protection, hourly wages, and access to social benefits. By analysing jointly seven EU countries, the authors compared fertility behaviours of part-timers earning hourly wages equivalent to those obtained in full-time positions to fertility behaviours of part-timers receiving lower remuneration. They concluded that only well-paid part-time jobs (i.e., those that pay similar hourly wages to full-time jobs) facilitate childbearing. Poor-quality jobs do not significantly increase the birth risk. Similar conclusion was drawn by Ariza et al. (2005) who compared childbearing behaviours of women employed full-time and part-time in eleven European countries and found that part-time schedules enhance fertility only in Belgium, Germany, Italy, Ireland, and the Netherlands, but not in Denmark, France, Greece, Portugal, Spain nor the United Kingdom.

3.3.3 Social Norms for Women's Roles

Apart from family policies and labour market structures, individual behaviour is also influenced by values and ideals for the 'correct' division of labour between women and men which dominate in a given society (Pfau-Effinger, 1998). By defining who should work and who should take care of children, they determine the intensity of the *cultural incompatibilities* between fertility and paid employment. Cultural incompatibilities are highest in the societies displaying low acceptance of mothers' employment, particularly mothers of small children. In these societies, therefore, women's labour supply is expected to be the lowest. Furthermore, where women are expected to stay at home with children while their earnings could contribute substantially to household income (because of low wages of men or high human capital of women), the opportunity costs of children will be large. As a result, women may eschew childbearing in order to participate in the labour force.

Empirical evidence on the impact of values and norms for working mothers on fertility and women's employment is scarce. Out of the few researchers who addressed this topic were de Laat and Sevilla Sanz (2006). Using the 1994 International Social Survey Programme, they first constructed an egalitarian index for eleven OECD countries. The index was based on respondents' responses to ten statements capturing the attitudes towards the division of household chores. Applying regression techniques they found that women living in countries with more egalitarian attitudes tended to have more children and were more likely to participate in the labour force. A similar finding, but only with respect to one of our variables of interest, was established by Algan and Cahuc (2006). The study was conducted for nineteen OECD countries. The attitudes towards working mothers were measured using the World Value Survey. Based on their macro-level regression model, the authors concluded that women's employment rate was higher in countries where there was a larger percentage of persons opposing the statement 'When jobs are scarce, men should have job priority over women'.

3.3.4 Living Standards

Living standards comprise the last dimension of the context we find relevant for studying fertility and labour market decisions. They determine the extent to which women are free to decide to have a certain number of children and to allocate their time between paid work, household duties and hobbies without being constrained by their economic position. In less affluent societies or during economic slowdown, women's work may be perceived as an important source of household income. Hence, low living standards are expected to increase women's labour supply. The empirical research provides findings largely consistent with this hypothesis (Colombino & Di Tommaso, 1996, Di Tommaso, 1999, Del Boca et al., 2005 for Italy; Shaw, 1994 and Del Boca et al., 2005 for UK; Hotz & Miller, 1988, Moffit, 1984, Macunovich, 1996, Taniguchi & Rosenfeld, 2002, and Budig, 2003 for USA).

The impact of living standards on fertility is less clear as parents may decide to invest their additional income in increasing the quality of the children they have instead of bearing additional children (Becker & Lewis, 1973). On the other hand, however, it is likely that couples living in poorer economic conditions fail to realise their fertility intentions due to economic constraints. If this is the case, one may argue that in poorer societies or countries experiencing economic slowdown, women's paid work might even be perceived as a pre-condition to family formation. Consistently with this view, Macunovich (1996) showed that, even in the U.S. context, the income effect of women's paid work on fertility tends to suppress the price effect during the times of economic slowdown, when husband's earnings are insufficient to satisfy the couple's material aspirations. Using similar arguments Hoem (2000) and Andersson (2000, 2002) explained the decline in Swedish fertility in the first half of the 1990s when Sweden was hit by economic recession and female unemployment increased markedly. Other researchers referred to the negative effect of economic slowdown or even crisis on fertility while explaining fertility decline in CEE countries right after the collapse of state socialism (Kotowska, 1999; Rychtarikova, 1999, 2000; Macura, 2000; Kotowska et al. 2008). In that context, by applying regression techniques to the macro-level data for 11 post-socialist countries, Macura (2000) showed that the deterioration in economic activity and decline in household income in that part of Europe were partly responsible for a decline in period fertility rates. A more in-depth individual-level analysis conducted by Billingsley (2010) showed that downward occupational mobility and a job loss experienced by Russian women in the 1990s led them to postpone transition to second birth.

3.3.5 *Interplay of Contextual Dimensions*

On the whole, the impacts of context on childbearing and women's labour market behaviours are well documented. The empirical studies in this field show that under certain institutional conditions (better childcare provision, short and flexible parental leave schemes, income transfers that do not impose high METRs), structural conditions (low barriers to the labour market entry, high flexibility of work arrangements), and cultural conditions (positive attitudes towards mothers' work) the price effect can be suppressed. This in fact means lower incompatibilities between fertility and women's work and hence higher fertility and women's labour supply. At the same time, living standards affect the income effect. The latter increases with a worsening of the economic situation in a country or the financial situation of a household.

Notwithstanding, some of the reviewed studies report insignificant impacts of the contextual elements on fertility and women's labour supply; sometimes, they even provide evidence that contradicts our expectations. This does not necessarily mean a failure of the theory to predict individual behaviours. According to Neyer (2006) and Neyer and Andersson (2008), it is possible that family and labour market policies, social norms, and living standards not only influence fertility and employment, but also interact with each other. In support of this argument, Neyer and Anderson (2008) gave as an example the reform of the Swedish parental leave system introduced in the mid-1980s. The so-called speed-premium policy conditioned women's right to preserving the parental leave benefit on giving birth to a subsequent child within a restricted period of time after a previous delivery. The introduction of the policy resulted in a substantial shortening of the birth intervals and in an increase in second and higher order birth intensities in the 1980s. In the following decade, however, when Sweden was hit by an economic recession, the total fertility rate fell dramatically although the speed-premium was still in force. This did not mean that the policy failed, but its impact was mitigated by worsening employment prospects among women. Since the level of a parental leave benefit in Sweden was tightly linked to women's earnings prior to birth, a decrease in employment resulted in the shrinkage of the population covered by the speed-premium policy. Interestingly, there was no decline in fertility rate in Finland at that time, although the country also experienced a severe worsening of economic conditions. This phenomenon is explained by an introduction of home-care allowances paid to parents who preferred to take care of a child themselves instead of using public services (Vikat, 2004; Neyer, 2006; Neyer & Andersson, 2008). These allowances could have been used by unemployed women as a partial compensation for the lost earnings in the period of limited employment opportunities. These two examples demonstrate that policies interact with economic developments and may bring different results under different conditions. Based on this finding, Neyer (2006) concluded that a mix of certain welfare-state policies, gender relations and labour-market structures might be much more conducive to fertility and women's labour supply than explicitly fertility-focused policies.

3.4 The Role of Preferences

Macro-contextual opportunities and restrictions are only one of the two components of decision-making, the one which was well described and operationalised within the price-of-time model. The other component are preferences. This component of human behaviour has so far been largely ignored by economists working in the field of fertility and women's labour supply. Preferences were assumed to be given and identically distributed across women and all efforts to explain differences in fertility behaviours were made by looking into differences in the contextual opportunities and constraints. As a result, motivational structures that in sociological and psychological research occupy a central place have been collapsed into a one-dimensional concept of utility. On the one hand, this approach has been widely accepted, if not strongly recommended, in the economic community: 'The economist has little to say about the formation of wants; this is the province of the psychologist. The economist's task is to trace the consequences of a given set of wants' (Friedman, 1962: 13). On the other hand, the approach received a strong criticism stemming not only from researchers representing other disciplines, but also from economists (Easterlin, 1976; Meeker, 1980; Robinson & Harbison, 1980; Bagozzi & van Loo, 1980, 1991; Siegers, 1991; Turchi, 1991; Pollak & Watkins, 1993; de Bruijn, 1999). It was argued that a failure to recognise the heterogeneity and nature of human preferences leads to wrong predictions of individual behaviour, particularly as regards fertility.

One of the few economists who recognised the role of preferences was Easterlin. In his work, he concentrated basically on material aspirations (Easterlin, 1976, 1980). His theoretical model of fertility behaviour, known as the 'relative income' model, presupposes that a couple's willingness to have children depends on their outlook with regard to reaching desired living standards. The main advantage of his approach over the price-of-time model is the assertion that material aspirations are not given but formed during the adolescence by experience of certain living standards at the parental home. If the aspirations can be easily met, the couple can afford the desired number of children. By contrast, a failure to reach the demanded standard of living leads to fertility postponement. Nonetheless, Easterlin's model failed to predict fertility behaviour in empirical tests (Ermisch, 1979; Pampel & Peters, 1995; Soja, 2005). One of the major drawbacks of this approach was its concentration on men's role in the labour market, neglecting the economic role of women.

Given the advantages and disadvantages of these two apparently competing academic perspectives, the 'relative income' and the 'price of time', Macunovich (1996) proposed to combine them into one theoretical framework. She assumed that a couple maximises its utility from a certain combination of consumptions goods and number of children of a given quality subject to the household's *relative* income. Consequently, in her theoretical model, the demand for children depends on the price of the woman's time and the household's material aspirations, proxied by the living standards experienced at the parental home.

Macunovich applied this theoretical model to explain the changes in fertility and female labour force participation in the United States in the years 1969–1993. The couple's material aspirations were measured at the aggregate level as the real average annual income of all families with at least one child under age 18 and with a head of household aged 45–54. The resulting empirical models had a very strong explanatory power.[2] They provided evidence that the extent to which men's wages are sufficient to meet the financial aspirations of the partners is largely decisive for women's fertility and labour market behaviours. A decline in male earnings relative to the desired living standards led females to resume economic activity. At the same time, the income effect of women's wages on fertility was increasing, outweighing the price effect. On the contrary, when the income earned by men was sufficient to reach the desired standard of living, the income effect of women's wages was reasonably lower and dominated by the price effect.

The model proposed by Macunovich constitutes an important extension of the classic price-of-time model as it relates childbearing decisions not only to the absolute income of the couple but also to the extent to which the income satisfies couple's material aspirations. Nevertheless, the shortcoming of the proposed approach is that it focuses solely on financial needs, disregarding the fact that human behaviour can be driven by a whole variety of human motives. Apart from the safety needs (a category which encompasses material aspirations) these motives can be physiological, belongingness and love, self-esteem, and self-actualisation. According to the theory of human motivation proposed by Maslow (1943, 1954) all these needs are organised in a hierarchical order with safety needs at a higher level than physiological needs. The needs that are higher in the hierarchy begin to drive individual behaviour once the lower order needs have been satisfied to a sufficient degree. Thus, once material aspirations are met, women may strive for self-esteem and self-actualisation, and these new motives will determine their childbearing and employment decisions, which may bring results contrary to the predictions of Macunovich's model. This might be particularly the case in the current Western societies where lower order needs have become largely met and individuals may aim at satisfying postmaterial needs (Inglehart, 1977, 1990). An increase in the importance of post-materialistic values is also to be expected in the former post-socialist countries of Central and Eastern Europe along with an improvement in living standards. At the beginning of the twenty-first century, however, they were still less widespread there than in the West (Kowalska & Wróblewska, 2008).

Against this background, Willekens (1991) developed a concept of *career orientations*. His underlying idea was that each person has a certain knowledge of the world and certain expectations about the sequence of events throughout life. Each person is also led by certain motives. This constitutes a basis upon which a

---

[2]The models explain over 90% of the variation in the labour force participation of women. Similarly strong explanatory power is achieved in fertility models.

person's life goals are formed. A predisposition to engage in certain activities in order to reach the life goals is called a career orientation. The career orientation of an adult can be quite stable since it is partly determined genetically and to some extent formed through experience in childhood and adolescence. Nevertheless, the orientation can also undergo certain modifications as an adult acquires new knowledge and develops new perceptions. The role of career orientation is to build a hierarchy of a person's life domains. The hierarchy is required for an individual to allocate resources in a proper way. Activities that are less important for achieving the person's life goals receive fewer resources (time and energy). For example, if the family takes a lower place in the hierarchy than employment, family planning is subordinate to the work schedule. In this study, we use the concept of career orientation when referring to situations in which women's basic (physiological and safety) needs are met.

Consistently with the concept of career orientation, Hakim divided women into three categories, differing in the level of family and work orientations (Hakim, 2000). *Family-centred* women give priority to marriage and motherhood. They tend to have big families and try to avoid employment unless they experience financial problems. By contrast, *work-centred* women are highly oriented to employment, invest continuously in their human capital, and have children only if these do not hamper their professional careers. The last group consists of *adaptive women*. Women of this type want to combine children with employment, without prioritizing either. They are over-represented in female-dominated occupations, in the public sector, and in part-time jobs. This group of women is most numerous in Hakim's view, accounting for about 40–80% of all women, whereas the other two groups constitute around 10–30% each.

This theoretical model, known under the term Preference Theory, attracted a great deal of interest but also critics in demographic and sociological literature. In general, empirical studies found the distribution of work-family preferences to resemble the distribution proposed by Hakim (e.g. Vitali et al., 2010). Nevertheless, the causal link between preferences and behaviours was questioned and some researchers even considered the theory as simplistic, arguing that differences in employment choices cannot be simply explained by the fact that the choices are made by different types of women (Crompton & Harris, 1998; McRae, 2003). Instead, one should look into contextual factors that shape these preferences since 'preferences may shape choices, but they do not [...] determine them' (Crompton & Harris, 1998: 131). We fully agree with these critical views that heterogeneity in preferences does not fully explain heterogeneity in behaviours. Consistently with the rational choice model we see final choices as a product of women's preferences and contextual opportunities and restrictions. In our view, neglecting one of these components of decision-making weakens the explanatory power of models explaining women's fertility and employment behaviours. Therefore, throughout this book we will refer to the concept of work and family orientations and will underline their importance for explaining women's choices additionally to the importance of contextual factors.

3.5 Measurement Problems and Selection Effects

Women of certain work-family preferences and acting in the environment that offers them certain opportunities but also imposes certain restrictions will develop strategies to deal with incompatibilities between fertility and market work in order to maximise their preferences. These strategies imply complete abandonment or temporary termination of one career in favour of the other, reduced involvement in one career as well as changes in the sequence and timing of events pertaining to each career. The choice of a strategy depends on woman's orientation towards family and paid work. For instance, women who do not plan to have children and who are oriented at work career may choose jobs with steep income profiles and promotion ladders, while women who are strongly family-centred may exit employment before the planned conception. Those who aim at combining the two careers may decide to take up a stable job which offers reasonable income security with a view to have a child in the future. They may also develop strategies that allow them to shorten career breaks between subsequent births, by either returning to work quickly after first birth or by deciding to have the second child right after the first (Ni Bhrolchain, 1986a, 1986b). All these examples tell us that women may adjust their current fertility (employment) behaviour to their future employment (fertility) plans. As a result, the observed sequence of fertility and employment outcomes does not represent a causal order. This poses a major difficulty to modelling fertility and employment behaviours if women's plans and orientations are unobserved by researchers which is often the case (Bernhardt, 1993; Ni Bhrolchain, 1993). As a result selection effects arise and they lead to a bias of the estimates of the conflict between childbearing and market work.

There might be two types of selection effect: negative (adverse) and positive. *Negative selection* refers to the situation in which women give up one activity (employment or childbearing) with the prospect of getting involved in the other. For instance, work-oriented women will tend to abandon having children since they plan to be heavily involved in economic activity, whereas the family-oriented will rather withdraw from employment prior to conception with a plan to have a child. By contrast, *positive selection* implies that women want to combine employment and childbearing and for this reason will undertake one activity (employment or childbearing) with a plan to get involved in the other in the future. Hence, if they expect that having children before entering a professional career will impede their chances in the labour market, they will tend to find a job first and will realise their fertility intentions only after their situation in the labour market is stable enough, i.e., when they have a job they can return to after birth. Positive selection is also likely to occur if material aspirations of women are not accounted for in empirical models.

The inability to establish a causal relationship between fertility and women's employment has been troubling researchers for the last three decades (Waite & Stolzenberg, 1976; Weller, 1977; Smith-Lovin & Tickamyer, 1978; Cramer, 1980; Lehrer & Nerlove, 1986; Klijzing, Siegers, J., Keilman, N., & Groot, 1988; Felmlee, 1993; Budig, 2003; Engelhardt et al., 2004; Schröder, 2005). Development of dynamic models, improved access to longitudinal data, and advancement in modelling techniques (including event history analysis) raised a hope of understanding the causal mechanism underlying fertility and women's labour market decisions. Nevertheless, the difficulty still lies in the unavailability of appropriate data (Bernhardt, 1993; Ni Bhrolcháin, 1993). If we had longitudinal data fully describing women's material aspirations, their orientation towards paid work and childbearing and any other women's plans regarding fertility and employment, using the simple event history model, we could probably easily measure the price and income effects, net of all other intervening factors. Such data, however, are currently unavailable. Attempts should be undertaken to make up for this deficiency. Interdisciplinary research could probably help in finding the way to a better measurement of human motives, while certain questions could be introduced into questionnaires to collect the necessary data. Such data, however, should be available from panel surveys, and this takes time. For the time being, other solutions need to be implemented. Among them dynamic models in combination with advanced statistical techniques that allow for capturing the unobserved factors have become more and more acceptable and widespread solution in social science.

3.6 Theoretical Framework: Summary and Implications for the Study

The objective of this study is to explore interdependencies between fertility and women's labour supply. For that purpose, we follow the recommendation of methodological individualism and take our empirical analyses down to the micro-level. Hence, our primary subject of investigation is women and the decisions they make. In order to operationalise the process of decision-making, we adopt the version of price-of-time model modified by Macunovich (1996). The modification lies in replacing the household's total income against which the household's utility is maximised with the relative income. According to this model women allocate their time between home production (including care) and market work by maximising the utility of the two activities. Their choice is constrained by the limited amount of financial resources they possess and the extent to which these resources meet their material aspirations. The final decision depends on the complex interplay between two effects: the price effect and the income effect. The former represents a conflict between childrearing and paid work. It is determined by the level of opportunity costs of parenting and hence implies that women's involvement in the labour market lowers the demand for children. The income effect operates in the opposite direction. *Disentangling the impact of the price effect from the income effect is an important step in understanding women's fertility and employment behaviours.*

The magnitude of both effects depends on the context in which fertility and employment decisions are made. Besides the micro-level context (household structure, household's economic situation) the macro-context constitutes an important determinant of women's choices. Four dimensions of the macro-context are considered to be particularly relevant for childbearing and employment decisions: institutional (family policies), structural (labour market structures), cultural (gender norms), and economic (living standards). The first three influence the magnitude of the price effect, whereas the latter affects the income effect. On the whole, the impacts of all contextual dimensions on childbearing and women's labour market behaviours are well documented in the literature. The majority of the reviewed empirical findings suggest that under certain institutional (better childcare provision, short and flexible parental leave schemes, paternity leaves, income transfers that do not impose high METRs), structural (low barriers to the labour market entry, high flexibility of work arrangements), and cultural conditions (positive attitudes towards mothers' work), the price effect can be suppressed. This gives an opportunity for an increase in fertility and women's labour supply. The income effect increases with a worsening of the living standards. Furthermore, it is notable that family and labour market policies, social norms, and living standards not only influence fertility and labour supply, but also interact with each other. *Identifying the influence of the context and its dimensions on fertility and women's labour supply is important for understanding the interdependencies between fertility and women's labour supply and consequently for designing effective public policies.*

Apart from the context, fertility and employment decisions are also determined by women's orientation towards family and paid work. The economic theory has so far accounted little for the variation in preferences (particularly for those referring to higher order needs), which is one of the reasons why it has been subjected to strong criticism in the recent two decades. Three issues need to be raised at that point. First, each woman has certain ideals of her involvement in paid work and the number of her children. Provided she has reached her desired family size, she has no reason to have a(nother) child, even if her income has unexpectedly increased. Second, it is doubtful that women's behaviours are only driven by material aspirations. It has been well documented in psychological research that once these lower-order needs are satisfied, women start to strive for self-esteem and self-realisation. The impact of the higher order needs on individual behaviour might be particularly important in post-modern societies. Third, women do differ in their orientations towards family and paid work, and these orientations play an important role in assessing the magnitude of the opportunity costs. Hence, the opportunity costs of having children are larger for a work-oriented woman than for a family-oriented one even if they earn the same wages and act in the same environment. *Accounting for women's orientations towards employment and family is another important step in understanding the interdependencies between fertility and women's work.*

Unfortunately, data on material aspirations as well as family and work orientations of women are often unobservable to researchers. This constitutes a serious obstacle to empirical research on the interdependencies between fertility and women's labour supply. The reason is that the observed sequence of events may not represent a causal order. For instance, the fact that labour force exit precedes birth does not necessarily mean that economic inactivity triggers childbearing. Given that women think prospectively and anticipate consequences of their actions, it is equally likely that the decision to have a child is made prior to the decision to terminate labour force participation. Such behaviour may be typical of family-oriented women for whom economic inactivity or professions with flat earning profiles or low advancement opportunities are most conducive to realising their fertility intentions. By contrast, work-oriented women, who decide not to have children (or to have only one child), may from the beginning of their employment careers choose professions with steep earning profiles and steep promotion ladders. Such inclination, to give up one activity (employment or childbearing) with a prospect of getting involved in the other, is called negative (adverse) selection. In contemporary advanced societies, positive selection is, however, more likely to be in force. This is due to the predominance of the adaptive women and the fact that some of the family-centred women work for pay. These women are interested in combining childbearing with paid work and hence may decide to enter the labour force before the planned conception. Altogether, this implies that women may select themselves into one activity before taking up the other and this effect is often not directly observed by a researcher. *Exploring the mechanism that drives this selection effect is another important step in understanding the interdependencies between fertility and women's labour supply.*

Summing up, the theoretical framework presented in this chapter lists four conditions for understanding the interdependencies between fertility and women's labour supply:

1. to disentangle the price effect from the income effect;
2. to control for the impacts of the context on fertility and women's labour supply;
3. to control for work- and family-orientations;
4. if data shortcomings make it impossible to account for some of the factors listed in conditions 1–3, then selection effects might occur. Exploring these selection effects may provide valuable information for understanding the interdependencies between childbearing and women's labour force participation.

In the following chapters, we follow these four conditions. In Chapters 4 and 5 we explore the impacts of the context on fertility and women's economic activity. Additionally, we review the existing studies on the topic and assess them critically in the light of this theoretical framework. In Chapter 6, using the data for Poland, we try to make up for the shortcomings of the available empirical studies. As expected, we lack data on women's material aspirations as well as their family and work orientations. As a response to this problem, we propose to use multi-process hazard model to take the selection effects into account.

Chapter 4
Macro-Context and Its Cross-Country Variation

4.1 Introduction

The context is a multi-dimensional and multi-level 'structure of institutions that embody information about opportunities and restrictions, consequences and expectations, rights and duties, incentives and sanctions, models, guidelines, and definitions of the world' (de Bruijn, 1999: 21). This information is continuously transmitted to individuals and defines the choice options they face. As described in Chapter 3 four dimensions of the macro-context are considered relevant to women's fertility and employment decisions: institutional (family policies), structural (labour market structures), cultural (gender norms), and economic (living standards). The first three influence the magnitude of the price effect, producing the so-called institutional, structural and cultural incompatibilities between childbearing and market work. The intensity of these incompatibilities depends on the extent to which mothers' work is socially accepted and institutionally supported and to which the labour market is prepared to accommodate female labour. The fourth dimension of the context affects the income effect.

This chapter provides the reader with an overview of the differences in the macro-context relevant for fertility and women's employment decisions across the EU member states, Norway, and Switzerland in the second half of the 2000s. First, we measure the intensity of the institutional, structural, and cultural incompatibilities between women's employment and fertility and provide a ranking of countries with respect to the conditions offered to women for combining the two activities. Second, we discuss the cross-country differences in the potential income effect. The indicators we present in this Chapter refer to the second half of the 2000s. We admit it would be ideally to discuss the conditions for work and family reconciliation over the longer time span, reaching back to the 1970s for Western Europe and 1990s for CEE. It would allow us to cover the time period of a changing cross-country correlation between LFP and TFR in Western Europe, decline in LFP and TFR in CEE in the 1990s as well as recent improvements in fertility in all EU member states. Time series data on contextual indicators of high quality are not available, however, especially the policy indicators. Therefore, our analysis is constrained to the most

A. Matysiak, *Interdependencies Between Fertility and Women's Labour Supply*, European Studies of Population 17, DOI 10.1007/978-94-007-1284-3_4,

recent years. Further studies are needed in the future to extend the analysis to the 1990s and 1980s.

The chapter is organised as follows. Sections 4.2, 4.3, 4.4, and 4.5 present the cross-country differences in family policies, labour market structures, cultural settings, and living standards, respectively. In Sections 4.2, 4.3, and 4.4 we build indicators that assess the magnitude of the potential institutional, structural and cultural incompatibilities between work and family and present country rankings with respect to each of them. Section 4.5 has rather a descriptive character and discusses the cross-country differences in living standards as well as their implications for women's motivation to work in the market. Finally, Section 4.6 provides a summary of our findings and a final ranking of countries analysed with respect to the potential work-family incompatibilities imposed by the macro-context in general (accounting for its three dimensions).

4.2 Family Policies

Family policies govern the rules of absence from the labour market as well as the access to social benefits and services. By offering women certain conditions for work and family reconciliation, they define the intensity of the institutional incompatibilities between the two activities. Not surprisingly has the cross-country variation in family policies been often referred to in discussions on the interrelationship between fertility and women's labour supply. These discussions have been so far largely centred on the Western countries and resulted in several country typologies with respect to the prevailing family policy models. In this section we briefly summarise the major conclusions drawn from this discussion (Section 4.2.1) and provide some information on the change in family policy model in CEE countries after the collapse of the socialist system (Section 4.2.2). Finally, we build a series of policy indicators that allow us to rank the old as well as the new EU member states plus Norway and Switzerland with respect to the intensity of institutional incompatibilities between women's employment and fertility (Section 4.2.3).

4.2.1 Western Countries – Overview of the Existing Welfare State Typologies

Family policies constitute an integral part of welfare policies and it is generally acknowledged in the literature that their impact on fertility and women's labour supply should not be discussed without considering the general organisation of the welfare-state setup (Neyer, 2006; Neyer & Andersson, 2008). Therefore, the Esping-Andersen's (1990, 1999) typology of welfare states into liberal (Anglo-Saxon countries), conservative (Continental and Southern Europe), and social-democratic (Nordic countries) represents one of the most important points of reference in the discussion on the differences in family policy models across the Western countries.

This typology was originally based on three dimensions characterising the welfare state: the relationship between the state and the market in providing welfare, the effect of policies on social stratification, and the level of 'de-commodification' – in other words, the extent to which the welfare state weakens a person's reliance on the market to afford a livelihood. After the critics of feminist scholars for proposing typology which is 'gender-blind' and 'inadequate for understanding the effects of state social provision on all workers' (Orloff, 1993: 317) Esping-Andersen introduced another dimension into his analysis – a de-familisation. It measures the extent to which welfare policies lessen individuals' dependence on the family. Adding this new dimension did enrich the discussion on welfare state but did not provide sufficient arguments to the father of the 'welfare triad' for changing the classification (Esping-Andersen, 1999: 94). For feminist scholars, on the contrary, accounting for the interaction between family policies and gender relations does modify the typology as the principles governing family policies can differ from principles underpinning welfare state policies. As a result, there emerged several alternative typologies of welfare states dealing explicitly with family policies and gender issues (Lewis & Ostner, 1995; Anttonen & Sipilä, 1996; Gauthier, 1996; Gornick et al. 1997; Letablier, 1998; Trifiletti, 1999; Korpi, 2000; Bettio & Platenga, 2004). The so-called family-policy, gender, or care regimes were distinguished on the basis of an analysis of the way the policies regulate partnership and parenthood, in particular on the availability of social services, maternity and parental leave provisions (duration, coverage, related benefits), and the income transfers directed to families. In most cases, these classifications correspond to the one proposed by Esping-Andersen (1990), although some exceptions occurring repeatedly throughout the works are also to be noticed.

An overview of the alternative typologies[1] shows that the Nordic countries consistently score highest in terms of their support to working mothers (e.g., Korpi, 2000: 147) and are often classified together (Lewis & Ostner, 1995; Anttonen & Sipilä, 1996; Gauthier, 1996; Letablier, 1998; Korpi, 2000; Bettio & Platenga, 2004). An anomaly in this group is Finland, due to its weaker provision of public childcare and longer parental leave provisions for mothers. The Scandinavian countries progressed very quickly with expanding the system of public childcare of high quality and currently are characterised by one of the best childcare arrangements for children of all ages in Europe. Well-developed childcare facilities are also to be found in France and Belgium. A different ideology underlies childcare provision in these two groups, however, which usually led researchers to classify them separately (Anttonen & Sipilä, 1996; Gauthier, 1996; Letablier, 1998; Bettio & Platenga, 2004). In the Nordic countries, family policies are mainly oriented at assuring gender equality in care and employment. As a result these countries are pioneers in introducing income-based parental leave benefits, which encourage individuals to

[1] Here we present only the major conclusions drawn from the review of the alternative typologies. More comprehensive overview of these typologies can be found in Meulders and O'Dorchai (2008) and Muszyńska (2007: 113–116).

establish a strong position in the labour market before entering parenthood, as well as in individualising rights to family benefits. Daddy quotas and paternity leaves, launched in the 1990s, were an outstanding feature of the Nordic family policy model for the whole decade and only recently have these solutions been slowly introduced in other European countries (O'Brien, 2009).

By contrast, to Nordic countries in France and Belgium low fertility is the main concern and family policies have mainly a pro-family and pro-natalist character (Gauthier, 1996: 203–204; Korpi, 2000: 147). Despite the very good public childcare provision these two countries lag behind Scandinavia as far as the solutions encouraging fathers to participate in childcare are concerned. France is additionally characterised by relatively high marginal effective tax rates imposed on a dependant spouse that discourages (full-time) employment of a secondary earner (OECD, 2001, 2003, 2004a). The remaining countries of the conservative welfare regime score much lower as regards support to the reconciliation of work and parenthood (Korpi, 2000: 147). The system of public childcare, particularly for the youngest children, is far worse developed there and in some countries, like Germany, the opening hours of public childcare slots are short and inflexible. Parental leave regulations differ across these countries, ranging from long leaves in Austria and Germany to short in the Netherlands and the Southern European countries. The common feature of these schemes is the low wage compensation (parental benefits are often means-tested and flat rate), although in recent years some countries have undertaken reforms in that respect (particularly Germany). Furthermore, Germany stands out in the conservative welfare regime as regards the exceptionally high marginal effective tax rates it imposes on dependant spouses (OECD, 2001, 2003, 2004a).

Among countries classified to the conservative welfare regime the support for working mothers is the weakest in the Mediterranean region. The family-policy model of Southern Europe is based on the conviction that families are the most relevant source of social support and they rarely fail. This strong familialism explains the residual nature of the Southern European family policy model. For this reason, the Mediterranean countries were often grouped separately from the Continental Europe in family policy typologies (Anttonen & Sipilä, 1996; Gornick et al. 1997; Letablier, 1998; Trifiletti, 1999; Bettio & Platenga, 2004). Indeed, the supply of care services in the Southern Europe is strongly limited (except for pre-school children in Italy and Spain), and informal care plays an important role there (Bettio & Platenga, 2004). The Mediterranean countries are also characterised by extremely low family allowances and residual parental leave schemes, compared to the Continental Europe (Gauthier, 1996: 167).

Very low support for working mothers is also provided in countries classified by Esping-Andersen as liberal. However, the ideology underlying this family-policy model is different there than in the Southern Europe. In the Anglo-Saxon countries it is rather the market than the family individuals are deemed to rely on and the state intervenes only when the market fails. For this reason, these countries were often considered separately in typologies of family policy models (Gauthier, 1996; Gornick et al., 1997; Korpi, 2000).

4.2.2 Central and Eastern European Countries

The family policy models in the Western countries have been evolving for a long time and are widely documented in the literature. The situation in the CEE, to which we now turn, is much less clear. This is because the family policy model in this part of Europe has been undergoing major changes since the breakdown of state socialism. Many decisions during the early phases of the transformation process were made under financial pressure, and there were neither sufficient time nor resources for creating long-term family policy strategies. Reforms were often a result of 'a compromise based on the institutional legacy of the old regime, the advice of international agencies, and the need for legitimacy and support from the middle class' (Rostgaard, 2004: 33). It is thus difficult to state whether CEE is following any of the Western European policy models or it is developing its own. It is also not clear whether all CEE countries will follow the same path or the heterogeneity within the group will increase over time. In the later passages of this Section we will demonstrate that the latter scenario seems to be more likely. Before, we outline major changes in the policies that were introduced after the breakdown of socialist regime.

During the period of state socialism, policies were strongly directed at forcing high levels of women's employment, so they strongly facilitated reconciliation of work and family. Well-developed public care arrangements for pre-schoolers and children of school age were designed to serve this goal. The enrolment rates in kindergartens at the end of the 1980s were as high as 80–90% (Rostgaard, 2004), and in East Germany even reached 100% (Matysiak & Steinmetz, 2008). Only Poland and Latvia lagged behind in that respect, with enrolment rates of around 50%. As regards younger children, a more traditional home care-based view prevailed, however. Consequently only 5–16% of under-threes, depending on the country, attended crèches at that time (again East Germany constituted an exception with a coverage rate of 80% in 1989). The low provision of public care services for the young was compensated by the extended parental leave system (with 3-year long leaves) and strong job guarantees. Since there was no competition in the labour market, the return to employment after birth was relatively easy. Nevertheless, parental leave was only available for women and hence it was they, not the fathers, who were perceived as the main care providers. Finally, the family policy model under state socialism was characterised by relatively generous social benefits with the entitlements rights tightly linked to employment (Rostgaard, 2004).

The financial constraints that were faced by all governments in the transforming economies led to major changes in this socialist family policy model. The results were substantial cuts in the provision of services and social benefits. The number of places in crèches and kindergartens fell substantially and the state subsidies for after-school care services were abandoned in the majority of the CEE countries (Muszyńska, 2007: 122). On top of that, public childcare institutions shifted some of the childcare costs to parents (around 2–15% of the average monthly wages, depending on the country (Rostgaard, 2004; OECD Family Database, 2004)). Currently, not more than 10% of children aged 0–2 attends crèches in that part of Europe, except for Estonia and Slovenia where these proportions exceed 30% (OECD Family Database, 2006). The enrolment rates in kindergartens are higher, 70–85%, with only Poland and Lithuania lagging behind the rest of the post-socialist countries in that respect (around 60%). Such enrolment rates are typical for the conservative and liberal welfare states. Gradually over the 1990s the governments were withdrawing their support to families granted in form of cash benefits. These became often means-tested, and their level deteriorated from 10–13% to below 7% of the average wages (Rostgaard, 2004). Only in recent years did some of the CEE countries adopt a more universal approach in the entitlement rights to family benefits (Estonia, Hungary, Latvia, Lithuania, and Romania). Not much has changed as regards parental leave legislation. The leaves remained long: in Czech Republic, Estonia, Slovakia and Poland they amount to three years, in Hungary and Lithuania to two years (OECD Family Database, 2006). Only in Latvia and Slovenia parents are entitled to a parental leave of maximum one year. Clear cross-country differences emerge, however, as regards the parental leave benefits: while Estonia, Hungary, Lithuania and Slovenia offer income-based parental benefits for at least part of the leave, the benefits granted in Czech Republic, Slovakia and Poland are based on a flat rate (and in the latter country they are additionally means-tested) (OECD Family Database, 2006). Paternity leaves are a novelty in the CEE region. By 2006 five of the post-socialist countries had statutory paternity leave entitlements lasting 1–3 weeks. These countries were Estonia, Hungary, Latvia, Lithuania and Slovenia.

To conclude, the family policy model emerging in the CEE in the 1990s was a mix of the conservative welfare state model, typical of the socialist past, and the liberal regime, whose elements were introduced during the transformation process (Rostgaard, 2004). Little attention was paid to easing the conflict between fertility and paid employment. The eradication of public childcare facilities together with the generous parental leave provision in terms of the leave duration suggested instead a shift towards support of the traditional male breadwinner model (Pascall & Manning, 2000; Pascall & Lewis, 2004). In recent years, however, clear cross-country differences started to emerge in the CEE family policy models. While Czech Republic, Slovakia and Poland seem to follow the conservative path, supporting the traditional male breadwinner model, the Baltic countries, Hungary, and Slovenia are introducing policy measures which are more oriented towards supporting employment of mothers and encouraging fathers to participate in childcare.

4.2.3 Institutional Incompatibilities Between Women's Employment and Childbearing in Europe: Country Ranking

This brief overview of the family policy models in Europe reveals clearly distinct approaches of policy makers to supporting employment of mothers and helping couples in realising their fertility intentions. As a result, the institutional incompatibilities between women's employment and childbearing differ across the European countries. In this Section we develop a quantitative index measuring the intensity of the institutional incompatibilities across the European countries which is next used for developing a country ranking.

Although there has been much discussion in research literature on the diversity of family policy models adopted in European countries, not many attempts have been made to measure the cross-country variation in public support to working mothers in a quantitative manner. In fact, we succeeded in locating only studies by Gornick et al. (1997) and Gornick and Meyers (2003) who approached that problem. The authors proposed an index of public support of employment for mothers which expresses the level of public support to working mothers quantitatively and can be used for building a country ranking. For constructing the index the authors made use of a wide range of policy indicators that capture childcare provision for pre-schoolers (including enrolment rates, quality of service, opening hours, costs to parents and statutory rights to childcare), after-school care, leave policies (full-paid weeks to mothers, paternity leaves and other incentives for fathers, availability of paid leaves after child's third birthday) and working time regulations. Their index was computed for twelve OECD countries. In this study we follow the approach of Gornick et al. (1997) and Gornick and Meyers (2003), but we aim at constructing an index for all EU member states. For that reason we are much more constrained in our choice of comparative policy indicators. After a review of several international policy databases freely accessible online from the perspective of the availability of comparative policy indicators and our research needs (among them OECD Family Database, Anne Gauthier's Comparative Family Policy Database, The Clearinghouse on International Developments in Child, Youth and Family Policies, GGP Contextual Database) we decided to select following five indicators:

- Childcare coverage for children aged 0–2, measured as the number of places in public (or publicly subsidised) childcare facilities per 100 of children aged 0–2 years (CARE 0–2);
- Childcare coverage for children aged 3 to school age, measured as the number of places in public (publicly subsidised) childcare facilities per 100 of children age 3–5 years (CARE 3–5);
- Marginal effective tax rates, measured as a relative difference in taxes paid and benefits received between single earner couples with the earner earning 200% of the average wage and dual earner couples with both spouses earning 100% of the average wage in the national economy (METR);
- Number of weeks in full-time equivalents available to mothers within maternity and parental leave schemes, measured as a product of a duration of leave in weeks and wage compensation received during the leave expressed in % of average national wage (MLEAVE);
- Leave provisions to fathers, measured as the number of available weeks multiplied by a binary variable equal to 1 if paternal rights of fathers are non-transferable and 0 otherwise (FLEAVE).

These five indicators cover the most important policy aspects that affect women's fertility and employment choices: availability of public care for pre-schoolers, availability of paid care leaves, incentives for fathers to participate in care and employment disincentives for secondary earners (often women) built in the tax and cash benefit systems. We regret to have no data on the quality of public childcare nor availability of after-school care, but we located no comparative indicators on these issues in international databases for all EU member states. Despite this fact, we found this selection of policy indicators to be fully appropriate and sufficient for describing institutional conditions for work and family reconciliation and hence for measuring the intensity of institutional incompatibilities between women's employment and childbearing.

The data on policy indicators enumerated above were extracted from international comparative policy databases. These databases hardly offer time series data, but rather focus on single time periods, usually most recent years. The exception is the Anne's Gauthier Comparative Family Policy Database. Nonetheless, at the time the study was conducted the database missed updated information on policies. More importantly, the data on childcare provision it offers refer exclusively to pre-primary education programmes (ISCED 0). Such data may not necessarily cover all childcare arrangements in a country for children aged 3 to school age and certainly do not cover data on childcare provision for the youngest children. For this reason, we decided to use policy data that correspond to a single time period only, despite the fact that it would be much more desirable from the perspective of our research objectives to use policy indicators that describe conditions for work and family reconciliation back in the 1980s or even 1970s. Having made this decision we extracted three out of five policy indicators (METR, MLEAVE, FLEAVE) from the OECD Family Database and the remaining two (CARE 0–2, CARE 3–5) from the policy database prepared under the Multilinks project.

The major advantage of the OECD Family Database is that it provides not only qualitative information on family policy measures, but also offers indicators that measure cross-country differences in policies in a quantitative manner. Detailed description of these indicators is available on the OECD website as well as in Thevenon (2010). We also planned to use this data source for extracting data on childcare provision in order to use one single database. Nonetheless, the OECD Family Database contains data on enrolment rates in all formal childcare arrangements, including private care. We found such data unsuitable to our needs for two reasons. First, they refer to childcare use rather than provision. Second, they lump together care provided by the state and the market. In our opinion, such indicators do not sufficiently measure the incompatibilities between women's employment and childbearing caused by a shortage of easily available care services. We found data on public childcare supply to be much more suitable for us. Such comparative data are collected under the Multilinks project. They are available in Saraceno and Keck (2008) and the methodology of their collection is described in Keck, Hessel, and Saraceno (2009). The policy indicators extracted from the OECD Family Database refer to time periods around 2006 and the childcare indicators from the Multilinks database to time periods around 2003. They cover all EU member states, apart from Bulgaria and Romania. Data on Norway are missing as well.

For constructing the index of institutional incompatibilities between women's employment and childbearing we proceeded in two steps. First, we rescaled the policy indicators we selected for our study so that they ranged from zero to one, assuming higher values the lower the public support for mothers' employment and the stronger the disincentives to participate in the labour force. For that purpose the minimum value assumed by a policy indicator was subtracted from all its values and these differences were further divided by the indicator range. The computed measures were further subtracted from one if they assumed higher values the better the policy support. Second, we computed an arithmetic average of the rescaled policy indicators. The arithmetic average constitutes an index of institutional incompatibilities between women's employment and childbearing:

$$\mathrm{IINC}_i = \frac{1}{5}\sum_j \left(1 - \frac{\mathrm{PI}_{ij} - \min\limits_i(\mathrm{PI}_{ij})}{\max\limits_i(\mathrm{PI}_{ij}) - \min\limits_i(\mathrm{PI}_{ij})} \right) \tag{4.1}$$

where PI_{ij} denotes the j-th policy indicator in country i. The *IINC* index assumes higher values the stronger the institutional incompatibilities between women's employment and childbearing.

Our computations confirm the already well known finding that the institutional incompatibilities between women's employment and fertility are weakest in the Nordic countries (Sweden, Denmark and Norway), followed by Belgium and France (Fig. 4.1). Only Finland deviates from this group and ranks close to the Netherlands. This is mainly due to its poorer childcare provision than in Scandinavia. Italy and Spain take a middle position in the ranking, close to the Netherlands, Finland and

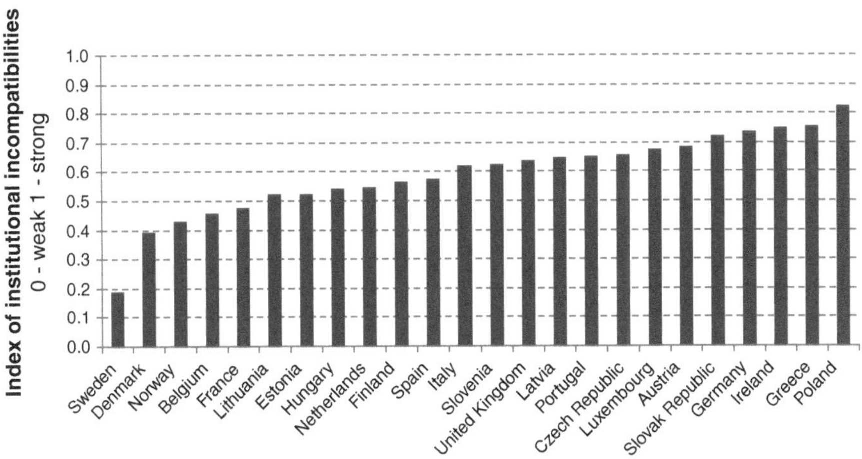

Fig. 4.1 Cross-country variation in institutional incompatibilities between women's employment and fertility, EU member states and Norway in the second half of the 2000s
Note: the presented index assumes higher values the stronger the institutional incompatibilities between women's employment and fertility.
Source: author's calculations on data from OECD Family Database and childcare indicators provided by Saraceno and Keck (2008).

the United Kingdom. These two Mediterranean countries earn this relatively good position thanks to the very good childcare provision for children aged three to school age and low marginal effective tax rates (see Fig. 4.2a–e). Among the Western European countries institutional incompatibilities between women's employment

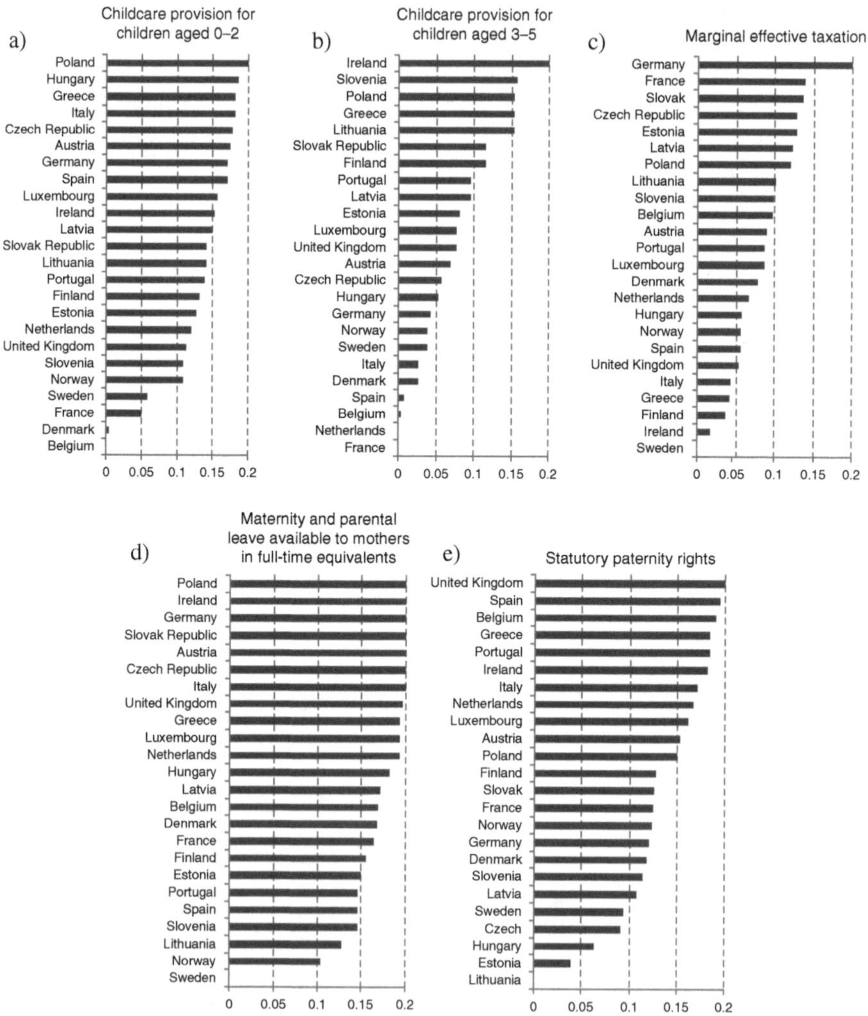

Fig. 4.2 Contribution of certain policy areas to the index of institutional incompatibilities between fertility and women's employment – country rankings in the components of IINC. (**a**) Childcare provision for children aged 0–2; (**b**) Childcare provision for children aged 3–5; (**c**) Marginal effective taxation; (**d**) Maternity and parental leave available to mothers in full-time equivalents; (**e**) Statutory paternity rights

Note: the figures present the five components of the index of institutional incompatibilities between women's employment and childbearing. They assume values ranging from 0 to 0.2, with higher values signifying weaker policy support.

Source: author's calculations on data from OECD Family Database and childcare indicators provided by Saraceno and Keck (2008).

and childbearing turn out to be strongest in the German-speaking countries (Austria and Germany). The two countries score low mainly because they provide no statutory paternity rights and display weak childcare provision for the youngest children. The position of Germany is additionally low due to high METRs.

Large variation in institutional incompatibilities between women's work and fertility is also found among the CEE countries. Consistently with what was concluded on the transformation in family policy models in this part of Europe after the fall of state socialism (see Section 4.2.2) the conditions for work and family reconciliation are poorest in Czech Republic, Slovak Republic and Poland (with Poland taking the last position in our ranking). By contrast, Lithuania, Estonia and Hungary score relatively high, taking positions between France and the Netherlands. The three post-socialist countries earn this relatively high position thanks to generous parental leave provisions in terms of duration and wage replacement as well as newly introduced statutory paternity rights. The remaining CEE countries – Latvia and Slovenia – are located in the middle of the country ranking, close to the United Kingdom.

Finally, we compared the intensity of the institutional incompatibilities between women's employment and fertility with country-specific fertility and women's labour supply rates. Indeed, stronger institutional incompatibilities tend to be observed in countries with low fertility and low to medium women's labour supply (Poland, Greece, Slovak Republic, Czech Republic, Germany or Austria), while weaker institutional incompatibilities are more typical for high fertility and high women's labour supply countries (Sweden, Norway, Denmark). Nevertheless, there are also countries that clearly deviate from this rule. These are particularly Italy and Spain, which take a middle position in our ranking but are characterised by low fertility and low women's labour supply, but also Lithuania and Hungary where low fertility persists despite the relatively weak institutional incompatibilities. Institutional factors are not the only source of tensions between women's employment and childbearing, however. Therefore, in the following sections we will assess the cross-country variation in work-family conflict imposed by the labour market structures and social norms for women's roles and will investigate how adding these contextual dimensions into the analysis modifies the country ranking.

4.3 Labour Market Structures

Another important element of the context that introduces variation in the relationship between fertility and women's work are the labour market structures. This issue is less often discussed in the literature, although in recent years some discussion on this topic has arisen, given the high labour market rigidities in Southern Europe in combination with low fertility and low female labour force participation (Adserá, 2004, 2005; Aaberge et al. 2005: 131–135). So far, however, labour market structures have been treated as a consequence of the welfare policies, and so they have been discussed as an integral part of the welfare regimes (e.g., Esping-Andersen, 1999; Muszyńska, 2007). Alternatively, only some of their elements, like high unemployment or part-time jobs, have been brought into the discussion on the interdependencies between fertility and women's labour supply (Jaumotte, 2003; Adserá, 2004, 2005; Aaberge et al. 2005: 131–135; d'Addio & d'Ercole, 2005). In this section we try to fill this gap and propose a measure of the incompatibilities between women's employment and childbearing imposed by the labour market structures.

Two characteristics of labour markets are highly relevant from the perspective of our study. These are flexibility of the work arrangements allowing for a relatively smooth adaptation of working hours to family responsibilities and the magnitude of the barriers to labour market entry. We quantify them by computing two types of indexes: the *labour market flexibility index* and the *labour market entry index*. These indexes are further used for assessing the intensity of the structural incompatibilities between fertility and women's labour supply in Europe in recent decades.

Flexibility of work arrangements has been widely recognised in the literature as an important factor affecting the intensity of tensions between women's employment and fertility. The opportunities to work part-time or to organise working hours in a flexible manner give mothers a chance to combine childrearing with paid work without forcing them to choose between the two activities. These work arrangements have not developed equally across Europe. While in some countries (the Netherlands, Germany, Norway, United Kingdom, Austria, Sweden) high proportions of women have been working part-time in recent decades, in others (mainly the CEE countries, but also the Southern European countries) these possibilities have been strongly limited (for more details see Chapter 2). Similarly strong cross-country differences are observed as regards the flexible working hours. According to the data from the Eurostat survey 'Reconciliation between work and family life' that was conducted in all EU member states in 2005, over 85% of women employed in the Netherlands were generally allowed to vary the start and the end of the working day, and 65% could take a day off for family reasons. For comparison, in Poland, a country which is at the other end of the spectrum, these figures amounted to 29 and 24%. In order to better assess the cross-country differences in the level of flexibility of the work arrangements, we propose to build the *labour market flexibility index (FLEX)* which is constructed on the basis of two indicators: proportion of women working part-time and an indicator of the opportunities to adjust the working hours to family responsibilities. Since these two labour market indicators can be correlated in the later step we use factor analysis for extracting the FLEX index.

The barriers to labour market entry are another characteristic of the European labour markets which is highly relevant to our study. They are generally strongest in countries with highly regulated labour markets, where strict rules on hiring and firing of the workers apply. Women experiencing child-related career breaks are more affected by the reduced hiring and least able to take advantage of the reduced firings than those who are already in employment, i.e., prime-aged men (Aaberge et al. 2005: 131–132; Adserá, 2004, 2005; OECD, 2004b). Therefore strong employment protection is often claimed to be responsible for high and persistent unemployment among females. Bearing this in mind, we propose the *labour-market entry index (ENTRY)*, which is computed on the basis of three labour market indicators: women's unemployment rate, excess women's unemployment, measured as a ratio of female to male unemployment rates, and excess women's long-term unemployment (12 months or more), expressed as a ratio of the proportion of long-term unemployed women and the proportion of long-term unemployed men. Again, these three labour market indicators are strongly correlated and it is more appropriate to extract the ENTRY index in the procedure of factor analysis than to sum the indicators.

The labour market indicators necessary for constructing the FLEX and ENTRY indices were retrieved from the Eurostat Statistics database. This data source provides time series data on unemployment and part-time employment and hence it should be possible to compute our indices for Western Europe since the 1980s and for CEE since the 1990s. Nevertheless, to be consistent with our analysis presented in Section 4.2 we decided to limit our computations to the second half of the 2000s. We used mean unemployment and part-time employment measures for the years 2005–2008 in order to account for any short-term fluctuations in the economic and labour market situation. The year 2009 was deliberately excluded from the analysis since the labour market indicators in this year might have been affected by the economic crisis. Only the data on the opportunities to adjust the working hours to family responsibilities refer to a single point in time. This kind of data is not available on an annual basis. We extracted it from the Eurostat survey 'Reconciliation between work and family life', conducted in 2005. The desired indicator was computed as an average answer to the two statements: 'Can you vary the start/end of the working day?' and 'Can you take a day off for family reasons?' (with the available answers coded as 2 – generally possible, 1 – rarely possible, 0 – not possible). Unfortunately, the survey was not conducted in Switzerland and hence we had to drop this country from our analyses.

The FLEX and ENTRY indices were obtained within the procedure of factor analysis. Principal component method was employed for extraction of factors. Within this procedure the original five labour market indicators were transformed into two components that explain 80.6% of the variance of the original data (see Table 4.1). After rotation using the Varimax method, the extracted components correspond to two dimensions of labour market structures: flexibility of work arrangements and barriers to the labour market entry. The country means computed for each factor constitute the FLEX and ENTRY indices, respectively. These two indices were further re-scaled to range from zero to one, with higher values signifying lower flexibility in work arrangements and stronger barriers to the labour market entry. This was achieved by subtracting the minimum index value from its all values and dividing these differences by the range assumed by the index. The re-scaled FLEX index was further subtracted from one so that it assumed higher values the more rigid the work arrangements.

In general, countries varied more in the flexibility of work arrangements than in the magnitude of the barriers to labour market entry (Fig. 4.3). According to the computed FLEX index the working hours over the years 2005–2008 were definitely most flexible in the Netherlands, but they were also relatively flexible in Austria, Belgium, Denmark, Norway, Luxembourg and Sweden. The lowest flexibility in work arrangements was found in all post-socialist countries and in particular in

Table 4.1 Factor analysis on labour market indicators

Variable	Principal components: Flexibility of work arrangements	Principal components: Barriers to labour market entry
Proportion of women employed part-time	**0.84**	–0.21
Opportunities to adjust working hours to family obligations	**0.92**	0.03
Women's unemployment rate	0.16	**0.92**
Excess unemployment among women	–0.49	**0.73**
Excess long-term unemployment among women	–0.21	**0.86**
Explained variance (%)	43.20	37.44
Cumulative (%)	43.20	80.65

Note: extraction method: principal components analysis; rotation method: Varimax with Kaiser normalisation
Source: author's calculations on the LFS data and data from Eurostat's survey 'Reconciliation between work and family life' extracted from Eurostat Statistics Database

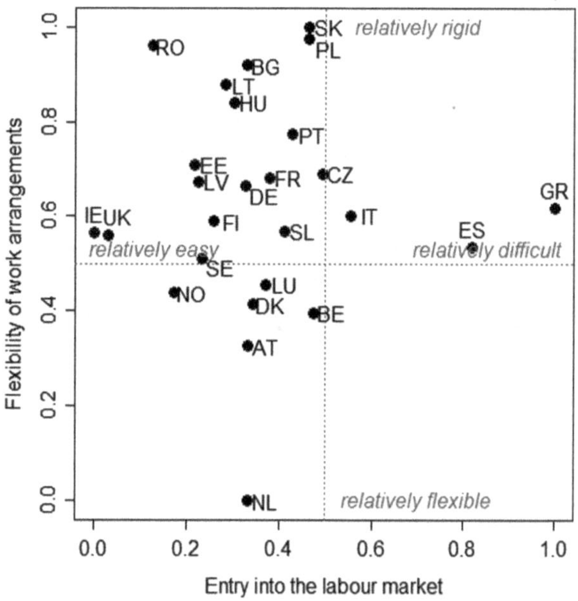

Fig. 4.3 The magnitude of the barriers to the labour market entry and flexibility of working hours in EU member states and Norway, 2005–2008
Note: the barriers to the labour market entry are measured with the ENTRY index and the flexibility of working hours with the FLEX index.
Source: author's calculations on the LFS data and data from Eurostat's survey 'Reconciliation between work and family life' extracted from Eurostat Statistics Database.

Slovakia, Poland, Romania, Bulgaria, Lithuania, and Hungary. The post-socialist countries displayed also relatively strong barriers to the labour market entry. The strongest barriers were found in Greece and Spain, however. By contrast, the entry to the labour market was the easiest in Ireland and the United Kingdom.

Finally, we computed an index of structural incompatibilities between women's work and fertility. It was defined as an arithmetic average of the rescaled labour-market entry index and the rescaled flexibility index:

$$\mathrm{SINC}_i = \frac{1}{2}\left(\frac{\mathrm{ENTRY}_i - \min(\mathrm{ENTRY}_i)}{\max(\mathrm{ENTRY}_i) - \min(\mathrm{ENTRY}_i)} + 1 - \frac{\mathrm{FLEX}_i - \min(\mathrm{FLEX}_i)}{\max(\mathrm{FLEX}_i) - \min(\mathrm{FLEX}_i)}\right) \quad (4.2)$$

The *SINC* index assumes higher values the stronger the conflict between childbearing and paid employment imposed by the labour market structures. It turns out that this conflict is least intense in the Netherlands, Ireland, the United Kingdom, Norway and Austria, followed by Sweden and Denmark, and strongest in post-socialist countries (except for Latvia, Estonia, and Slovenia) as well as in Southern Europe. It is particularly pronounced in Greece, Slovakia, Poland and Spain (Fig. 4.4). Furthermore, one can notice that countries where the structural incompatibilities are stronger (CEE and Southern European countries) display lower fertility and often also lower (or moderate) women's labour supply than countries where the structural incompatibilities are weaker. Nevertheless, there are also exceptions from this rule such as France with highest fertility in Europe but moderate structural incompatibilities or Austria, a country of low fertility where the labour market structures seem to be favourable to work and family reconciliation.

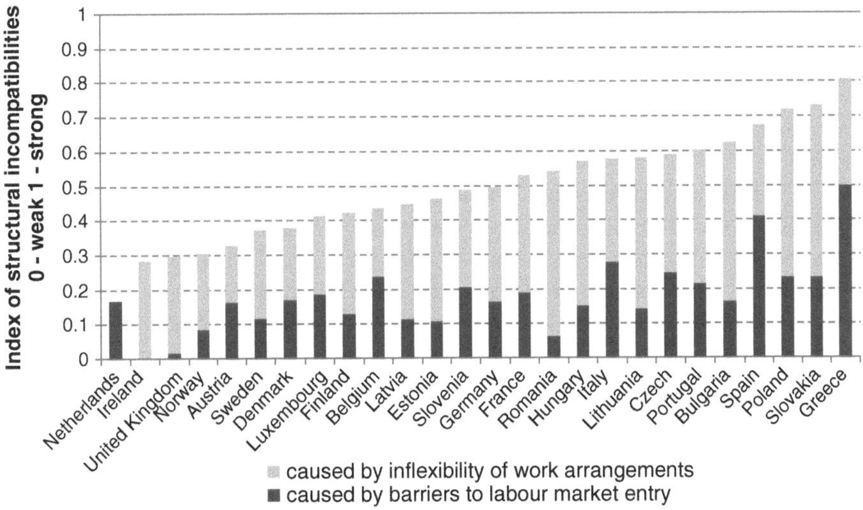

Fig. 4.4 Cross-country variation in structural incompatibilities between women's employment and fertility, Western Europe and Central and Eastern Europe, 2005–2008
Note: the presented index assumes higher values the stronger the structural incompatibilities between women's employment and fertility.
Source: author's calculations on the LFS data and data from Eurostat's survey 'Reconciliation between work and family life' extracted from Eurostat Statistics Database.

4.4 Social Norms for Women's Roles

Social norms and values defining the roles of women in a society are another important dimension of our study. By assigning certain responsibilities to women and men they establish who should work and who should take care of children. In this sense, the norms and values constitute another source of the incompatibilities between fertility and women's work, known as the cultural incompatibilities, imposed on those who are expected to provide care.

The cross-country differences in the intensity of these incompatibilities have already been explored by several researchers. One of the very first attempts was the study by Treas and Widmer (2000). Using the ISSP 1994 data, the authors investigated the cross-country patterns in attitudes towards married women's employment at four stages of the family life-cycle: (1) after marriage but before any children are born, (2) when there is a child under school age at home, (3) after the youngest child starts school, and (4) after the children leave home. The analysis revealed a widespread support for women's employment in all countries under study, but at the same time it showed large cross-country differences as to the opinions on employment of mothers. In general, employment of mothers was found to be most accepted in the work-oriented countries (Canada, East Germany, Israel, the Netherlands, the United States, and two Nordic countries: Norway and Sweden) and least in the motherhood-centred countries (CEE countries: Bulgaria, the Czech Republic, Hungary, Poland, Slovenia; Ireland, and Spain). Part-time employment was established to be most often seen as a solution to employment of mothers with school-aged children in the so called family-accommodating country cluster (Anglo-Saxon countries: Australia, Great Britain, New Zealand, Northern Ireland; Continental Europe countries: Austria and West Germany, as well as Italy, Japan, and Russia).

While the study by Treas and Widmer (2000) deals with opinions on the issues of whether women should work at all and if so, at what stages of the family life-cycle they should work, it does not look at the general ideology underpinning these beliefs. This gap was filled by Lück and Hoffäcker (2003), who identified two dimensions along which the views whether and when women should work are formed: family-orientation (acceptance of the traditional male breadwinner model) and job-orientation (support for the dual-earner family model).[2] This analysis showed that the traditional male breadwinner is most accepted in post-socialist countries, followed by the Southern Europe and Continental Europe (excluding the Netherlands). People were found to be least positive about the traditional role of women in the Anglo-Saxon countries (including Ireland), the Nordic countries, and finally the Netherlands. Interestingly, the former socialist countries took also the leading position on the job-orientation scale. The authors explained this phenomenon with relatively large financial necessities of the households in CEE countries.

Another important contribution to the analyses of the cultural settings with respect to fertility and women's labour supply was provided by Philipov (2008). He proposed to disentangle the family-orientation dimension into two components: the gender-role ideology, referring to the beliefs about the ultimate role of women,

---

[2] A similar analysis that additionally involved country grouping was conducted by Muszyńska (2007).

and the consequences for the family, measuring the perceptions of the impact of women's work on children's and family well-being. Both indicators were constructed based on a set of statements asked in the International Population Policy Acceptance Study (IPPAS)[3] and the validity of the statement selection for describing gender ideology and consequences for the family was confirmed using factor analysis. Unfortunately, the country coverage of the survey used was not as large as that of ISSP 1994, and so the comparison was possible only for ten European countries (Austria, Cyprus, Estonia, Germany, Hungary, Italy, Lithuania, the Netherlands, Poland, and Romania).

In this Section we aim at ranking the European countries with respect to the intensity of the cultural incompatibilities between women's paid work and fertility. For that purpose we identified latent factors that underpin the opinions on women's roles as mothers and income providers as well as determine the social norms on whether mothers should work or not. The identified latent factors were next used for country ranking. For measuring the opinions on mothers' work we followed the approach proposed by Philipov (2008), but we used data coming from the European Value Study (EVS). To the best of our knowledge, this survey covers the largest range of European countries among all other attitudinal surveys available, asking at the same time questions on gender roles which are necessary for our analysis. EVS has been conducted every nine to ten years since 1981. The first wave was carried out only in 14 European countries (only the Western countries). In following rounds data collection was gradually extended to the rest of Europe. In this study we use data from the fourth wave which was conducted around 2008 and which covers all countries of our interest. By choosing the last wave we are consistent with our analyses conducted in Sections 4.2 and 4.3 which also employed data from the second half of the 2000s.

Using the EVS data we selected four statements that may describe respondents' perceptions of gender roles as well as their beliefs on the consequences of women's work on the family and children's well-being:

- A working mother can establish just as warm and secure a relationship with her children as a mother who does not work,
- A pre-school child is likely to suffer if his or her mother works,
- A job is alright but what most women really want is a home and children,
- Being a housewife is just as fulfilling as working for pay.

The answers to these statements were measured on a 4-point scale (strongly agree, agree, disagree, and strongly disagree), with codes ranging from 1 to 4. Low codes correspond to answers expressing agreement with the traditional gender roles and the view that women's work has negative consequences on the family and children's well-being. Factor analysis was run on this data with principal component method used for extraction of factors. Within this procedure, the original

[3]See Appendix, Table A.1 for more detailed information on IPPAS.

Table 4.2 Factor analysis on the indicators on social norms for women's roles

Variable	Principal components	
	Gender-role ideology	Consequences for the family
A working mother can establish just as warm and secure a relationship with her children as a mother who does not work (1=strongly disagree, 4=strongly agree)	–0.07	**0.87**
A pre-school child is likely to suffer if his or her mother works (4=strongly disagree, 1=strongly agree)	0.34	**0.75**
A job is alright, but what most women really want is home and children (4=strongly disagree, 1=strongly agree)	**0.73**	0.32
Being a housewife is just as fulfilling as working for pay (4=strongly disagree, 1=strongly agree)	**0.85**	–0.07
Explained variance (%)	35.26	34.57
Cumulative (%)	35.26	69.83

Note: extraction method: principal components analysis; rotation method: Varimax with Kaiser normalisation
Source: author's calculations on EVS 1999

four variables were transformed into two components that explain around 69.8% of the variance of the original data (see Table 4.2). After rotation using the Varimax method, the extracted components fully correspond to the dimensions distinguished by Philipov (2008): the acknowledged gender role ideology and perceived consequences of women's work for the family. They take higher values the stronger the rejection of the traditional gender roles and the less prevalent the opinion on the negative consequences of women's work for the family.

In the next step the mean factor values were computed for each country, yielding the Gender Role Ideology Indicator (GRI) and Consequences for the Family Indicator (CF). These two indicators were further rescaled into two comparable indictors ranging from zero to one. This was achieved by first subtracting the minimum value of an indicator from its all values and later by dividing the obtained differences by the indicator range. The values of the indices constructed in this way give the position of a certain country in the country ranking according to acknowledged gender role ideology and perceived consequences of mother's work for the family. They were further subtracted from one so that their higher values signified more traditional views on gender roles and more serious concerns about the consequences of mothers' employment for children's well-being. An arithmetic average of the two indices yields the overall index of cultural incompatibilities between women's work and fertility (*CINC*). It assumes higher values the stronger the cultural incompatibilities between the two activities.

$$\mathrm{CINC}_i = \frac{1}{2}\left(\frac{\mathrm{GRI}_i - \min(\mathrm{GRI}_i)}{\max(\mathrm{GRI}_i) - \min(\mathrm{GRI}_i)} + \frac{\mathrm{CF}_i - \min(\mathrm{CF}_i)}{\max(\mathrm{CF}_i) - \min(\mathrm{CF}_i)}\right) \tag{4.3}$$

The cross-country differences in the intensity of cultural incompatibilities as measured by the index are presented in Fig. 4.5. It becomes clear that cultural incompatibilities are strongest in post-socialist countries (with Lithuania and Poland taking the leading positions, followed by Estonia, Romania, Hungary, Latvia, and Czech Republic) and some of the Mediterranean countries (Italy and Greece). Among the Western European countries cultural incompatibilities are also relatively strong in Switzerland and Austria. Ireland, Portugal, Slovenia, Bulgaria, and Great Britain take the middle position in the ranking. The weakest cultural incompatibilities between women's employment and fertility were found in Nordic countries, Germany, the Netherlands, and France. The high position of Germany in our country ranking is somewhat suprising and it might be partly driven by the fact that we merged data for East and West Germany. Besides, our findings are in general consistent with those achieved by Lück and Hoffäcker (2003), suggesting that people in Southern Europe and CEE countries are more likely to support the traditional male breadwinner family model than the citizens of the Nordic countries, Great Britain or the Netherlands as they more often acknowledge traditional gender roles and perceive employment of mothers as a threat to children's well-being.

It is also noteworthy that traditional gender ideology does not always go in hand with serious concerns about family well-being. In fact, the opinion that women reach self-fulfilment mainly thanks to family and children is widely shared in countries

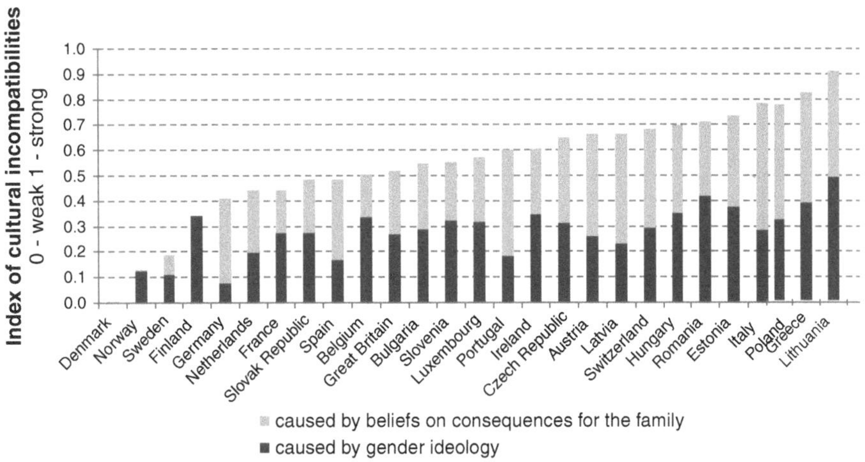

Fig. 4.5 Cross-country variation in cultural incompatibilities between women's employment and fertility, EU member states, Norway and Switzerland around 2008
Note: the presented index assumes higher values the stronger the incompatibilities between women's employment and fertility.
Source: author's calculations on EVS 2008.

like Finland, France or Belgium, but the fears that mother's employment would have negative consequences for the family are not serious there. Contrary situation prevails in Germany or Portugal where cultural incompatibilities are largely driven by the belief that women's involvement in the labour market would imprint negatively on children's well-being.

Finally, we compare the intensity of cultural incompatibilities with women's labour force participation rates and fertility at the macro-level. It turns out that low cultural incompatibilities tend to be indeed found in countries characterised by high fertility and high women's labour supply (Denmark, Finland, Sweden, the Netherlands), while strong incompatibilities seem to co-exist with low fertility and low or at most medium levels of women's labour supply (Italy, Greece, the post-socialist countries). However, there are also clear exceptions from this rule like Spain or Germany that according to our indices display relatively weak cultural incompatibilities between work and family but also low fertility.

4.5 Living Standards

Living standards are the last element of the context which we find highly relevant for employment and fertility decisions. Contrary to family policies, labour market structures, and gender norms that influence the indirect costs of having children, living standards affect the direct costs. They determine the extent to which people are free to decide to have a certain number of children and to allocate their time between household duties and paid work without being constrained by their economic situation. In countries with higher living standards, people may be more likely to reach the desired family size and women do not feel compelled to work for financial reasons, but they can choose between staying at home and working for self-fulfilment. Hence, by influencing the income effect, living standards further mediate the relationship between fertility and women's employment.

The impact of living standards is rarely taken into account in the discussion and empirical analyses on the interdependencies between childbearing and women's labour supply. This might be done as long as we compare the Western countries where financial situation of the households is relatively good and on average there are no substantial cross-country differences in that respect. Once the CEE countries are included in the comparative framework, the differences in living standards should be no more disregarded. Although the gap in the living standards between the Western and Eastern Europe has been gradually narrowing over the 1990s and 2000s the financial conditions of the CEE citizens still clearly deviate from those experienced by the Western Europeans. To illustrate these differences we present a couple of objective and subjective indicators of living standards. For instance, as it is shown in Fig. 4.6, the average annual consumption expenditures of households in Purchasing Power Parities exceed 15,000 EUR all over the Western Europe, except for Portugal and Spain, whereas in CEE they usually fall below 7,000 EUR with the exception of Slovenia. East Europeans tend to be also less often satisfied with their living standards and salaries they earn than West Europeans (Figs. 4.7 and 4.8).

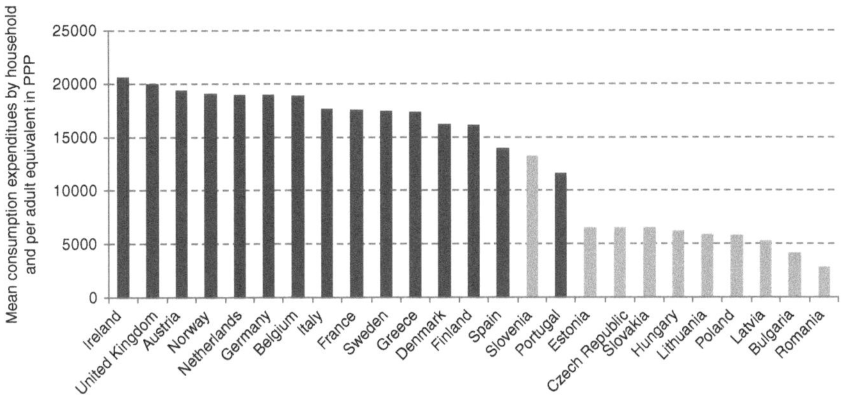

Fig. 4.6 Mean consumption expenditures by household and per adult equivalent in Purchasing Power Parities, EU member states and Norway, 2005
Source: Eurostat Statistics Database.

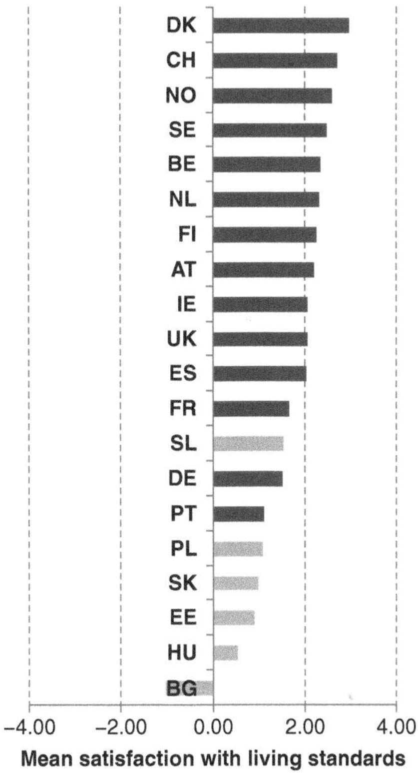

Fig. 4.7 Satisfaction with living standards
Note: the figure presents average responses to the statement 'How satisfied are you with your present standard of living?' The answers to the question were coded on a 10-point Likert scale: -5 'extremely dissatisfied' to 5 'extremely satisfied'.
Source: author's calculations on European Social Survey (2006).

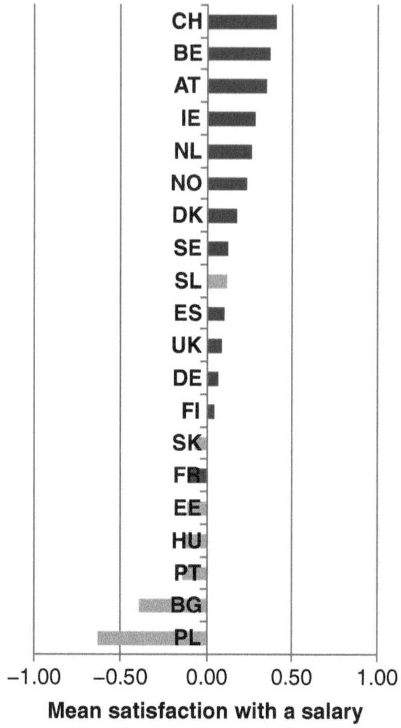

Fig. 4.8 Satisfaction with salary
Note: the figure presents average responses to the statement 'Considering all your efforts and achievements do you feel you get paid appropriately?' The answers to the question were coded on a 5- point Likert scale: -2 'strongly disagree' to 2 'strongly agree'.
Source: author's calculations on European Social Survey (2006).

The lower living standards of families in CEE countries may trigger employment of women as well as of mothers. This may explain the finding by Lück and Hoffäcker (2004) that people in former socialist countries display higher support for dual earner model despite traditional views on women's roles. An implication of this finding might be a stronger income effect of women's employment on fertility in CEE than in Western Europe. In other words, facing the financial constraints, women in post-socialist countries may be more motivated to take up employment it if they wish to increase their family size (investment in the number of children) and later to maintain the family (investment in the quality of children).

4.6 Final Country Ranking

So far we have discussed the cross-country variation in the macro-context in which fertility and women's labour supply decisions are made looking at each context dimension separately. In this Section we build a final ranking of countries with respect to the intensity of the overall incompatibilities between work and care imposed by family policies or lack thereof, labour market structures and social norms for gender roles. We also discuss how the cross-country differences in living standards may mediate the influence of work-family tensions on women's labour supply rates.

In order to assess the overall intensity of incompatibilities between fertility and women's employment at the country level a general index of incompatibilities was built. This index is a simple arithmetic average of the three indices of tensions between childbearing and women's paid work proposed in previous sections of this Chapter (namely the indices of institutional, structural, and cultural incompatibilities), after they were re-scaled to range from zero to one[4]:

$$INC_i = \frac{1}{3}\left(\frac{IINC_i - \min(IINC_i)}{\max(IINC_i) - \min(IINC_i)} + \frac{SINC_i - \min(SINC_i)}{\max(SINC_i) - \min(SINC_i)} + \frac{CINC_i - \min(CINC_i)}{\max(CINC_i) - \min(CINC_i)}\right) \quad (4.4)$$

The index assumes higher values the stronger the overall incompatibilities. It could not be calculated for few countries for which any of the partial indices were not computed due to lack of data, i.e. Bulgaria, Romania, and Switzerland. According to the index the incompatibilities between women's employment and fertility are weakest in Sweden, Denmark and Norway (Fig. 4.9). In these three countries public policies are in fact most supportive to employment of parents and the social norms for gender roles are least traditional. They are also characterised by fairly weak structural incompatibilities between women's paid work and childbearing. In our ranking of overall incompatibilities between work and care Sweden, Denmark and Norway are followed by the Netherlands and Finland where the conflict between employment and fertility is slightly stronger, mainly due to less supportive public policies. It is notable that Nordic countries and the Netherlands

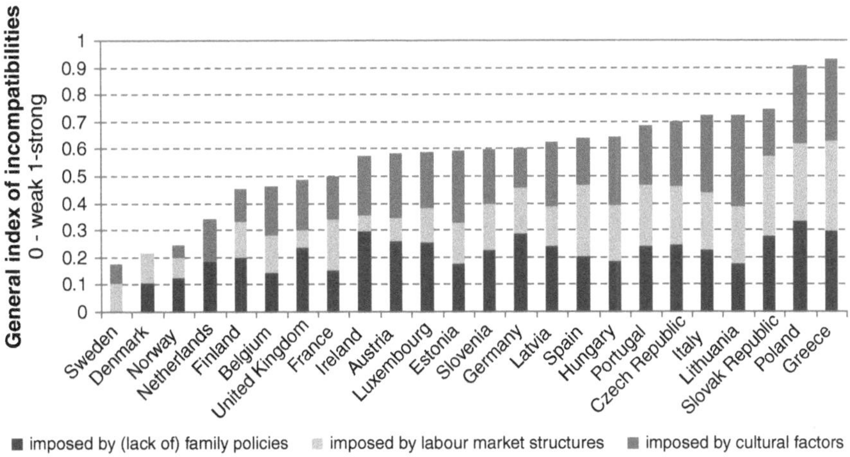

Fig. 4.9 Cross-country variation in overall incompatibilities between women's employment and fertility, EU member states and Norway in the second half of the 2000s
Source: author's calculations.

[4]The single indices were rescaled so that the same weight is given to each of them.

display one of the highest levels of women's labour supply in Europe (belong to the high-LFP cluster as distinguished in Chapter 2) and are also characterised by high fertility. Belgium, the United Kingdom, and France take the subsequent positions in our ranking of incompatibilities between work and care. Among these three countries Belgium and France score relatively good on the institutional dimension, but display relatively strong structural incompatibilities. Exactly the opposite was observed for the United Kingdom. These three countries are characterised by medium women's labour supply and relatively high fertility (compare Chapter 2). Ireland, Austria and Luxembourg take the subsequent positions. They are all characterised by stronger institutional and cultural incompatibilities than countries that take higher positions in the ranking, but score very well on the structural dimension. Moderate incompatibilities between work and care were found in Estonia, Slovenia and Germany. The remaining positions in the ranking are taken by the CEE and Southern European countries, i.e. the low fertility countries differing in women's labour supply rates. In Latvia, Spain, and Hungary the conflict imposed by the macro-context is slightly stronger than in Germany. The situation is already worse in Portugal, Czech Republic, Italy, Lithuania, and Slovakia and the worst in Greece and Poland. It is also notable that countries where the general work-family incompatibilities are strongest score very poorly on all three dimensions considered: institutional, structural, and cultural.

In general, the weaker the incongruities between fertility and women's employment imposed by the macro-context the higher the total fertility, women's labour supply as well as women's employment (Fig. 4.10a–c). This strong correlation between our general index of incompatibilities and total fertility/women's labour supply justifies our approach that taking the multi-dimensionality of the context into account is more appropriate than focusing on one context dimension only. Nevertheless, there are also countries where total fertility or woman's labour force participation clearly deviate from the level that would be expected on the basis of the intensity of the incompatibilities between work and care. These are, for instance, France and Ireland. In these two countries total fertility is even higher than in Nordic countries but the general index of incompatibilities points out that incompatibilities between work and care are stronger there than in Norway, Sweden or Denmark. Furthermore, the labour force participation and employment of women in Slovenia is far higher than in Austria, Germany, Luxembourg or Ireland, although the work-family incompatibilities imposed by the context are comparable in these countries. Similar conclusions are to be drawn from comparing Lithuania, Slovakia, Czech Republic or Poland to Italy and Greece. There can be several explanations for this state of affairs. First, there might be some other country-specific factors apart from the incompatibilities between women's employment and fertility that affect the two variables. One of them can be the living standards. The generally lower living standards in CEE countries may explain higher labour force participation and employment of women in Slovenia, Lithuania, Czech Republic, Slovakia or Poland than in Western European countries characterised by similarly intense incongruities between work and care. This explanation does not seem to hold for all post-socialist countries, in particular not for Hungary. Second explanation for the

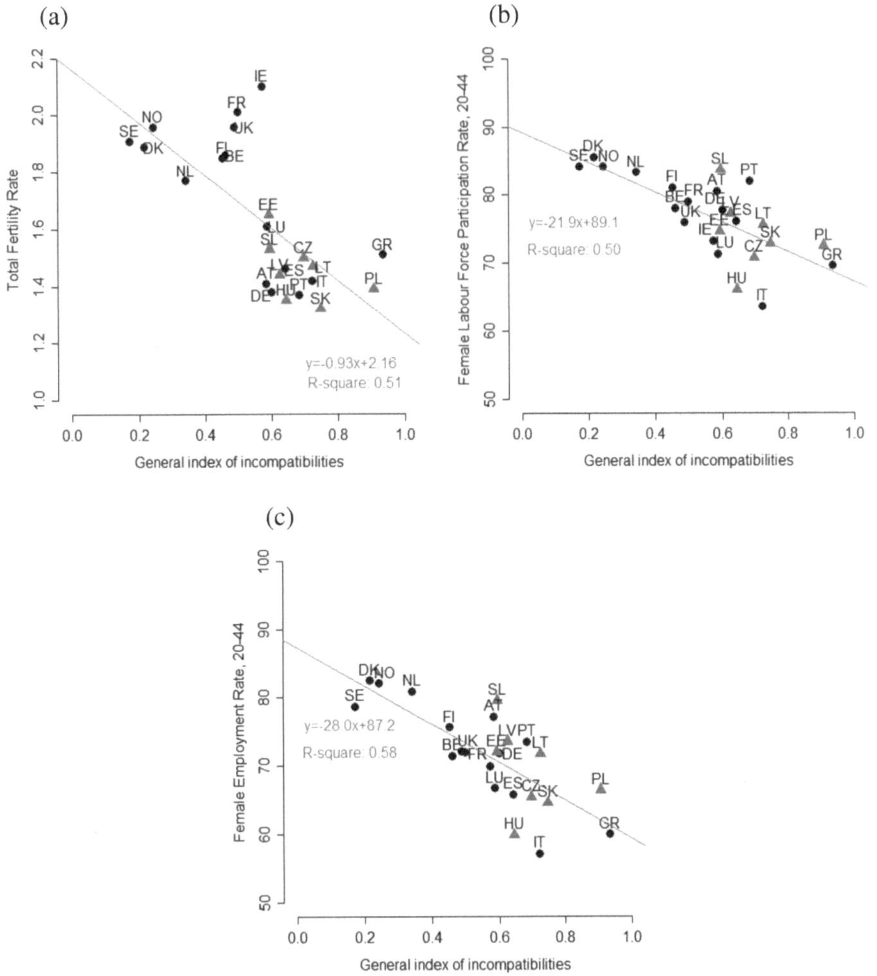

Fig. 4.10 Cross-country variation in the incompatibilities between women's paid work and fertility imposed by the macro-context and (**a**) total fertility rate; (**b**) women's labour force participation rates; (**c**) women's employment, EU member states and Norway 2008
Source: author's calculations.

deviation of total fertility and women's labour supply rates from the level expected on the basis of the intensity of the incompatibilities between paid work and care in a given country refers to the weaknesses of our method for measuring the conflict. The advantage of the adopted approach is that it allows us to measure the intensity of the conflict imposed by the macro-context in a quantitative manner and to rank the countries. The problem is that it assumes the three dimensions of the context that generate the incompatibilities to be equally important for fertility and labour supply decisions and it disregards interactions between policies, labour market structures and social norms. Future research should attempt to relax these assumptions. Finally, Fig. 4.10a–c refer to the macro-level and demonstrate simple correlations between the country-specific incompatibilities and total fertility/women's labour supply rates. Future research should investigate the effect of the index on the individual fertility and employment behaviours.

The indices computed in this Chapter measure the intensity of incompatibilities between paid work and fertility imposed by the macro-context in the second half of the 2000s. A question that appears at that stage is whether and how the country ranking was changing over time. We were not able to address this question since we lacked data on comparative policy indicators reaching back to the 1990s and 1980s for European countries. We can suspect that the position of some countries in the ranking, such as Nordic countries, France, Begium, was relatively stable as these countries were pioneers in developing public support for working mothers and Nordic countries additionally aimed at ensuring gender equality in care and in the labour market. Similar conclusion can be drawn with respect to Southern European countries that have always been described in the literature as institutional laggards, characterised additionally by rigid labour markets and traditional opinions on women's roles. Some countries could have changed their position, however. These countries could have been the Netherlands that experienced an enormous improvement in women's labour supply since the 1970s, advancing from the low-LFP to high-LFP country, and the United Kingdom where development of public support for working mothers have been enforced by EU regulations. The situation has certainly changed in CEE. Future research is needed to measure the intensity of the incompatibilities between work and care imposed by the macro-context in a dynamic perspective. The gradual development of contextual comparative databases and foremost family policy databases, such as the Family Policy Comparative Database developed by Anne Gauthier or the database constructed under the Multilinks project, opens new opportunities for the future research in this field. The comparative data from such databases should allow to compute the proposed indices for several points in time and for studying the dynamics of the incompatibilities between work and care in connection with the dynamics in fertility and women's labour supply.

Chapter 5
Macro-context and the Cross-Country Variation in the Micro-level Relationship Between Fertility and Women's Employment

5.1 Introduction

It is widely acknowledged that European countries differ strongly in the conditions offered to working parents to combine paid employment and childcare. Our analysis conducted in Chapter 4 demonstrates that in the second half of the 2000s these conditions were undoubtedly best in Scandinavian countries, followed by the Netherlands, Finland, Belgium, the United Kingdom, and France. In such countries as Ireland, Austria, Luxembourg, Estonia, Germany, and Latvia the incompatibilities between women's employment and childrearing imposed by the macro-context were already stronger. The institutional, structural and cultural environment was found to be least favourable to work and family reconciliation in Southern European countries and remaining former socialist countries, such as Hungary, Czech Republic, Lithuania, Slovakia and Poland. Among them, Poland and Greece displayed extraordinarily high incompatibilities between work and care. Europe is also strongly divided as regards the level of living standards which are better in the West than in the East in the objective as well as subjective terms.

The macro-context shapes the individual fertility and employment choices by influencing the opportunity costs of childbearing, but also by defining the opportunities of childbearing and childrearing in single-earner couples. In general, the economic theory of fertility and women's labour supply predicts the opportunity costs of childbearing to be higher where the support to working parents is lower. In such countries working women are hypothesised to be more likely to postpone transition to motherhood and experience more difficulties with employment (re-)entry due to an inability of organising childcare. Furthermore, those who succeed in re-entering employment after first birth are expected to be less likely to progress to their second child. Consequently, one should expect the micro-level relationship between childbearing and women's employment to be more negative in countries where the conditions for combining the two life spheres are worse. In the light of the

This chapter is a modified version of the article prepared together with Daniele Vignoli: Matysiak, A., & Vignoli, D. (2008). Fertility and women's employment: A meta-analysis. *European Journal of Population, 24*(4), 363–384.

A. Matysiak, *Interdependencies Between Fertility and Women's Labour Supply*, European Studies of Population 17, DOI 10.1007/978-94-007-1284-3_5,

information presented in Chapter 4 it should be thus most negative in those Southern and CEE countries where our general index of incompatibilities indicated strong tensions between work and family and least negative in Scandinavian countries.

The country-specific conditions for work and family reconciliation are not the only factor that may influence women's fertility and employment behaviours, however. Another factor are the country living standards and the extent to which material aspirations of the individuals are unsatisfied. Consistently with the theoretical arguments presented in Chapter 3 women's employment may constitute an important condition for the entry to motherhood and the increase in family size beyond parity one in countries where living standards are lower and material aspirations of the couples remain largely unsatisfied. In such countries mothers can be also strongly motivated to resume employment fairly quickly after birth. Such situation may take place in CEE countries. Hence, the micro-level relationship between fertility and women's employment in this part of Europe might be inflated in comparison to Western countries provided that the economic situation of the households and material aspirations of the couple are not taken into account in empirical models.

The expectations presented above could be verified in two ways. The first possibility would be to conduct a cross-country comparative analysis on micro-level longitudinal data, while the second would be to review the abundant micro-level empirical evidence on the topic. The problem with the first approach is the lack of an international comparative dataset that could provide required data, in particular as regards the post-socialist countries. For instance, the European Community Household Panel (ECHP), which is otherwise well suited for this type of analysis, is available for EU-15 only and covers a relatively short period of time (1994–2001). Another dataset that could be used is the Family and Fertility Survey (FFS). Admittedly, it includes the CEE countries, but for the majority it covers mainly fertility and employment histories realised during the socialist period.[1] A release of the Generations and Gender Survey data for public use will certainly change this situation, but this is a matter of a future. Apart from the international, there are also many national data sources, but they are neither easily accessible nor harmonised. Therefore, for the purpose of our study we decided on the second approach.

Although several reviews of the studies researching the interdependencies between fertility and women's work have been already conducted (Spitze, 1988; Willekens, 1991; Schröder, 2005), the character of these works is narrative. This means that they do not provide a quantitative assessment of the effect of interest standardised for the across-study differences. Therefore, in this study we go one step further and adopt a quantitative approach. This means that, instead of conducting a narrative literature review, we apply meta-analytic techniques. In this methodological framework, the single study estimates of the impacts of fertility on women's employment and vice versa constitute statistical units of observation, and the original study characteristics are used for standardising these estimates for the across-study differences. In this way, we are able to assess the variation in the effects

[1] FFS in the majority of the CEE countries was conducted in the first half of the 1990s.

of interest with respect to the contextual settings, net of the differences in the method applied, control variables employed, sample selected, etc. Finally, it is important to note that the effect estimates that are produced within the meta-analytic framework have higher external validity than those obtained in an individual study due to the generality of results across various research works (Shadish, Cook, & Campbell, 2002). Hence, the adopted analytical approach is not only superior to the narrative literature review, but it has a certain advantage over conducting a cross-country comparative analysis that would rely on single estimates.

The meta-analysis presented in this chapter was initially conducted together with Daniele Vignoli.[2] Its results are published in the *European Journal of Population* (see Matysiak & Vignoli, 2008) where we demonstrated the variation in micro-level relationship between fertility and women's employment across the Esping-Andersen's welfare regimes. In this book, we make us of the meta-database constructed together with Daniele Vignoli, but we investigate how the micro-level relationship differs across countries that vary in the intensity of work-family tensions as measured by the general index of incompatibilities. We focus only on European countries. Finally, we also slightly change the specification of our meta-regression models and employ an upgraded Stata module for meta-regression. Compared to the module used by Matysiak and Vignoli, it provides an opportunity to use a Knapp-Hartung modification of the variance of the estimated coefficients (Knapp & Hartung, 2003).

This chapter consists of seven sections, including this introduction. Section 5.2 introduces the method of meta-analysis. Section 5.3 describes the study selection criteria while Section 5.4 briefly reviews the collected research works with an emphasis on methodological aspects. In Section 5.5 we provide information on meta-analytic techniques applied in this paper. The results are presented in Section 5.6, followed by Section 5.7, which summarises and discusses the findings.

5.2 Meta-Analysis as a Quantitative Literature Review

Meta-analysis or, in other words, a quantitative literature review, has been developed in order to synthesise, combine, and interpret the abundance of empirical evidence on a certain topic. It offers a clear and systematic way to compare the results of various studies standardised for the differences in the methodological approaches applied and types of data used. Originally it was developed in medical and epidemiological research, but recently it has been increasingly employed in the social sciences (Vemer et al. 1989; Amato & Keith, 1991; Waldorf & Byrun, 2005; Weichselbaumer & Winter-Ebmer, 2005; Wagner & Weiss, 2006).

[2]The work was conducted when Anna Matysiak and Daniele Vignoli were resident PhD students at the Max Planck Institute for Demographic Research. Together they carried out the literature search, constructed the meta-sample, built the meta-database, and ran the analyses. Matysiak was in charge of the effects of young children on mothers' employment, Vignoli the effects of women's employment on fertility.

In order to conduct a meta-analysis, papers researching a topic of interest are collected in a systematic manner. First, estimated coefficients are selected across studies and recalculated in a standardised way into comparable indicators (i.e., effect sizes). The indicators reflect the magnitude of the association in each study. Next, they are combined into single summary indicators that measure the true underlying effect or in other words the parameter of interest. If the computed effects contain a large amount of heterogeneity, regression techniques should be applied. Within this analytical framework, the dependent variable denotes the effect sizes and all methodological features of a particular study can be used as control variables.

As a method designed for surveying empirical findings, meta-analysis has several advantages over the standard narrative literature review (see e.g., Stanley, 2001). The first is its quantitative character. While a standard narrative literature review consists of commentary on the findings of previous research, meta-analysis allows for a quantitative assessment of the effect of interest. Second, it provides researchers with the opportunity to standardise the studied effects for the country examined, the method of analysis applied, the control variables employed, the sample selected, etc. Not only does it help to explain wide across-study variations in research findings, but it also enables the evaluation of the merits of different research methods, designs, data, and country-specific contexts. Third, meta-analysis requires inclusion of all papers available worldwide meeting pre-defined criteria, which minimises the risk of literature selection bias. The quality and reliability of these papers is taken into account by weighting the original estimates by the inverse of their standard errors. It can also be controlled for in the meta-regression framework. Papers cannot, however, be highlighted or discarded from the review for any methodological or data-related reasons, a decision that may be taken in a narrative literature overview subject to the reviewer's individual assessment of the papers.

Meta-analysis has limitations, however. First, it is much more confined in its range than a traditional literature review, which can cover a very broad range of studies (i.e., without pre-defined criteria) and even include studies that are only marginally related to the phenomenon under investigation. Second, since publishers tend to accept studies that report significant results, there might be a bias to the estimated effect size; in the worst case, it may be even impossible for the meta-analyst to locate a sufficient number of relevant studies on the topic (the so-called 'file-drawer' problem). Finally, a common problem is that researchers often do not report results required for conducting a meta-analysis (i.e., standard errors or t-statistics). It is thus necessary to make assumptions in order to overcome the lack of information.

5.3 Meta-Sample

In order to carry out a meta-analysis, a necessary preliminary step consists of constructing one's own meta-data. The principle of completeness drives the choice of the original papers. Our search strategy, following Stuck et al. (1999), consisted of three stages: first we used Current Contents and EconLit, universal research databases[3]; second, we checked the references in existing articles; third, we asked experts for their recommendations. Given that Current Contents covers articles published in 1990 and thereafter, all selected studies were limited to this publication period.

In our meta-study we focused on two types of effects: the impact of women's employment on childbearing and the impact of young children on women's entry into employment. We conducted an overview of available research works concerning EU member states, Norway, and Switzerland. The search was performed in the 7 months from April 2006 to October 2006. In order to collect a representative sample of high quality studies, we focused solely on reviewed articles and chapters in books and monographs, leaving out working papers and internal research reports. Our systematic search was conducted using a specific combination of selected general keywords (work, fertility, childbearing, transition, progression, labour market, employment, etc). We limited our selection to papers that clearly explored women's transition to birth and to employment. Amongst them, only research works that adopted a life-course perspective for analysing the interdependencies between the two activities were accepted. Thus, we restricted the search to longitudinal studies. We ended the search at saturation point – in other words when, combining the different keywords and adding new ones, we obtained articles already selected.

Furthermore, we decided to exclude papers where the transition to employment after childbirth was analysed, the reason being that in these papers the age of the child is the process time, and that the calculated baseline intensities, even if reported, do not measure the effect which we focus on in our study, i.e., the effect of young children versus older ones or no children on women's employment entry.

English, German, Italian, and Polish-language articles were considered. We are quite certain of having a representative sample of existing studies, possibly with a bias towards English-language literature. Omission of studies published in other languages may cause an under-representation of some countries in our analysis. This is a common problem in the literature reviews. On the other hand, however, we did not locate many of them in the literature sources we used.

At the end of the selection process, we came up with 25 papers on the transition to childbirth and 16 papers on employment entry (for the list of selected articles see Appendix, Table A.4). Some authors presented an analysis of more than one independent sample or studied more than one transition in the same paper. These estimates were treated as independent and were all included into our analysis. We accepted the estimates from final models only. When the same author published two papers using the same dataset and the same model specification, an average estimate was calculated based on the reported outcomes. However, when the same dataset was used, but a different model was estimated, we included both estimates in order to avoid the possibility of a study selection bias.

---

[3]Current Contents and EconLit, provided by the Ovid service, give access to complete bibliographic information and table of contents of over 7,600 of the world's leading scholarly journals and to more than 2,000 book series covering all disciplines. They cover items published since 1990.

Overall, the search procedure gave us a total of 67 effects of employment on fertility and 37 effects of young children on entry into employment (see Tables 5.1a and 5.1b). After collecting the articles, two separate datasets were constructed: one for the transition to childbearing, the other for the transition to work.

The collected studies encompass fairly large selection of European countries although for some countries no studies meeting our pre-defined criteria were located (e.g., Austria, Greece, Ireland, Portugal, and many post-socialist countries) and consequently they are not included in the meta-analysis. The country coverage is presented in Table 5.2. The numbers in brackets represent the number of effects located for each country. The selection of studies for investigating the effect of women's employment on childbearing is much broader, covering different regions

Table 5.1a Meta-sample: transition to employment

Type of transition		Number of estimates	Countries
From:	*Into:*		
Unemployment	Employment	3	France (1), Finland (1), Denmark (1)
Inactivity		7	Italy (1), France (1), Denmark (1), Germany (3), Finland (1)
Non-employment		10	the Netherlands (7), Germany (3)
Unemployment	Full-time employment	–	–
Inactivity		3	UK(1), Germany(1), Denmark (1)
Non-employment		9	Netherlands (5), Germany (4)
Unemployment	Part-time employment	–	–
Inactivity		1	Germany (1)
Non-employment		4	Germany (4)

Notes: non-employment is defined as unemployment as well as inactivity. Studies covering periods prior to 1990 refer to West Germany

Table 5.1b Meta-sample: transition to childbirth

Type of transition	Number of estimates	Countries
First parity	41	Flanders (2), France (5), Netherlands (2), Germany (5), UK (2), Italy (5), Spain (5), post-socialist Hungary (1), post-socialist Czech Republic (1), Norway (2), Sweden (7), Finland (4)
Second parity	12	France (2), Italy (2), Spain (1), Finland (2), Sweden (5)
Third parity	13	France (2), Italy (2), Spain (1), Finland (2), Norway (2), Sweden (4)
Joint transition to first and higher parities	1	UK (1)

Note: studies covering periods prior to 1990 refer to West Germany

Table 5.2 Meta-study country coverage

Effect of children aged 0–6 on women's employment		Effect of women's employment on childbearing	
Country	Cohorts	Country	Cohorts
Denmark (3)	1940s–1970s	Belgium-Flanders (2)	1950s–1970s
Finland (2)	1930s–1970s	post-socialist Czech Republic (1)	1970s–1980s
France (2)	1930s–1970s	Finland (8)	1950s–1980s
Germany (16)	1920s–1980s	France (9)	1950s–1970s
Italy (1)	1940s–1970s	Germany (5)	1950s–1980s
the Netherlands (12)	1920s–1970s	post-socialist Hungary (1)	1970s–1980s
the United Kingdom (1)	1920s–1970s	Italy (9)	1950s–1980s
		the Netherlands (2)	1960s
		Norway (4)	1930s–1960s
		Spain (7)	1940s–1980s
		Sweden (16)	1940s–1970s
		UK (3)	1950s–1980s

Note: studies covering periods prior to 1990 refer to West Germany Number of effect sizes in parentheses

of Europe (Nordic, Western, Southern, Central and Eastern). The selection of countries for investigating the effect of children on women's employment entry is far narrower and it is widely concentrated in two countries: the Netherlands and Germany. Furthermore, we located no single study investigating the effect of young children on mothers' employment entry in post-socialist countries and only one for a Southern European country, namely for Italy.

The collected studies differ also in birth cohorts they cover. In general the studies investigating the effect of women's employment on childbearing were conducted on younger cohorts, mainly born in the 1950s through the 1970s, but there also studies encompassing women born earlier, in the 1940s, and later, in the 1980s. The birth cohorts covered by the studies on the impact of young children on mothers' employment entry more often reach back to the 1930s and even 1920s and rarely extend to 1980s.

5.4 Critical Review of the Collected Studies

Before we proceed with our meta-study, some remarks should be made as to the methodological aspects of the collected research works. Our discussion is led by three out of the four conditions for understanding the interdependencies between fertility and women's labour supply formulated against the theoretical framework presented in Chapter 3 (Section 3.6), namely:

1. Disentangle the price effect from the income effect;
2. Control for work- and family-orientations;

3. If data shortcomings make it impossible to account for some of the factors listed in conditions (1) and (2), then selection effects might occur. Exploring these selection effects may provide valuable information for understanding the interdependencies between childbearing and women's labour force participation.

The overview of the collected studies shows that the clear majority do not meet the conditions listed above. First, the income effect is often not disentangled from the price effect. The collected studies fail to control directly for women's material aspirations and only some introduce variables describing the financial situation of the household, such as husband's earnings or non-labour income. Second, the orientations of women towards family and work are rarely taken into account. Altogether, out of 43 accepted papers only 12 incorporate variables describing the financial situation of a woman in an empirical model,[4] one paper takes women's preferences into account, and four control for unobserved characteristics of women, but assuming no correlation between unmeasured characteristics and model regressors.

A failure to control for important determinants of childbearing as well as women's employment entry and to allow for the correlation between unobserved characteristics and model regressors leads to selection effects. Consequently, the obtained estimate can either underestimate or overestimate the real conflict between fertility and women's employment, depending on the type of selection effect. Existence of negative selection leads to an overestimation of the conflict, since women select themselves into inactivity before the planned conception or give up childbearing in favour of their intended professional career. Positive selection, by contrast, results in underestimation of the price effect, as women decide to take up a job with the prospect of having a child or choosing to conceive, provided they will be able to resume employment after birth. Positive selection is very likely to occur if women's material aspirations are not taken into account.

The unavailability of data describing women's material aspirations or career orientations towards family and paid employment calls for other more innovative and non-standard solutions to be applied to account for selection effects. Among promising solutions are advanced statistical techniques that allow for capturing the unobserved factors and their correlation with model regressors. It appears, however, that attempts aimed at controlling these effects are rarely found in practice. Only one of the papers collected tackles this issue, by estimating fertility and employment jointly in a common maximum-likelihood framework. Additionally, we located four other papers where there was an attempt to account for selection. They were all based on instrumental variable methodology. As they were all conducted for the US they were not included in our analysis.

On the whole, this short review of the collected studies shows that the micro-level relationship, the variation of which we are studying, is composed of several

[4]Researchers mainly used partner's labour market status or partner's education as a proxy for partner's earnings. Only six papers directly used the variable 'partner's income', and only three controlled for household income.

effects: the price effect, reflecting the conflict between fertility and paid employment, and selection effects, caused by a failure of the researchers to control for women's material aspirations (income effect) as well as work and family orientations. This fact should be taken into account while interpreting the findings from our meta-study. Given that the Western economies are largely homogenous with respect to the magnitude of the income effect and that the post-materialistic values are relatively equally spread there (at least if compared to CEE countries), we attribute the differences in the micro-level relationship between fertility and women's work to the differences in the conflict between the two activities. More caution is required once we incorporate the CEE countries into our analysis as they display worse living standards, and materialistic values play a more important role there than in the West (compare Kowalska & Wróblewska, 2008).

5.5 Meta-Analytic Techniques

5.5.1 Effect Size Estimates

Our effect size estimates are the log odds ratios, the log relative risks, and the estimates of the OLS regressions measuring the impacts of women's employment on fertility and the impacts of young children on women's employment entry, respectively.

In order to study the influence of women's employment on childbearing, we selected the estimates of being employed or, if this was not possible, being employed full-time versus being inactive, unemployed, or non-employed.[5] The inversely coded effects (e.g., non-employment versus employment) were recalculated.

Our analysis of the effects of fertility on women's employment focused on children aged 0–6. This was the most frequent age interval in which the age of children was classified. Many authors, however, used other age intervals. In order to maintain coherence across studies, we fitted spline functions to all coefficients that referred to the influence of the age of children on women's entry into employment for each study. The size of the coefficient was the Y-axis value. We placed the mid-points of the reported age intervals on the horizontal axis. Given the parameters of the spline function, we were able to calculate the coefficient for the mid-point of the required age interval.

Another problem we encountered while calculating the effects of children on women's employment was the different reference categories used by researchers. The majority of authors defined the reference category as 'having no children', but some used 'having no children younger than' a certain age. We accepted both types of papers, but in the case of the latter we did so only if the age limit was at least seven. Furthermore, the variable describing the age of the child was defined differently across the studies. The most frequent solution was to analyse the effect of

[5] Non-employment is defined as unemployment as well as inactivity.

the age of the youngest child. However, in some cases, older children were categorised together with the youngest child (having children in the given age interval). There were also papers where age of children was interacted with number of children (number of children in a given age interval). We accepted all three solutions. The effect sizes were later standardised for the definition of the age of a child and the type of reference category in the meta-regression framework.

5.5.2 Summary Indicators

The effect size estimates as discussed above were used to compute the summary indicators that describe the magnitude of the relationship of interest. For that purpose, a random-effect model was used as a point of departure. This model assumes that the variance of the effect size estimates is a sum of two components: the within-study variance (a sampling error) and the between-study variance (caused by across-study differences). Let $\hat{Y}_i$ be an estimate of effect size Y_i in study i and Y be the true underlying effect size (in other words, the parameter of interest). Then:

$$\hat{Y}_i = Y_i + \varepsilon_i, \quad \varepsilon_i \sim N(0, {\sigma_i}^2) \tag{5.1}$$

$$Y_i = Y + \eta_i, \quad \eta_i \sim N(0, \tau^2) \tag{5.2}$$

where ${\sigma_i}^2$ is the within-study variance, τ^2 is the between-study variance, and ε_i and η_i are mutually independent, normally distributed error terms.

Under the random effects model, the estimator of the true effect is computed as a following summary indicator:

$$\hat{Y} = \frac{\sum_{i=1}^{n} w_i \hat{Y}_i}{\sum_{i=1}^{n} w_i}, \text{ where } w_i = \frac{1}{\hat{\sigma}_i^2 + \hat{\tau}^2} \tag{5.3}$$

where $\hat{\sigma}_i^2$ and $\hat{\tau}^2$ are the estimates of the within- and between-study variance components respectively. Hence, $\hat{Y}$ is an estimate of the parameter of interest, describing the magnitude of the studied effect. In analytical terms, it is defined as a weighted mean of effect size estimates $\hat{Y}_i$ with higher weight given to studies in which estimates have lower variance (that is, are more precise).

Computing the summary indicator $\hat{Y}$ requires ${\sigma_i}^2$ and τ^2 to be estimated. Let us first start with the within-study variance component. It is commonly assumed that individual studies provide good estimates of ${\sigma_i}^2$(Biggerstaff & Tweedie, 1997; Konstantopoulos, 2006). Consequently ${\sigma_i}^2$ is measured as a squared standard error of the parameter as reported in the study. A problem often encountered by meta-analysts is the lack of standard errors or other statistics allowing a direct calculation of standard errors (e.g., t-statistics or at least p-values). This problem arose also in our analysis, mainly with reference to the papers on transition to childbirth. Following the literature on meta-analysis, we made the following assumptions: When the result was marked significant and no other details were available, we set the p-value equal to 0.05. When the result was not significant and the upper limit for significance assumed by the author was 0.1, we set the p-value at 0.45, and when the upper limit was 0.05, we used a p-value equal to 0.475. When the significance was marked with asterisks only, we assumed the p-value to be equal to the mid-point of its interval.

Estimating the between-study variance τ^2 is slightly more complicated. One may start by assessing whether τ^2 is indeed significantly different from zero. A statistical test designed for that purpose was proposed by Cochran (1954). It is based on the test statistic Q that measures the extent to which the estimates of individual effect sizes vary around the estimate of the underlying effect size computed under the assumption that $\tau^2 = 0$:

$$Q = \sum_{i=1}^{n} w_i^* (\hat{Y}_i - \hat{Y})^2, \text{ where } \hat{Y} = \frac{\sum_{i=1}^{n} w_i^* \hat{Y}_i}{\sum_{i=1}^{n} w_i^*} \text{ and } \quad w_i^* = \frac{1}{\sigma_i{}^2} \tag{5.4}$$

Under the hypothesis of homogeneity ($\tau^2 = 0$) Q follows a χ^2_{n-1} distribution. Large values of Q lead to a rejection of the hypothesis of homogeneity and the $\hat{\tau}^2$ has to be computed. DerSimonian and Laird (1986) propose a point estimate $\hat{\tau}^2_{DL}$ of τ^2:

$$\hat{\tau}^2_{DL} = \max\left\{0, \frac{Q-(n-1)}{\sum_{i=1}^{n} w_i^* - \sum_{i=1}^{n} w_i^{*2} / \sum_{i=1}^{n} w_i^*}\right\} \tag{5.5}$$

The relative importance of the between-study variance can be assessed by using the statistic I^2:

$$I^2 = \frac{\hat{\tau}^2}{\hat{\tau}^2 + \sum_{i=1}^{n} \sigma_i^2} \tag{5.6}$$

This statistic describes the proportion of total heterogeneity in the effect size estimates which can be attributed to the between-study variance (Higgins, Thompson, Deeks, & Altman, 2002).

In our meta-study we expect large between-study variation. The source of the variation lies in the differences in the contextual settings, in which the employment and fertility decisions are taken, as well as in the peculiarities of the original studies in terms of the methods applied, the data looked at, sample restrictions, cohorts covered, the types of the transition studied, the definitions of the reference category of the investigated coefficient, or any other variations in the effect measurements (see Section 5.5.1). Hence, estimating the mean effect size for each contextual setting using formulas (5.3) and (5.5) may not be satisfactory, particularly if there is also variation in the effect size estimates between the identified country groups. A straightforward solution to this problem is to estimate a meta-regression.

5.5.3 *Meta-Regression*

Our meta-regressions take the following form:

$$Y_i = \sum \alpha_j w_{ij} + \sum \beta_k c_{ik} + \sum \vartheta_l v_{il} + \sum \theta_n s_{in} + \sum \delta_p m_{ip} + \eta_i + \varepsilon_i, \qquad i = 1, 2, ..., n, \tag{5.7}$$

where Y_i is the effect size corresponding to study i, w_{ij} are a set of dummies for the country j and c_{ik} for the cohort k, v_{il} represent l control variables for the type of the transition and measurement of the studied effect (e.g., birth order, type of employment, type of non-employment, definition of the reference category, definition of the child's age variable, etc.), s_{in} stand for n dummies controlling for the sample selection (taking value 1 if the sample was restricted only to a certain group of women), m_{ip} denote p variables standardising for the method and type of the data. The parameters $\alpha_j, \beta_k, \vartheta_l, \theta_n, \delta_p$ were estimated stepwise, using the standard maximum likelihood method. First, we introduced country into the model. It was followed by controls for the cohort, type of transition and measurement of the studied effect, the sample selected, the method applied and the type of the data used. At each stage, the reduction in the between-study variance was measured by comparing the estimate of τ^2 before and after adding the successive covariates. The adjusted R^2, measured as $100\% \cdot (1 - \tau^2(\text{full model})/\tau^2(\text{with no covariates}))$, provides us with the information on the extent to which our meta-model succeeded in reducing the between-study variance. Furthermore, the robustness of the meta-regression estimates is verified by conducting a sensitivity analysis. Namely, we estimated the same models on the samples reduced randomly by 10%. Minor differences in the estimates prove that the outcomes are reliable.

5.6 Empirical Findings

Table 5.3 presents the summary indicators of the impact of women's work on birth risk and the impact of children aged 0–6 on mothers' employment entry respectively. They are computed based on the studies accepted for meta-analysis according to formula 5.3.

The indicators suggest that both effects are significantly negative. The effect of women's employment on childbearing equals to -0.19 ($p = 0.000$), whereas the

Table 5.3 Mean effect sizes

	Number of studies	Summary indicator			Homogeneity Test		Between-study variance	
	N	$\hat{Y}$	t-stat	p-value	Q	p-value	$\hat{\tau}^2_{DL}$	I_2
Effect of women's employment on fertility	67	−0.19	−4.30	0.000	759.6	0.000	0.073	91.2
Effect of children aged 0–6 on women's employment entry	37	−0.33	−10.7	0.000	194.2	0.000	0.085	81.5

Note: the table includes the random effect estimates
Source: author's calculations

effect of children aged 0–6 on mothers' entry into employment amounts to −0.33 ($p = 0.000$). These effects vary considerably across the studies, however. More specifically, in both cases the between-study variance constitutes over 80% of the overall heterogeneity in the effect size estimates. One of the most important sources of heterogeneity may be the macro-context in which employment and childbearing decisions are taken. But the differences may also result from the across-study differences in the methods applied, the data examined, the sample restrictions imposed, the type of transitions studied, and the reference categories or definitions employed for the child's age variable. In order to deal with this problem, we applied meta-regression techniques.

In the first step we introduced only the country into our meta-regressions. As a reference category we used the country where the incompatibilities between women's employment and fertility imposed by the context are the strongest, provided that we succeeded in collecting a reasonably high number of studies for this country. As a result, in our meta-regression on the effect of women's employment on fertility our reference category is built by Italy for which we have nine effect sizes. As we collected only one study investigating the effect of young children on women's employment entry in Italy, in our second meta-regression we refer to Germany (16 effect sizes). The corresponding meta-regression estimates are presented in Tables 5.4 and 5.5 in columns M1. As the univariate analysis whose results were presented in Table 5.3 suggests that the micro-level relationship between fertility and women's employment is negative we interpret positive coefficients in the meta-regression to represent a weakening of the negative relationship. Similarly, negative coefficients are interpreted to display intensification of the negative effect.

Introducing only a country into our meta-regressions reduced the between-study variances by around 25% in both models. The model findings are not consistent with our expectations. The effects of women's employment on fertility do not vary significantly across countries. There is some significant cross-country variation in the effects of young children on mothers' employment entry suggesting that compared to Germany the effects are less negative in Denmark and France. The between-study

Table 5.4 Effect of women's employment on fertility: meta-regression estimates

Variable name	Variable categories	M1	M2
Country	Norway	0.01	0.51*
		(0.25)	(0.30)
	Sweden	0.20	0.32*
		(0.21)	(0.16)
	Finland	0.22	1.06***
		(0.20)	(0.28)
	Netherlands	−0.75**	0.33
		(0.33)	(0.37)
	France	0.23	0.16
		(0.24)	(0.18)
	Belgium	−0.36	0.91**
		(0.33)	(0.41)
	United Kingdom	−0.42	0.49
		(0.27)	(0.62)
	Germany	−0.06	0.55**
		(0.27)	(0.27)
	Spain	−0.23	−0.37**
		(0.22)	(0.16)
	Italy	ref.	ref.
	post-socialist Hungary	0.93	2.48***
		(0.58)	(0.72)
	post-socialist Czech Republic	0.07	0.57*
		(0.48)	(0.34)
Birth cohort	>=1960		−0.44***
			(0.15)
	< 1960		ref.
Method	Continuous time		0.57*
			(0.34)
	Discrete		ref.
Parity progression	Parity one		0.05
			(0.35)
	Parity two		0.06
			(0.33)
	Parity three		−0.03
			(0.32)
	All parities		ref.
Constant		−0.20	0.09
		(0.16)	(0.32)
adj-R^2		0.248	0.694
number of studies		67	67

Note: *** < 0.01, ** < 0.05, * < 0.1. Standard errors are reported in parentheses. The results are standardized for the construction of the variable describing the effect of employment on childbearing and the sample selected
Source: author's calculations

Table 5.5 Effect of children aged 0–6 on women's employment entry: meta-regression estimates

Variable name	Variable categories	M1	M2
Country	Denmark	0.73**	2.93***
		(0.29)	(0.67)
	Finland	−0.23	1.96***
		(0.30)	(0.67)
	France	0.58*	1.04**
		(0.29)	(0.40)
	The Netherlands	−0.17	2.15***
		(0.24)	(0.66)
	The United Kingdom	0.27	0.28
		(0.42)	(0.41)
	Germany	ref.	ref.
	Italy	1.37	0.01
		(7.52)	(7.52)
Type of transition	from unemployment		−0.02
			(0.18)
	from inactivity		0.52**
			(0.21)
	from non-employment		ref.
	to full-time job		0.20
			(0.19)
	to part-time job		0.76***
			(0.18)
	to any job		ref.
Birth cohort	>=1960		−1.15**
			(0.48)
	<1960		ref.
Method	continuous		1.56**
			(0.59)
	discrete		ref.
Constant		−0.67***	−1.39**
		(0.13)	(0.51)
adj-R^2		0.232	0.972
number of studies		37	37

Note: *** < 0.01, ** < 0.05, * < 0.1. Standard errors are reported in parentheses. The results are standardized for the construction of the variable describing the effect of children on mothers' employment entry
Source: author's calculations

variance is still high, however, constituting around 87 and 65% of the overall variation in the effects of women's employment on fertility and the effects of young children on mothers' employment entry respectively. The cross-country variation in the effect sizes presented in columns M1 is thus unlikely to represent the variation in true effect sizes. The model estimates are probably affected by differences in various study characteristics mentioned above.

Therefore, in the second step we introduced all other variables that, in our opinion, might strongly contribute to the increase in between-study variance, e.g. the cohort, the type of transition, the type of reference category of the effect sizes, the sample selection, and the method applied. Due to the low number of observations, it was unfortunately not possible to introduce many characteristics of original studies (in particular in the meta-study of the effect of fertility on women's employment entry) and we had to limit ourselves to the most important ones. For this reason we were not able to study in detail the effect of the control variables employed in the original studies on our effect sizes. Despite this limitation our findings show that after the introduction of the covariates the between-study variance declined by 69% in the meta-regression explaining the variation in the effects of women's employment on fertility and by 97% in the meta-regression of the effects of young children on mothers' employment entry relative to the between-study variance in the same meta-regressions without any covariates (columns M2 in Tables 5.4 and 5.5). Using these model specifications we carried out sensitivity analyses in order to verify the robustness of our estimates. Namely, we reduced each sample randomly by 10% and estimated both models with the same covariates. The outcomes remained stable, suggesting that our findings are reliable (see Appendix, Tables A.5 and A.6). Altogether the substantial reduction in the between-study variance as well as the robustness of our estimates to the sensitivity test led us to the accept these model specifications as our final models.

Our findings on the cross-country variation in the micro-level relationship between fertility and women's employment are only partly consistent with our expectations. On the one hand, both our meta-regressions indicate that the effect sizes in Norway, Sweden, Finland and Denmark are significantly higher than in Italy and Spain which means that they are less negative. This implies that women are less likely to postpone entry to motherhood when employed in the Nordic countries than in the South. Furthermore, they are also more likely to enter employment after birth and more likely to give birth to another child after re-entry. It is, however, surprising that the conflict between women's employment and fertility experienced by women is weakest in Finland.

Our findings suggest also that employment has relatively little negative impact, if any, on childbearing behaviours of women in Belgium. This is in line with our expectations as we showed in Chapter 4 that the incompatibilities between women's employment and fertility imposed by the macro-context are not strong there. The situation of the Netherlands and France is already less clear. According to our estimates employed women in these two countries are as likely to postpone childbearing as women in Italy or Spain. At the same time mothers in France and the Netherlands experience less problems with employment entry than mothers in Germany or Italy. Exactly, the opposite is to be found in Germany where it is relatively difficult for women to re-enter employment, but employed women do not postpone entry to motherhood on such a large scale as in Italy. Mothers of young children seem to experience relatively serious difficulties with employment entry in the United Kingdom. In the same country women's employment seems to be a serious barrier to childbearing. Employed women are most likely to postpone births in

Spain, however. The estimates of our first meta-regression suggest that the impact of women's employment on fertility is even more negative there than in Italy.

On the basis of our findings we cannot tell much on the tensions between women's employment and childbearing experienced by women in post-socialist countries. We only collected two studies for this part of Europe for the period following the fall of state socialism. These two studies investigate the impact of women's employment on fertility in Czech Republic and Hungary. They suggest that this impact is far less negative than in Italy (in particular in Hungary) despite the fact that the incompatibilities between women's employment and childbearing are similarly intense in these three countries. This finding might be driven by the income effect that is supposed to be stronger in post-socialist countries than in Italy.

Some of our findings are surprising in the light of the information on the expected intensity of incompatibilities between women's employment and fertility presented in Chapter 4. The most astonishing are the results for the Netherlands where according to the general index of incompatibilities the conditions for work and family reconciliation are relatively good as well as for Spain and the United Kingdom which score better on the index than Italy. The evidence for France and Germany, although mixed depending on the meta-regression we look at, may suggest simply that the conflict is more intense there than in Nordic countries and less than in Southern Europe. Comparing the evidence brought by meta-regressions with the general index of incompatibilities between women's employment and fertility one should be careful, however. The empirical studies we collected cover childbearing and employment choices of women made in the 1970s through 1980s and 1990s to 2000s whereas the index is based on the data from the second half of the 2000s. Using the index in this analysis would be proper if we assumed that the cross-country variation in incompatibilities did not change over time. While it is probably true for many countries (for instance for Nordic versus the Southern European countries) it may not be the case for the Netherlands or the United Kingdom where the public support for working mothers is likely to have improved to a larger extent than in other Western economies.

Apart from the assessment of the variation in the studied effects across countries and contextual settings, our analysis provides an opportunity to evaluate temporal change in the micro-level relationship between fertility and women's employment as well as to assess the merits of certain research designs. As regards the first issue, our findings suggest that mothers born after 1960 tend to experience larger difficulties with employment entry than mothers born before that year. Likewise, younger cohorts of women are more likely to postpone childbearing when employed than older cohorts. We address these findings in more detail in the discussion.

As far as the research method is concerned, we did not have many options for selection of the covariates. All studies included in the analysis employed event-history techniques, applying continuous or discrete time models. As already mentioned, very few studies controlled for unobserved characteristics of women. Therefore, as regards the method, we only included variables testing the influence of the continuous versus discrete time models on the effect sizes in both meta-equations. Our results show that in both cases analysed, the models with continuous time tend to yield higher effect size estimates than models with discrete time. This finding is consistent with that of Zhang and Yu (1998: 1690), who show that if the event of interest is relatively frequent, the odds ratios tend to underestimate the relative risk if it is below one.

Finally, our meta-models control also for the type of transition. It turns out that for young mothers it is more difficult to enter employment if they are unemployed than inactive. It is possible that inactive women in some studies are women on parental leaves which would explain this finding. For mothers, it is easier to take a part-time job than a full-time one. We do not find any variation in the effect of women's employment on fertility with respect to the number of children a woman already has.

5.7 Discussion

In Chapter 4 we discussed the cross-country differences in the intensity of the potential incompatibilities between fertility and women's work and the magnitude of the potential income effect imposed by the macro-context. The objective of the research described in the present chapter was to investigate the cross-country variation of the micro-level relationship between fertility and women's employment and to verify whether it is consistent with the cross-country differences in the work-family incompatibilities imposed by the macro-context as well as the cross-study differences in the living standards.

We addressed these issues by making use of the numerous micro-level empirical findings on the interdependencies between childbearing and women's employment, published in peer-reviewed journals, book chapters, and monographs. We focused on two effects: the effect of women's work on fertility and the effect of young children on women's employment entry. In order to synthesise, combine, and interpret the abundance of empirical estimates, we employed meta-analytic techniques. This enabled us to assess the variation in the effects of interest with respect to the country covered, net of the differences in the research design. An important advantage of our analytical approach over conducting a cross-country comparative analysis is that meta-analytic estimates have higher external validity than those obtained in a single study, due to the generality of results across various research works. The disadvantage of the approach, however, is that we had to rely on existing research works with all their methodological shortcomings. The most important one is that the collected studies mostly do not control for women's material aspirations or for their work and family orientations. This means in practice that the yielded estimates do not reflect the conflict between childbearing and paid employment but rather a mix of a price effect, income effect, and further selection effects. This is less of a problem if we compare Western economies. Since they are largely homogenous with respect to the magnitude of the income effect, and as the post-materialistic values are relatively equally spread there, the variation in the micro-level relationship between childbearing and women's employment may be basically attributed to the differences in the contextual incompatibilities between the two activities. Nevertheless, once we incorporate the CEE countries into our analysis, we should be more cautious in our interpretation.

The first and main finding of our meta-study is that the impact of employment on fertility in the majority of the collected studies was on average negative, and vice versa. At the same time, however, we found a large variation in the magnitude of the analysed impacts across countries. As regards the *Western European countries*, it is clear from our study that the micro-level relationship between fertility and women's employment is least negative in the Nordic countries and most negative in the Southern European countries (Italy and Spain). This implies that women are less likely to postpone entry to motherhood when employed in the North than in the South. Furthermore, they are also more likely to enter employment after birth and more likely to give birth to another child after re-entry. The findings for other Western European countries are more ambiguous. They show that the conflict between fertility and employment experienced by women in France, the Netherlands, and Germany, i.e. Western European countries except for Nordic and Southern for which we collected most empirical studies, is stronger than in the North and weaker than in the South, but it is difficult to conclude on the ranking of these countries in that respect. We can only say that it is easier for mothers of young children to enter employment in France and the Netherlands than in Germany. In Germany, by contrast, employment of women hinders fertility to a lower extent than in France and the Netherlands. Furthermore, our analysis showed that the conflict between fertility and women's employment experienced by women in the United Kingdom is as strong as in Italy.

Our findings for Western Europe are quite in line with what would be expected on the basis of the general index of incompatibilities between fertility and women's employment developed in Chapter 4 despite the fact that the index was computed for the second half of the 2000s and the meta-analysis presented in this Chapter refers to studies that investigate women's employment and fertility behaviours since the 1970s. One of the reasons for this consistency might be that the cross-country variation in the incompatibilities between work and care has been relatively stable over time. Countries that are now most advanced in supporting women's employment and where the opinions on women's roles are least traditional, i.e. the Nordic countries, are probably those which pioneered in supporting labour market integration of mothers as well as gender equality. Likewise, the institutions and labour markets in Southern European countries which currently lag behind the Nordic countries on all contextual dimensions relevant to women's employment and fertility choices were long resistant to the ongoing social change. Nonetheless, there are also countries for which the results of our meta-analyses deviate from what would be expected on the basis of the general index of incompatibilities between women's employment and fertility. These are particularly the Netherlands and the United Kingdom for which our meta-study indicates presence of a stronger conflict than one could predict on the basis of the general index of incompatibilities. A possible explanation for this inconsistency might be that these two countries made a remarkably serious progress in terms of reducing the tensions between women's work and fertility.

In particular, the Netherlands succeeded in developing exceptionally flexible work arrangements while the United Kingdom introduced the system of statutory maternity and parental leaves in the 1990s forced by the EU legislation. Despite these exceptions our findings seem to suggest that employed women were more likely to postpone childbearing and mothers were less likely to enter employment in countries where the institutional, structural and cultural conditions are less favourable to work and family reconciliation than in countries where the overall incompatibilities between fertility and women's paid work imposed by the macro-context are weaker.

The findings for *the post-socialist countries* are different. In spite of the fact that the incompatibilities between fertility and women's labour supply in that part of Europe are exceptionally strong the two empirical studies we located identify no significantly negative relationship between the two variables at the micro-level. Given the importance of materialistic values in this part of Europe, strongly pragmatic attitudes towards women's work, large instability of employment in the transforming labour markets, and the rising consumer aspirations (probably unmet due to worse living standards compared to Western economies), we believe that the observed positive effect of women's work on childbearing results from a strong income effect. Driven by a need to contribute to the household income, women in this part of Europe are strongly oriented towards participating in the labour force and may even perceive employment as a pre-condition to childbearing. This explains the relatively high economic activity of women in CEE, observed also among mothers with children aged 5+ (see Chapter 2). At the same time, however, women do experience strong difficulties in combining paid work with caring for young children. This difficulty is reflected in low labour market participation rates of mothers of under-fives, as it was presented in Chapter 2. If women are expected to earn income and at the same time cannot combine market work with care duties, they will obviously tend to postpone or even give up further childbearing. We investigate the interrelationship between women's fertility and employment choices in a post-socialist setting more thoroughly in the following Chapter 6 where we present an empirical study conducted for Poland, i.e. the country where the institutional, structural, and cultural conditions for combining work and care are the worst among all CEE countries.

Our meta-study revealed one more finding which calls for an explanation. Namely, both meta-regressions showed that the younger cohorts of women, born largely after 1960, experienced stronger conflict between fertility and employment than the older cohorts, born prior to 1960. This finding was established, net of the cross-country differences in the contextual settings. In our opinion, a complex interplay of two factors is responsible for this state of affairs. First, it is likely that the price effect in Western economies has intensified. This is possible despite the changing attitudes towards working mothers and evolving family policies aimed at supporting working parents. In fact, these developments could have been counterbalanced by the transformations in the labour markets imposed by globalisation processes. Increasing competition and employers' rising demands for mobility and availability of workers led to the instability of employment contracts and raised the uncertainty about the future well-being of the families (Kotowska, 2004, 2005; Mills & Blossfeld, 2005). Women and the youth became most exposed to the globalisation processes. Equipped with less work experience and unprotected by internal labour markets, they are likely to end up in precarious and low-quality employment such as fixed-term contracts, irregular working hours, or jobs characterised by low occupational standing and poor access to training. Second, it is very likely that the occupational aspirations of women have increased with a rise in women's educational attainment and that the professional career has gained in importance relative to the family career. As a result, women might be currently less eager to consent to a career break that would have been easily accepted by their mothers. Since the consequences of such work interruption are much more severe today than in the past, in terms of human capital lost or advancement opportunities foregone, the conflict between childbearing and paid employment experienced by women might have intensified.

Both the regional and temporal variation of the studied effects suggest that the institutional, structural, cultural, and economic factors have been important in determining the interrelationship between fertility and women's employment. This finding, established at the micro-level, supplements the research work of Brewster and Rindfuss (2000), Rindfuss et al. (2003), Kögel (2004) and Engelhardt et al. (2004) – i.e., that country-specific effects influence the correlation between fertility and women's labour supply at the macro-level. It remains to be established which contextual factors affect women's fertility and employment decisions in particular. Finally, our meta-study emphasises the necessity to better control for women's material aspirations as well as their work and family orientations while modelling fertility and labour market behaviours of women. The consequences of omitting such variables from the analysis are discussed more deeply in Chapter 6.

Chapter 6
Women's Employment in Post-Socialist Poland: A Barrier or a Pre-condition to Childbearing?

6.1 Introduction

Interdependencies between fertility and women's employment in post-socialist countries are largely unexplored. In fact, in our meta-study presented in Chapter 5 we located only two empirical studies that employed longitudinal perspective to investigate the micro-level relationship between the two variables. These two studies provide evidence contrary to what was found for Western Europe. Even though the institutional, structural, and cultural incompatibilities between childbearing and women's labour supply in CEE are exceptionally strong, the micro-level relationship between the two variables is not significantly negative. One reason for this state of affairs can be that we simply located too few studies for post-socialist countries and that the other would yield strongly negative effect sizes. Another explanation is that there are some other country-specific factors despite the incompatibilities between work and care that affect women's fertility and employment decisions and these factors play a particularly important role in the CEE setting. One of them can be the lower living standards leaving the material aspirations of Eastern Europeans unsatisfied to a larger extent than in the West of Europe and consequently driving mothers' determination to participate in the labour force. In this Chapter we aim to take a closer look into the interdependencies between fertility and women's labour supply in one of the CEE countries. For that purpose we selected Poland as it displays the strongest overall incompatibilities between work and care among all post-socialist countries and comparing to all EU member states takes the second position in our ranking, following Greece (compare Chapter 4). These incompatibilities are reflected in poorly developed childcare facilities, remarkable objection to employment of mothers with young children, exceptionally strong unemployment pressure, and notably rigid working hours. Choosing this country for analysis gives us thus an opportunity to illustrate women's decision-making in the situation when childbearing and employment are in a strong conflict but at the same time when

A shorter version of this chapter was published as a research article: Matysiak, A. (2009). Employment first, then childbearing: Women's strategy in post-socialist Poland. *Population Studies: A Journal of Demography, 63*(3), 253–276, published by Taylor and Francis, Ltd http://www.informaworld.com.

A. Matysiak, *Interdependencies Between Fertility and Women's Labour Supply*, European Studies of Population 17, DOI 10.1007/978-94-007-1284-3_6,

women's earnings are necessary for a decision to have a child.[1] Note, however, that our empirical findings cannot be fully generalised to all post-socialist countries.

Investigating the interdependencies between fertility and women's employment in post-socialist Poland is only one of two objectives we formulate in this chapter. The second one is to illustrate that a failure to account for the unobserved characteristics of women, such as material aspirations or work and family orientations, leads to endogeneity bias to the estimate of the conflict between fertility and women's employment. We propose to eliminate this bias by modelling fertility and women's employment jointly, using the multi-process hazard model.

We start our discussion by describing the macro-context in which fertility and employment decisions were made after the collapse of state socialism in Poland (Section 6.2). The section is divided into four parts, each corresponding to one of the four dimensions of the context we distinguished in Chapter 3. We then move on to present developments in fertility and women's labour supply (Section 6.3). As well as portraying the time trends, we also provide some information on women's preferences regarding family formation and employment. In our discussions in Sections 6.2 and 6.3 we do not go beyond the period following the collapse of state socialism up to 2006 as the individual survey data used for in-depth analyses cover exactly this period. In Section 6.4 we discuss the methodological developments aimed at eliminating the endogeneity bias. Section 6.5 describes our data, and Section 6.6 introduces the modelling approach. The results are presented in Section 6.7, followed by Section 6.8, which summarises and discusses the findings.

6.2 Contextual Opportunities and Restrictions

6.2.1 Economic Developments and Living Standards

The economic transformation that started in Poland in 1989 resulted in a serious reorganisation of the state and the society, and consequently led to a profound change in the conditions of gaining an income and participating in the labour force. The withdrawal of the state from its role as an employer as well as provider of financial support and social services, accompanied by the establishment of private companies, resulted in an increase of individual responsibility for one's economic well-being. The household became more dependent on its own resources, in particular on the ability to earn income (Kotowska, 1999; Kotowska et al. 2008).

At the same time, securing the income turned out to be much more difficult than in the past. The economic reforms of the early 1990s and the changes in the structure of labour demand led primarily to a substantial worsening in living standards. In the 'black years' of 1990–1993, the GDP fell by 13% and the employment rate declined from 71.5% in 1988 to 58.9% in 1993. At the same time, unemployment,

[1] The empirical study presented in this Chapter was also published as a research article in *Population Studies* (see Matysiak, 2009).

a previously unknown phenomenon, spread rapidly, reaching 14.4% in 1993 (see Table 6.1). This negative trend reversed in the period 1994–1998, when Poland experienced an average economic growth of 5.9% annually and the unemployment rate declined to 10.9% in 1998. The following years again brought a slowdown in economic development, however. The difficulties of finding and maintaining employment at that time were further intensified by an influx of the numerous cohorts of the post-war baby boomers' descendants to the labour market. As a result, in 2003 the overall unemployment rate hit the record value of 20%. Only from 2003 onwards has Poland been able to follow a path of fast economic growth, accompanied by significant improvements in the labour market.

These transformations in the labour market led to substantial changes in income distribution and consequently to an increase in economic and social inequalities. Rising poverty and social stratification was combined with social exclusion of specific groups and a decrease in the feeling of social security. Hardly any protection from poverty was offered to individuals (Kotowska et al. 2008). As a consequence, households faced a situation in which their responsibility for maintaining the family increased, while at the same time it became much more difficult to earn the income. These conflicting developments were not necessarily a hallmark of the early 1990s. They continued over time although gradually resulting less from economic restructuring and more from globalisation processes and increasing consumer aspirations. According to Kotowska (1999) and Kotowska et al. (2008) social reaction to such developments manifested in an increase in the importance of economic factors for family-related decisions, like marriage or childbearing. In fact, the Population Policy Acceptance Study[2] conducted in Poland in 2001 confirms that high direct costs of children are perceived as an important barrier to childbearing (Abramowska et al. 2003).

6.2.2 Family Policies

Since the beginning of the 1990s, the state has been reducing its support to families in terms of financial transfers as well as provision of social services. The undertaken reforms of family policies were largely imposed by the deficiencies in the state budget and were not introduced in response to the changing conditions of living and working as a family (Balcerzak-Paradowska et al. 2003; Kotowska et al. 2008).

Major changes were implemented in the system of income transfers directed to the families. The previously universal system of family benefits was transformed into a selective system, targeted at parents in the highest need. As a consequence, the majority of benefits (i.e., parental leave benefit, child benefit) became means-tested. Further attempts to reduce social expenditures resulted in diminishing the benefit levels in real terms as well as tightening the eligibility criteria (e.g., by lowering the income thresholds) (Balcerzak-Paradowska et al. 2003: 191).

[2]See Appendix, Table A.1 for detailed information on the survey.

Table 6.1 Labour force indicators, Poland 1988–2006

		1988	1993	1998	2003	2006	1988	1993	1998	2003	2006	1988	1993	1998	2003	2006
Indicator	Age	Men					Women					Total				
Labour force	15–24	49.1	46.2	41.0	38.2	37.5	39.3	38.3	33.7	30.5	30.7	44.3	42.2	37.3	34.4	34.2
(% of	25–34	95.3	95.5	93.9	92.9	92.8	73.6	75.4	74.3	77.0	77.0	84.6	85.6	84.2	85.0	85.0
Population)	35–44	94.9	93.7	92.1	92.2	92.1	84.1	85.1	82.6	83.6	81.9	89.5	89.4	87.3	87.9	87.0
	45–54	85.9	83.4	81.4	78.1	80.2	75.9	72.5	71.6	69.1	68.7	80.8	77.8	76.4	73.5	74.3
	55–64	63.7	47.6	44.5	41.8	42.6	42.7	28.9	25.7	23.9	20.3	52.3	37.5	34.3	32.2	30.7
	Total	79.0	75.7	72.8	70.2	70.1	64.0	62.1	59.7	58.4	56.8	71.5	68.8	66.1	64.2	63.4
Employment	15–24	49.1	33.3	32.2	22.1	26.9	39.3	25.9	25.2	17.0	21.0	44.3	29.5	28.6	19.6	24.0
(% of	25–34	95.3	83.3	85.8	75.4	81.3	73.6	60.8	63.7	59.8	65.6	84.6	72.2	74.9	67.7	73.5
Population)	35–44	94.9	83.4	84.7	78.6	83.2	84.1	73.7	73.3	68.4	71.2	89.5	78.5	79.0	73.5	77.2
	45–54	85.9	75.9	75.6	65.9	71.1	75.9	65.8	65.8	59.0	60.3	80.8	70.7	70.6	62.4	65.6
	55–64	63.7	44.4	41.7	36.8	38.4	42.7	27.1	24.3	21.5	19.0	52.3	35.1	32.3	28.6	28.1
	Total	79.0	65.9	65.8	56.7	60.9	64.0	52.1	52.2	46.2	48.2	71.5	58.9	58.9	51.4	54.5
Part-time	15–24	NA	7.9	6.8	11.8	9.5	NA	9.1	10.1	17.6	17.9	NA	8.4	8.3	14.4	13.2
employment	25–54	NA	3.3	2.9	3.3	2.9	NA	5.7	6.2	6.9	7.3	NA	4.4	4.5	5.0	5.0
(% of	55–64	NA	18.0	22.0	14.9	11.5	NA	32.1	33.8	24.7	25.2	NA	22.8	26.5	18.7	16.3
employment)	Total	NA	5.3	5.2	5.4	4.7	NA	7.5	8.1	9.0	9.5	NA	6.3	6.5	7.1	6.9

Table 6.1 (continued)

Indicator	Age	1988	1993	1998	2003	2006	1988	1993	1998	2003	2006	1988	1993	1998	2003	2006
		Men					Women					Total				
Temporary employment (% of employment)	15–24	NA	NA	12.6	52.5	65.4	NA	NA	11.6	55.1	69.7	NA	NA	12.2	53.7	67.3
	25–49	NA	NA	4.4	17.3	25.3	NA	NA	3.5	14.6	22.7	NA	NA	4.0	16.0	24.1
	50–64	NA	NA	6.7	12.2	18.6	NA	NA	4.9	7.3	13.9	NA	NA	5.9	9.9	16.5
	Total	NA	NA	5.9	20.4	28.5	NA	NA	4.7	17.4	26.0	NA	NA	5.4	18.9	27.3
Unemployment (% of Labour force)	15–24	0.0	28.0	21.5	42.1	28.3	0.0	32.5	25.2	44.3	31.6	0.0	30.0	23.2	43.0	29.8
	25–34	0.0	12.8	8.6	18.9	12.4	0.0	19.4	14.2	22.3	14.9	0.0	15.7	11.1	20.4	13.5
	35–44	0.0	11.0	8.0	14.7	9.7	0.0	13.4	11.3	18.2	13.1	0.0	12.1	9.6	16.3	11.3
	45–54	0.0	9.0	7.1	15.7	11.3	0.0	9.4	8.1	14.6	12.1	0.0	9.2	7.6	15.2	11.7
	55–64	0.0	6.7	6.2	12.0	9.8	0.0	6.3	5.5	10.2	6.2	0.0	6.5	5.9	11.2	8.5
	Total	0.0	13.0	9.5	19.3	13.1	0.0	16.1	12.6	20.8	15.1	0.0	14.4	10.9	20.0	14.0
Long-term unemployment	Total	0.0	36.4	32.5	48.6	49.0	0.0	41.6	41.8	50.8	52.0	0.0	39.1	37.4	49.7	50.4

Note: data on part-time employment are based on self-assessment, but persons who usually work more than 40 h per week are classified as full-time employed
Source: 1988 – data from population census ILO LABORSTA database, 1992–2006 – LFS data from OECD Employment Database; except for data on temporary employment which was extracted from Eurostat Statistics Database; data retrieved 3 January 2008

In parallel to weakening financial support for the families, the role of the state in providing childcare services substantially declined. After 1989, the responsibility for operating childcare institutions was shifted from the level of central administration to local authorities. Although childcare provision in Poland was already far from sufficient under the socialist regime the financial shortages of local authorities led to its further worsening. Over the years 1989–2003, the number of places in crèches dropped by 76% and in kindergartens by 25%. No increases in the number of places were recorded since that time. As a result, the coverage rates in Poland are among the lowest in the EU – in 2006, only 2.4% of the under-threes and 61.9% of pre-schoolers attended public day care centres.[3] Furthermore, local authorities aiming to reduce expenditures shifted part of the upkeep costs of childcare institutions (about 30–40%) onto parents. These costs included, for instance, fees for meals, contributions to parents' committee funds, and charges for services beyond the minimum educational program, like foreign languages, music lessons, or sport activities (Balcerzak-Paradowska et al. 2003: 204–205). It was calculated that in 2000 such additional payments accounted for 19% of women's net average wages and 38% of the minimum net wage if only one child was to be sent to kindergarten (Balcerzak-Paradowska et al. 2003: 217).

We now turn our attention to maternity and parental leave provisions. From 1924, employed mothers were entitled to a maternity leave of 16 weeks upon first birth and 18 weeks upon each successive birth[4] as well as to a maternity benefit fully compensating the wage loss. In the meantime, there were only temporary changes in the duration of the leave – in 1999, the leave was extended and in 2002 cut back to pre-1999 levels.[5] The first 14 weeks of the leave are compulsory for the mother, and since 2001 a father can make use of the remaining time. It is notable that a mother can shorten her maternity leave and return to work 14 weeks after birth provided that the father takes advantage of the leave. There is no other opportunity for the mother to shorten the maternity leave and for those mothers whose partners are unemployed the whole maternity leave is compulsory. Up to 2006 Poland had no statutory paternity leave arrangements.

After maternity leave, a parent may take advantage of the parental leave (since 1968). It is granted for a maximum of 36 months; a parent who makes use of it is protected from job loss and receives a legal guarantee to return to work in an equivalent position to the one held prior to birth. From 1981 onwards, parents meeting an income criterion have been entitled to a flat-rate parental leave benefit. Parental leave, as introduced during state socialism, did not meet the conditions of labour

[3]In fact, the coverage rate for children aged 3–6 has been continuously increasing since 1992, but this effect is entirely caused by a decline in the number of children.

[4]In 2008, maternity leave was prolonged to 18 weeks upon first birth and 20 weeks upon higher-order birth; in 2009 it was further prolonged to 20 weeks, irrespectively of birth order. It is longer in case of a multiple birth.

[5]In 1999, the leave was extended to 20 weeks and in 2001 to 26 weeks.

force participation under the market economy. Its major drawback was its inflexibility. Nevertheless, only in the second half of the 1990s and early 2000s were some reforms to the parental leave law introduced to adjust it to the EU regulations. Since 1996, fathers have been entitled to the leave; from 2002 onwards, the right to the leave can be replaced by the right to work part-time; and since 2003, the leave can be divided into four parts. Beginning in 2003, parents on leave can also undertake educational or professional activities as long as these do not limit their ability to take care of a child. Nevertheless, a survey conducted in 2005 shows that less than 10% of parents on parental leave made use of these entitlements (Matysiak, 2007a: 377).[6] The non-congruency of the parental leave to the conditions of labour force participation under the market economy is well reflected in the take-up rates. In 2005, only 50% of mothers and merely 2.6% of fathers entitled to the leave made use of it. Women who took parental leave were more likely to be low-educated, and almost 70% of them were entitled to parental benefit (Matysiak, 2007a: 375). Economic factors dominate among the reasons for not taking advantage of the leave (22%), although respondents also mention the negative effects of a career break on employment prospects or simply preference for work (17% each) (Matysiak, 2007a: 376).

In general, the Polish family policies as very unsupportive of the dual-earner model. Parents are forced to withdraw from economic activity for the period of care, unless they can rely on relatives. In fact in 2005, around 40% of working mothers reported that relatives took care of their children aged 14 or less during office hours, while only 20% made use of day care centres (Matysiak, 2007a: 369). Lack of statutory paternity rights and compulsory character of the maternity leave indicate additionally that care of an infant is perceived to be a female task. Comparing the Polish family policies to the policies in other EU member states we found in Chapter 4 that the institutional support to working parents in Poland is the worst in the whole EU. Poland earns this low position mainly due to the poorest childcare provision for the youngest children as well as those aged three to school age, no incentives for fathers to stay at home to take care of a child and low wage compensation during the parental leave.

6.2.3 Labour Market Structures

In Chapter 4 we proposed an index of structural incompatibilities between fertility and women's work. It was based on two other indicators measuring the magnitude of the barriers to the labour market entry and flexibility of the work arrangements. Based on this index, it turns out that among the EU member states, Norway

[6]The data come from a representative survey, 'Reconciliation of family and work' carried out in 2005 on the LFS sample (see Appendix, Table A.1).

and Switzerland only Greece and Slovakia are characterised by stronger structural incompatibilities than Poland (see Section 4.3). Both components of the index point to strong structural conflict between family and work in Poland. First, for some social groups, like the youth or women, it is exceptionally difficult to find a job. Second, the possibilities for adjusting the working hours to family responsibilities are highly limited.

Under the market economy, the barriers to labour market entry in Poland have been particularly large for the youth. While in 1988 44% of persons aged 15–24 were employed, in 1993 this percentage amounted to 29.5% and in 2003 to 19.6% (Table 6.1). At the same time, the unemployment rate in this age group jumped to 30% in 1993. After it fell to 23.2% in 1998 it doubled within the next 4 years, reaching levels twice as high as the total unemployment rate. Only in recent years has the situation of school graduates improved as Poland entered a path of fast economic growth. In 2006 Poland still displayed the highest joblessness among the youth in the EU, however. What is worse, labour market entrants in Poland have been also severely exposed to instability of employment contracts. After the law on temporary employment was liberalised in 2001, the percentage of the youth employed on a temporary basis increased rapidly and reached almost 70% by 2006.

Apart from the youth, women also face large barriers to labour market entry. Over the years 1992–2006, the unemployment rate of females was constantly 2–3% points higher than that of males (Table 6.1). Even larger differences were observed for persons aged 25–34. In this age group, the unemployment gap oscillated between 5.5 and 7.2% points until 2001, after which year it declined to the levels of 2.5–3.5. Women were also more likely to experience long-term unemployment (longer than one year). This was particularly true in the years 1994–2000, when the incidence of long-term unemployment was 20% higher for females than for males. The relatively larger difficulties experienced by women in finding a job and remaining employed were confirmed by micro-level studies, controlling for education level and family situation as well as job characteristics (Góra, 1996; Sztanderska & Grotkowska, 2007).

Besides large barriers to labour market entry, Poland is also characterised by very low flexibility of work arrangements. Since the beginning of the 1990s, the proportion of women working part-time oscillated between 7.5 and 10% (4.7 and 6% for men), while the EU-15 average exceeded 30%. The part-timers were mainly persons in pre-retirement and early retirement age and not women in the reproductive ages, as is commonly observed in Western Europe. Hence, the nature of part-time employment in Poland was different from the West. Analyses by Matysiak (2007a, 2007b) suggest that this form of employment is not undertaken for the purpose of combining motherhood with paid work, but rather constitutes a mere alternative for those who cannot find a full-time position. Having children does not increase the risk of taking a part-time job; in fact, only 5% of employed mothers are interested in reducing the number of working hours. This low interest in part-time employment is to be attributed to economic factors – over 60% of women and 72% of men in full-time positions reject the possibility of reducing the number of working hours because it

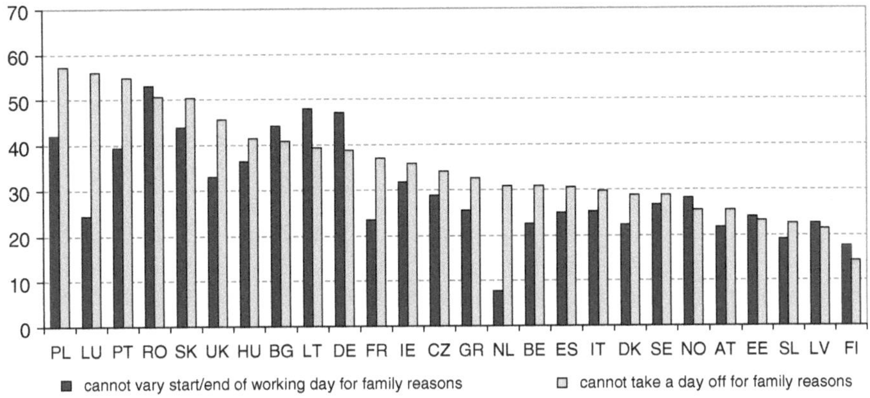

Fig. 6.1 Flexibility of working hours, % of those who cannot vary the start/end of working day or take a day off for family reasons
Source: Author's calculations based on the Eurostat Statistics Database.

would lead to lower earnings. At the same time, over 30% of part-timers admit that they accepted this form of employment since they could not find a full-time job.[7]

Finally, the working hours in Poland are exceptionally rigid compared to other EU member states. According to the data from the Eurostat's survey 'Reconciliation of family and work', conducted in all EU member states in 2005, as many as 42% of the employees are not allowed to vary the start and the end of the working day, and 57% cannot take a day off due to family reasons (Fig. 6.1). For comparison, for the EU-15 these figures amount to 30 and 36% and for Finland, where one of the lowest pair of values are recorded, to 17 and 14% respectively.[8]

6.2.4 Social Norms for Women's Roles

During state socialism, female labour force participation was ideologically supported by the state, and the dual-earner family model was widely socially accepted. A hallmark of this system was, however, that women were not only expected to earn income, but contrary to men they were also perceived as main care providers (Kotowska, 1995; Siemieńska, 1997). This led to the adoption of the so-called dual-earner/female double-burden model. This traditional perception of gender roles still prevails in Poland today.

---

[7]The provided percentages are computed by Matysiak (2007a, 2007b) based on three representative surveys conducted in the second quarter 2005: the Polish Labour Force Survey, the 'Reconciliation of family and work' ($N = 37{,}849$ aged 15–64) and the 'Reconciling family, work and education' ($N = 5{,}564$ aged 18–64) – see Appendix, Table A.1 for more information on the surveys.

[8]The data come from the Eurostat Statistics Database.

As we showed in Chapter 4, Poland displays the strongest cultural incompatibilities between women's employment and fertility after Lithuania and Greece. Poles perceive women's roles very traditionally, often expressing the beliefs that what women really want are home and children and that most women would be happy to be housewives. What is, however, very typical of Poland are the concerns about the negative repercussions of mother's employment on the well-being of children. These concerns are present also in other European countries, but they are definitely most often expressed in Poland (compare Fig. 4.5 in Chapter 4). The traditional perception of gender roles and the serious concerns about well-being of children when the mother works are probably major factors underpinning the exceptionally strong objection to women's employment if there are pre-school children at home which prevails in Poland. Nearly 60% of respondents interviewed within the International Social Survey Programme in 2002 (ISSP, 2002) think that mothers of young children should stay at home. It is the highest proportion among the EU member states, Norway, and Switzerland. For comparison, the proportion sharing this opinion in the remaining CEE countries was in on average 41% and in Sweden it was only 19% (Fig. 6.2). The support for women's work increases as children reach the school age. Still, the proportion of those who oppose it is the highest in Poland and amounts to 25% against 16% in the remaining CEE countries and 2% in Sweden.

Despite these traditional beliefs on women's social roles Polish women are expected to contribute to the household income together with men. Similar belief is present in other post-socialist countries. The coexistence of these contradictory social norms on women's involvement in the labour market in the CEE countries demonstrates a pragmatic attitude to women's family and economic roles, providing

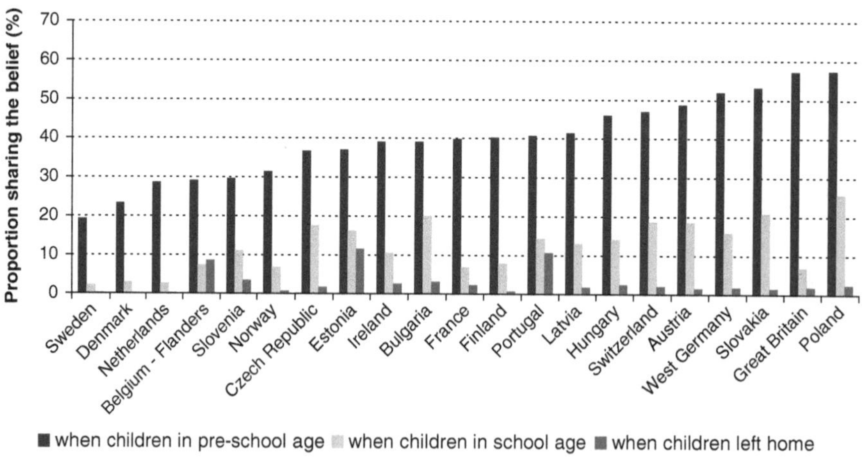

Fig. 6.2 Proportion claiming that a mother should stay at home, by age of children, EU member states, Norway, and Switzerland 2002
Source: Author's calculations on ISSP 2002.

evidence of the prevalence of the dual earner/female double burden family model: if there are young children at home women should withdraw from employment to take care of a child, but in other cases they should swiftly take up a job to contribute to the household income.

6.2.5 *Contextual Opportunities and Restrictions: Concluding Remarks*

The changes brought about by economic transformation and later by globalisation processes, reflected in rising labour market competition, led to a substantial intensification of the conflict between childrearing and market work. Although family and labour market policies could have mitigated some of the difficulties women face, not much was done in that respect. In fact, the state even limited its support for working mothers, by reducing expenditures on public childcare. The lack of social services has been compensated by long parental leave schemes that do not respond to the needs of many women, in particular the better educated who wish to remain economically active after childbirth. Furthermore, no incentives encouraging fathers to withdraw from employment temporarily to take over part of the family obligations were built in the Polish family policy model. The underlying assumption of this model is thus that childcare is a female task. Additionally to weak public support offered to working parents, the incompatibilities between childrearing and paid employment are intensified by strong barriers to labour market entry and inflexible work arrangements and low social acceptance of the labour force participation of mothers. At the same time, however, the increasing instability of employment, strong unemployment pressure, and rising individual responsibility for one's economic well-being provide a strong rationale for women's economic activity. Indeed, an opinion that females should contribute to the household budget is shared by a large part of the society, placing a double burden on women.

6.3 Developments in Fertility and Women's Labour Supply

Against this background description of the macro-context in which fertility and women's labour force decisions are made, we present in this section the changes in women's behaviours in these two spheres of life which took place after the collapse of state socialism. Our discussion is supplemented by available data on women's orientations towards family and paid work.

6.3.1 *Changes in Fertility Patterns and Women's Orientations Towards Family*

Poland was experiencing a decline in childbearing already in the early 1980s. At the beginning, this downward trend was relatively slow, but it accelerated substantially

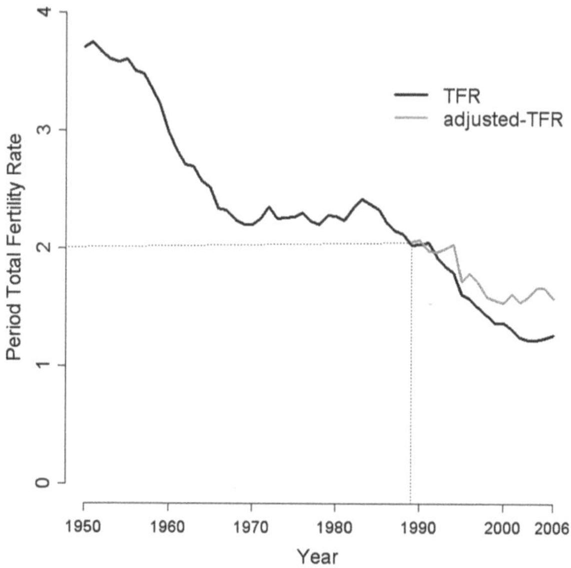

Fig. 6.3 Period total fertility rate, Poland 1950–2006 Source: TFR – Central Statistical Office of Poland, adjusted-TFR – Tymicki (2008).

after the onset of the economic transformation. While in 1983, the last year before the decline in childbearing was observed, the TFR amounted to 2.4, in 1989 it was 2.07, and by 2003 reached 1.22 (Fig. 6.3). This means that over 14 years of economic transformation, Poland moved from the high fertility to the lowest-low fertility countries. Only in recent years has a slight improvement in childbearing been recorded, with the TFR rising to 1.27 in 2006.

The observed decline in fertility reflects quantum as well as tempo effects. According to the estimates by Sobotka et al. (2005), postponement of childbearing was a major factor responsible for a decline in TFR in the first years of the economic transformation. With time, the quantum effects gained in importance, however. Altogether, over the years 1990–2002 around 48% of births were lost due to quantum and 52% due to tempo effects. Similar conclusions can be drawn based on the adjusted-TFR. This measure indicates that the total fertility would be higher by 0.2–0.3 children per woman in the whole period after 1993 if the distortions caused by the changes in the tempo of childbearing were eliminated. This means a total fertility of 1.58 in 2006.

Fertility postponement led to important shifts in fertility patterns by age. In 1989, women aged 20–24 were characterised by the highest childbearing intensities. Since 1998, the highest fertility has been recorded among women aged 25–29. Increases in childbearing intensities have also been observed among women aged 30–34 (see Fig. 6.4). To illustrate this shift in fertility into higher ages, we compare the contribution of births to TFR for different age groups of women in 1989 and 2006. While at the beginning of the economic transformation children born to women aged 20–24, 25–29, and 30–34 accounted for 36, 30, and 18% of all births, in 2006 these

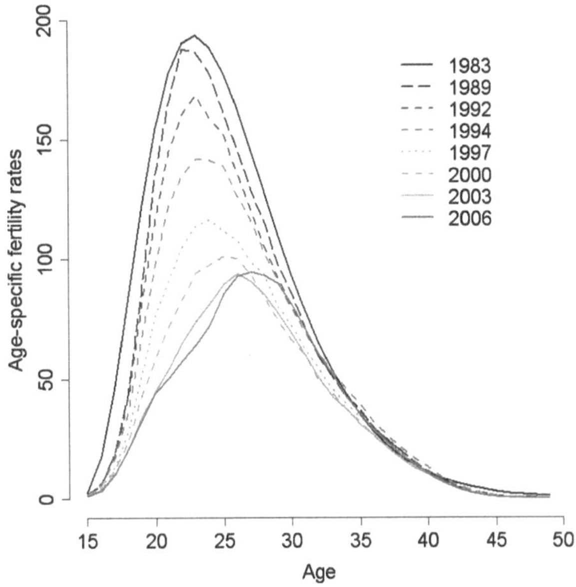

Fig. 6.4 Age-specific fertility rates, Poland 1983–2006
Source: CSO data, calculations by Tymicki (2008).

figures were 25, 37, and 23%, respectively.[9] As a result, the mean age at first delivery rose from 23.3 to 25.7 years, and the average interval between first and second birth lengthened by one year and a half (Tymicki, 2008).

Despite the negative developments in fertility, family and children still have an important position in the value system of the Poles. Among the countries participating in the Population Policy Acceptance Study, the Poles, together with the Lithuanians and the Hungarians, appeared to set a relatively high priority on marriage, while they strongly opposed de-institutionalisation of the family and relatively often expressed a belief that children, family, and home ensured happiness and self-fulfilment (Pongracz & Spèder, 2008; Stankuniene & Maslauskaite, 2008). Hence, it is not surprising that people in Poland would like to have more children than they have in reality. According to the data from the Eurobarometer survey of 2006, the gap between the actual and desired number of children by women aged 25–34 is 0.86, which is at the EU-25 level. Only 2% of women aged 15–39 with no children do not plan to have any offspring, whereas as many as 84% intend to have at least two children. The figures for the EU-25 amount to 11 and 63%, respectively (Testa, 2006a). Yet, these relatively high fertility intentions of Polish women seem to be very sensitive to economic conditions. The IPPAS conducted in Poland during the economic slowdown yielded a lower number of intended children, mainly due to an increase in the percentage of undecided (see Table 6.2).

[9] Author's calculation based on CSO data.

Table 6.2 Intended number of children, women with no children

Country	Data source	No children	One	Two	Three	Four or more	Don't know	Total
Poland	IPPAS 2001 (women aged 18–39)	8.6	8.0	41.4	8.0	0.8	33.1	100.0
Poland	Eurobarometer 2006 (women aged 15–39)	2.0	15.0	58.0	10.0	4.0	12.0	100.0
EU-25	Eurobarometer 2006 (women aged 15–39)	11.0	9.0	43.0	13.0	3.0	20.0	100.0

Source: Testa (2006a) and author's calculations on PPAS 2001

6.3.2 Transformations in the Labour Market and Women's Orientations Towards Paid Work

Under state socialism, women's participation in paid employment was relatively high. In 1988, 64% of women aged 15–64 and 74% of women aged 25–34 were employed. Women's employment was facilitated by high demand for their labour, generated by the labour-intensive economy and low productivity. Additionally, low wage policy led to the situation in which two incomes were necessary for maintaining a family. Despite the traditional perception of gender roles, the conflict between childbearing and paid employment was probably low at that time. Strong job guarantees, a right-to-a-job ideology as well as public childcare provision made it possible to combine motherhood with market work. This situation changed dramatically after the collapse of state socialism. Opening of the Polish economy to the global markets led to a rise in labour market competition and consequently to a rapid increase in employers' requirements regarding skills, mobility, and flexibility of workers. As a consequence, the conflict between the time spent with the family and the time devoted to work-related activities, including investments in human capital, was severely intensified (Kotowska, 2004, 2005). Although the social policy could have developed some instruments directed at supporting reconciliation between family and work, exactly the opposite tendency was observed. Given the gradual eradication of public support for working parents in combination with large barriers to the labour market experienced by females, rigid work arrangements, and traditional attitudes towards working women, one could expect that under the new conditions of labour force participation, the involvement of women in paid employment would deteriorate much more than in the case of men.

These expectations were not fulfilled, however. Comparing data from 1988 and 1992 reveals that, in the first years of the economic transformation, women's employment rate deteriorated by 1.2% points less than that of men (Fig. 6.5). Furthermore, this gender gap in the absolute rate of decline widened over time and in 2006 amounted to 2.4% points. Even larger gender differences were observed among persons aged 25–34, i.e., those in the highest reproductive ages. Although in the early 1990s the employment rate of women in this age group fell by 1% points more than the one for men, in the years 1994–1998 women benefited from

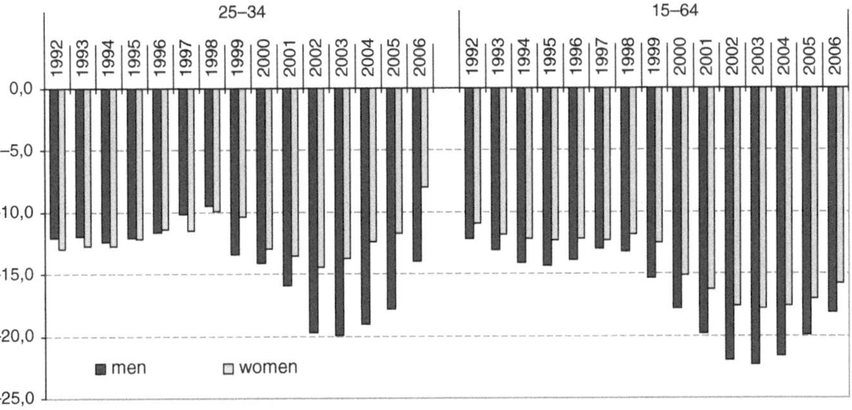

Fig. 6.5 Absolute rate of decline in employment rate relative to 1988, by gender
Source: Data for 1992–2006 drawn from the Labour Force Survey, data for 1988 from the Population Census; data extracted from the OECD Employment Database 10 October 2008.

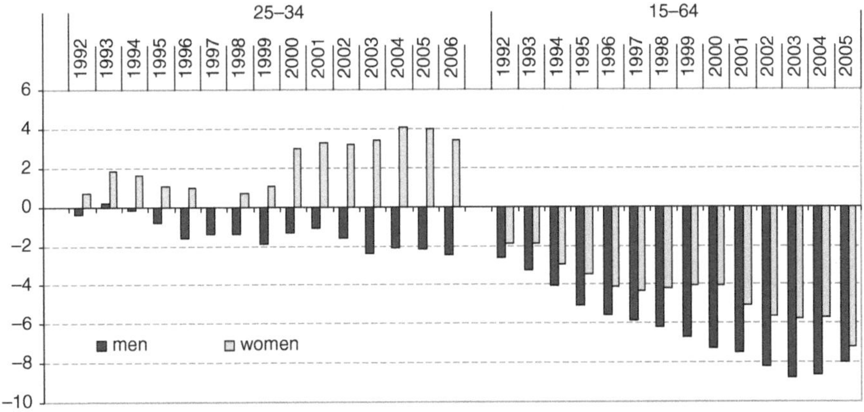

Fig. 6.6 Absolute rate of decline in labour force participation rate relative to 1988, by gender
Source: Data for 1992–2006 drawn from the Labour Force Survey, data for 1988 from the Population Census; data extracted from the OECD Employment Database 10 October 2008.

increases in employment to a larger extent and lost much less during the economic slowdown of 1998–2003. Altogether, in 2006 the employment rate of females aged 25–34 was 8% points lower than in 1988, while for men this difference amounted to 14% points. Moreover, looking at the changes in labour force participation, one can notice that women aged 25–34 in fact increased their economic activity while among men a decline was observed (Fig. 6.6). The high determination of women to find a job and to remain employed is also reflected in the data stemming from opinion surveys. For instance, the survey 'Reconciling family, work and education' conducted in 2005 showed that, among working women aged 20–49 who declared that they provided care to family members, only 6% said that the best solution to mitigate the tensions between professional and care duties would be to give up a job. Similarly, only around 10% of non-working women admitted the voluntary character of their inactivity. These findings do not change if we limit our observation only to mothers of young children (Matysiak, 2007b: 387, 394).

The data presented here clearly indicate a strong motivation of women to participate in paid employment despite the difficulties in combining work with family duties. Given the economic developments described, as well as the severe deterioration of men's employment, one could expect financial necessities to be mainly responsible for this determination. The data from the survey 'Reconciling family, work and education' support this belief. In this survey, employed respondents were presented with a list of statements describing the consequences of exiting employment. They were asked to evaluate each statement on a 5-point Likert scale, taking into account the relevance of the consequence for their personal situation. The scale ranged from −2 (completely unimportant) to +2 (very important). The financial aspects of paid employment as well as a fear of being unable to resume employment were assessed as the most important reasons for remaining in employment (Fig. 6.7). Interestingly, there are no substantial gender differences in that respect, which suggests that economic motives for being employed are as important for women as for men. Note, however, that apart from material aspirations, other higher-order motives also seem to drive people's decisions to work. These are largely a desire for independence as well as a search for personal development and self-fulfilment.

Based on these developments, it was hypothesised in the literature that women, motivated by a desire to have a job but at the same time experiencing difficulties with fulfilling this wish, developed certain strategies in order to reach their goal. One of

Fig. 6.7 Motives for paid work among the employed aged 25–44, Poland 2005
Note: Each of the statements was evaluated on the scale ranging from −2 (strongly disagree) to +2 (strongly agree). Mean answers are presented in the figure.
Source: Author's calculations on data from the survey 'Reconciling family, work and education'.

them was increased participation in education (Sztanderska, 2005: 46). Although educational attainment rose strongly for both sexes, this process was much more pronounced for women. As a result, in 2006 the ratio of female to male university graduates aged 25–34 was 3:2.[10] The rationale behind this strategy lies in the protective character of education against unemployment and inactivity. For instance, in 2005 the gender employment gap for university graduates was close to zero, compared to 20% points for those with vocational education in favour of men (Kotowska & Sztanderska, 2007: 35). Fertility postponement is suggested in the literature as another adjustment strategy developed by women in order to get a job and remain employed (Kotowska et al. 2008). Strong cultural, institutional, as well as structural incompatibilities between family and work threaten the prospects of labour market (re-)entry after birth and may encourage women to delay fertility decisions until they establish a stable position in the labour market. This hypothesis presupposing that women postponed childbearing until they entered employment is tested in the following sections. We address it separately for women with no children and women who already had their first child, thereby allowing us to obtain a deeper insight into the reconciliation strategies of women. In other words, we verify not only whether the selection operated before the first birth but also whether women who had given birth tended to enter or re-enter the workforce before conceiving another child.

6.4 Endogeneity of Fertility and Women's Work: Methodological Developments

In Chapter 3, we concluded that the interdependencies between fertility and women's employment could not be well understood unless one accounted for women's material aspirations as well as their orientations towards family and paid work. If doing so is not possible, selection effects might occur and what we interpret as a conflict between childbearing and women's employment is in fact a mix of a price effect and selection effects. We distinguish two types of selection effects. *Negative selection* refers to the situation in which women give up one activity (employment or childbearing) with a prospect to get involved in the other. By contrast, *positive selection* implies that women want to combine employment and childbearing and for this reason will undertake one activity (employment or childbearing) with a plan to get involved in the other in the future. Hence, if they expect that having children before entering a professional career will impede their chances in the labour market, they will tend to find a job first and will realise their fertility intentions only after their situation in the labour market is stable enough, i.e., they have a job they can return to after the birth. Positive selection is very likely to occur

[10] According to the LFS data, in 1992 the percentage of university graduates among persons aged 25–34 amounted to 8.7 for women and 7.1 for men. In 2006 these figures were 33.1 and 22.1, respectively.

if we do not control for material aspirations or if the majority of women are adaptive. In fact, the hypothesis that is tested in this chapter pre-supposes positive selection.

In reality, controlling for household's economic situation, contextual opportunities and restrictions as well as women's orientations towards family and paid work is often not possible due to data unavailability. Since all these factors influence fertility as well as women's labour supply, omitting them from analysis of the impact of childbearing on economic activity or vice versa leads, in statistical terms, to an endogeneity bias in the estimation of the relationship between women's labour supply and fertility. This means that the labour market status (child status) variable in the model of fertility (female labour force participation) is not only correlated with the dependent variable but also with its error term. The endogeneity bias may lead to an overestimation or underestimation of the conflict between childbearing and women's economic activity. The former takes place if the negative selection is in force, whereas the latter is a consequence of the positive selection.

The problem of endogeneity of fertility and women's labour supply is not new to the social sciences. Some attempts were made to account for it even in the 1980s. These efforts were undertaken mainly by economists. With the objective of estimating the direct impact of fertility on female labour force participation, net of women's intentions, needs, and life-goals, they aimed at computing the effect of an unplanned child on women's work. The instrumental variables estimation method was proposed to deal with this issue in the first stage. This method requires replacing variables describing fertility with instrumental variables, i.e., exogenous to women's labour supply but highly correlated with fertility. Assuming that the biological capacity to bear children is mostly unaffected by the couple's choice, Rosenzweig and Schultz (1985) tried to estimate the couple-specific fecundity and to use it as an instrument. An even more innovative approach was suggested by Rosenzweig and Wolpin (1980), who treated twins in the first birth as an unplanned child outcome and compared the labour force participation of mothers with 'twins first' to the labour force participation of other mothers. Angrist and Evans (1998) and Carrasco (2001) suggested using sibling sex composition as an instrument as demographic literature brought evidence for an increased propensity of parents with two children of the same sex to progress to the third child. The idea underlying this approach was to eliminate the bias in the estimates of the impact of children on labour force participation caused by fertility planning. Although all these studies were undoubtedly considered as innovative, at the same time they illustrate serious difficulties with finding proper instruments. The proposed instrumental variables are either not available and hard to estimate (like couple specific-fecundity) or their use results in a serious sample selection (mothers, mothers of at least two children) or the number of studied events is very low (multiple births).

These problems with modelling fertility and women's employment led to the conclusion that the variables should be analysed jointly (Ermisch, 1990; Del Boca & Locatelli, 2006). Hence, in a number of studies, researchers investigated the impact of a set of observed and unobserved exogenous determinants on the probability of having a newborn and being employed at the same time (Di Tommaso, 1999; Francesconi, 2002; Del Boca, 2002; Del Boca et al. 2005). These studies do not yield any estimates of the effects of fertility on employment and vice versa, since they assume that all fertility and employment outcomes are results of decision-making, and thus are caused by a set of exogenous factors, and the observed relationship between the two variables is spurious. Given that some women may become pregnant against their plan, may be infecund, lose a job, experience an unforeseen promotion or unexpected job satisfaction, the proposed approach is not satisfactory.

In this study, we do not have data describing women's financial or higher-order needs pertaining to either family or employment. Given the methodological developments we have presented, we propose to model childbearing and women's work jointly, but we allow the possibility that some of the fertility and employment outcomes are unexpected. This is achieved by estimating a multi-process hazard model developed by Lillard, Brien, and Waite (1995) and Lillard and Panis (1996). This method allows for controlling for the unobserved woman-specific preference for work and children in the fertility as well as employment equations. In this way, the bias in the impact of fertility (women's employment) on women's employment (fertility) caused by endogeneity is eliminated, and a direct relationship between the two variables is estimated. The advantage of the multi-process hazard model over the instrumental methodology is that it does not require searching for instruments, and it does allow for an assessment of the correlation between the person-specific unmeasured heterogeneity components (Lillard & Panis, 1996). To the best of our knowledge, this method has so far been used for studying interdependencies between fertility and women's employment only for the United Kingdom (Aassve et al. 2006). The multi-process hazard model we employ is described in detail in Section 6.6. Before that, in Section 6.5 we provide brief information on the data used in the analysis.

6.5 Data

The data for our analysis are derived from the Employment, Family and Education Survey. This is a retrospective survey conducted in October and November 2006 on a representative sample of 3,000 women born in 1966–1981 and their partners. The survey was prepared at the Institute of Statistics and Demography (Warsaw School of Economics) under the project 'Cultural and structural conditions of female labour force participation in Poland', financed by the Ministry of Science and Higher Education and coordinated by Professor Irena E. Kotowska. Instead of the traditional method of collecting retrospective data, a life history calendar method was applied (Freedman et al. 1988). The dataset contains respondents' education, employment, partnership, fertility, and migration histories since the age of 15, recorded on a monthly basis. Unfortunately, since over 50% of partners refused to participate in the survey, we decided to conduct our analysis using only the data for women, with the cost of losing the information about men.

In our study we focused on women born 1971–1981. These women were 8–18 years old in 1989 and 25–35 in 2006. Thus, the majority of their reproductive and employment careers took place under the new market conditions. For each woman, we created four detailed event histories: having first child, having second or higher-order child, entering and exiting employment. Women with incomplete event histories, those who experienced multiple births or had any foster or adopted children were dropped from the sample. As a result, out of 2,185 women born 1971–81, a total of 2,090 were selected for the study.

The dataset we used divides the labour market status of a woman into four categories: employed and working for pay, employed but on maternity leave, employed but on parental leave, and not employed (unemployed and inactive). For the purpose of our study, we grouped women into two categories: employed and non-employed. The employed are women who work in the market (including the self-employed and helping family members) as well as women on maternity leave, since maternity leave is obligatory in Poland. By contrast, the non-employed are women who are on parental leave, are unemployed, or inactive. Mothers who gave birth during the parental leave and hence automatically started the maternity leave are counted as not employed either. The decision to treat women on parental leave as non-employed was made for several reasons. First, parental leave, in contrast to maternity leave, is not mandatory in Poland. Second, it is unpaid for the majority of potential beneficiaries because of the low income threshold of entitlement to parental benefit. Third, the take-up rates are relatively low, suggesting that it is not an attractive option for parents who would rather search for other solutions for organising care. Finally, this approach seemed to be more appropriate to us given our aim of assessing the magnitude of the conflict between fertility and paid employment.

Finally, a woman is classified as exiting employment when she becomes not employed. Therefore, cases when a person remains continuously employed but changes a job, switches from part-time to full-time or from temporary to permanent contract, are not counted as changes in employment status.

6.6 Multi-process Hazard Model

In this section we introduce the statistical method we propose for analysing the interdependencies between fertility and women's employment. First, we specify a set of single-process hazard models. In the second step, a multi-process hazard model is presented.

In order to analyse interdependencies between fertility and women's employment we specify four intensity regression models. They describe transition to first birth, transition to second or higher-order birth, employment entry, and employment exit, respectively:

$$\ln\{h^{C1}(t)\} = \sum_{l} y_l^{C1}(t) + \sum_{m} z_m^{C1}(t - t_{0m}) + \alpha^{C1} e(t) + \sum_{n} \beta_n^{C1} x_n + \sum_{s} \gamma_s^{C1} w_s(t)$$
$$+ \varepsilon + \mu^{C1} \tag{6.1}$$

$$\ln\{h_i^{C2+}(t)\} = \sum_l y_l^{C2+}(t) + \quad +\alpha^{C2+}e(t) + \sum_n \beta_n^{C2+}x_n + \sum_s \gamma_s^{C2+}w_s(t) \\ +\varepsilon + \mu_i^{C2+} \tag{6.2}$$

$$\ln\{h_j^{EN}(t)\} = \sum_l y_l^{EN}(t) + \sum_m z_m^{EN}(t - t_{0m}) + \alpha^{EN}p(t) + \sum_n \beta_n^{EN}x_n + \sum_s \gamma_s^{EN}w_s(t) \\ +\xi + \mu_j^{EN} \tag{6.3}$$

$$\ln\{h_k^{EX}(t)\} = \sum_l y_l^{EX}(t) + \sum_m z_m^{EX}(t - t_{0m}) + \alpha^{EX}p(t) + \sum_n \beta_n^{EX}x_n + \sum_s \gamma_s^{EX}w_s(t) \\ +\eta + \mu_k^{EX} \tag{6.4}$$

where h^{C1} and $h_i{}^{C2+}$ are the hazards of first and subsequent conceptions respectively (measured 7 months before birth), $h_j{}^{EN}$ denotes the hazard of employment entry for non-employment spell j, and $h_k{}^{EX}$ stands for the hazard of employment exit for employment spell k. The subscript for an individual was suppressed for simplicity.

Each woman was observed from the age of 15. At this age, a woman starts to be at risk of conceiving her first child. Once the child has been born, the woman becomes at risk of conceiving the second child, and after the second child has been born, she becomes at risk of third conception, and so on. Transitions to second or higher-order child were specified within one hazard function, separately from the transitions to first child. The in- and out-of-employment transitions were defined similarly, with the difference that they are mutually exclusive. At age 15, all women are out of employment. Once a woman takes up a job, she falls under the risk of exiting employment and as soon as this happens, she becomes exposed to entering employment again. The observation was censored at the date of the interview.

The baseline log hazards were composed of multiple clocks of duration dependence, each represented by a piecewise linear spline $y(t)$ or a conditional piecewise linear spline $z(t-t_0)$ starting from an origin t_0 relevant to each individual. A piecewise linear spline function $y(t)$ is a vector of $n+1$ spline variables whose slope coefficients vary across intervals separated by n nodes. By specifying several piecewise linear spline functions of time, all defined as above but differing in the number of node points and width of the between-node intervals, the formulation allows for a variety of patterns of duration dependence (for more details see Lillard, 1993; Lillard & Waite, 1993).

The baseline log hazard of first conception was specified as a sum of time elapsed since age 15, calendar time since 1986, and time since completing education, whereas the baseline log hazard of second or higher-order conception is composed of calendar time elapsed since 1988 (the earliest year when first children were born to women) and time since the birth of the previous child. Current age, calendar time since 1986, and time since employment exit built the baseline hazard of employment entry. The same set of time-related factors, with time since employment entry replacing time since employment exit, made up the baseline hazard of employment exit. Additionally, we introduced work experience in the fourth equation.

Several endogenous and exogenous covariates were assumed to shift the baseline hazards proportionally. The endogenous covariates are a binary variable denoting employment, *e(t)*, in the hazard of first as well as higher-order conceptions, and a variable indicating birth order in the hazards of employment entry and exit, *p(t)*. The set of exogenous time-constant covariates, *x*, includes variables describing woman's social background, proxied by education level of parents, and her age at previous birth (only in the equation describing the transition to second or higher-order conception). The time-varying covariates, *w(t)*, are woman's education level, her work-experience (in the equation for employment entry), urban/rural place of residence, and order of the conception, non-employment and employment episode in the repeated-event equations respectively. Additionally, a set of covariates on woman's job characteristics is introduced into the equation modelling the intensity of employment exit.

Due to data unavailability, some important factors determining women's fertility and labour market decisions cannot be incorporated into our models. Among others, these are the material aspirations of women as well as their orientations towards family and work. One of the solutions for measuring the material aspirations would be to adopt the concept of relative income. Following Macunovich (1996), it could be computed by dividing the income earned by individuals born in the 1970s by the income of their parents. Such data are not available for us, however. Nor does our survey provide us with any information on household economic situation, which could serve as a proxy for material aspirations. In order to eliminate the possible selection bias caused by these data shortcomings, we decided to capture the woman-specific unobserved heterogeneity in a different manner. Thanks to the fact that each woman was observed over several conception, employment, and non-employment spells, it was possible to divide the unobserved heterogeneity pertaining to each of the analysed processes into two components: person-specific, denoted by ε, ξ, and η, and transition-specific, represented by μ^{C1}, μ_i^{C2+}, μ_j^{EN}, μ_k^{EX} (e.g., Keiding, 1998). The unobserved heterogeneity components ε, ξ, and η were assumed to be constant across all conception, non-employment, and employment spells respectively and to follow normal distributions with zero means and standard deviations of σ_ε, σ_ξ, and σ_η. They represent woman-specific unobserved propensities to have a child, to enter and to exit employment correspondingly. Hence, by incorporating ε into our models of first and higher order conception hazards, we accounted for woman-specific orientation towards family. Likewise, including ξ and η into the models of employment entry and exit respectively we controlled for women's material aspirations and orientation towards market work.

The common approach to studying interdependencies between fertility and women's employment is to model the Eqs. (6.1), (6.2), (6.3), and (6.4) separately as *single-process hazard models*. An assumption that underlines such model specification is that the random effects ε, ξ and η are mutually uncorrelated. Nevertheless, fertility is not only determined by women's orientations towards family, but also by material aspirations as well as orientations towards paid work. Likewise, employment transitions are influenced by women's orientations towards family, additional to material aspirations and orientations towards market work. Hence, a lack of the correlation between the unobserved propensity to have children and to enter / exit employment seems to be very unrealistic. Yet, a failure to account for this correlation, if it exists, leads to an endogeneity bias in the estimation of the impacts of women's employment on conception risk and the impact of birth order on employment transitions. Therefore, following Lillard et al. (1995), we estimated the Eqs. (6.1), (6.2), (6.3), and (6.4) jointly, by allowing for pair wise correlations between woman-specific unobserved heterogeneity terms. The joint distribution of the random effects is assumed to be normal:

$$\begin{pmatrix} \varepsilon \\ \xi \\ \eta \end{pmatrix} \sim N\left(\begin{pmatrix} 0 \\ 0 \\ 0 \end{pmatrix}, \begin{pmatrix} \sigma_\varepsilon^2 & \rho_{\varepsilon\xi} & \rho_{\varepsilon\eta} \\ \rho_{\xi\varepsilon} & \sigma_\xi^2 & \rho_{\xi\eta} \\ \rho_{\eta\varepsilon} & \rho_{\eta\xi} & \sigma_\eta^2 \end{pmatrix}\right) \tag{6.5}$$

The specification given by (6.1), (6.2), (6.3), (6.4), and (6.5) represents a *multi-process hazard model*. Additionally to single-process hazard models, it requires the correlations between the random terms ε, ξ and η to be estimated. If fertility and employment are endogenous, the correlation between the woman-specific unobserved propensity to have children, ε, and the woman-specific unobserved propensity to participate in paid employment, ξ and η, is significant ($\rho_{\varepsilon\xi} \neq 0$ and $\rho_{\varepsilon\eta} \neq 0$). Furthermore, the correlation sign defines the selection type. *Positive selection* takes place if the woman's unobserved propensity to have children, ε, is positively correlated with the woman's unobserved propensity to enter employment, ξ, but negatively correlated with the propensity to exit employment, η, ($\rho_{\varepsilon\xi} > 0$ and $\rho_{\varepsilon\eta} < 0$). In the opposite case, i.e., if $\rho_{\varepsilon\xi} < 0$ and $\rho_{\varepsilon\eta} > 0$, we have to do with *negative selection*. Finally, a correlation between ξ and η is also possible since women's choices between employment and non-employment are very likely to be driven by the same set of unobserved characteristics.

Three important steps precede the estimation of the parameters of the multi-process hazard model. First, a likelihood conditional on the observed variables and the random effects has to be derived for each of the four processes. These conditional likelihoods are denoted as $L(\alpha^{C1}, \beta_n^{C1}, \gamma_s^{C1}|\varepsilon)$, $L(\alpha^{C2+}, \beta_n^{C2+}, \gamma_s^{C2+}|\varepsilon)$, $L(\alpha^{EN}, \beta_n^{EN}, \gamma_s^{EN}|\xi)$, and $L(\alpha^{EX}, \beta_n^{EX}, \gamma_s^{EX}|\eta)$. Each of them is a product of individual intensities. For each of the analysed events, the individual intensities are independent, conditional on the woman-specific unobserved heterogeneity component, but are correlated in the aggregate because of the random term.

In the second step, the joint conditional likelihood is derived. Similarly as before, conditional on all observed covariates as well as on the vector of the random effects the hazard of first conception, the hazard of second and higher order conceptions, the hazard of employment entry and the hazard of employment exit are independent, and there is also no correlation across women's conception spells, non-employment and employment spells. Consequently, the joint conditional likelihood is a product of the conditional likelihoods of the four processes.

Our estimates are based on the joint marginal (unconditional) likelihood. It was computed in the third step. The joint marginal likelihood is defined as an integral of the joint conditional likelihoods times the marginal density of the three heterogeneity components. It is obtained by 'integrating out' the random effects (ignoring subscripts):

$$\begin{aligned} &L\left(\alpha^{C1}, \beta_n^{C1}, \gamma_s^{C1}, \alpha^{C2+}, \beta_n^{C2+}, \gamma_s^{C2+}, \alpha^{EN}, \beta_n^{EN}, \gamma_s^{EN}, \alpha^{EX}, \beta_n^{EX}, \gamma_s^{EX}, \varepsilon, \xi, \eta\right) \\ &= \int\int\int\int \left[L\left(\alpha^{C1}, \beta_n^{C1}, \gamma_s^{C1} | \varepsilon\right) \cdot L\left(\alpha^{C2+}, \beta_n^{C2+}, \gamma_s^{C2+} | \varepsilon\right) \cdot L\left(\alpha^{EN}, \beta_n^{EN}, \gamma_s^{EN} | \xi\right) \right. \\ &\qquad \left. \cdot L\left(\alpha^{EX}, \beta_n^{EX}, \gamma_s^{EX} | \eta\right) \cdot f(\varepsilon) \cdot g(\xi) \cdot h(\eta)\right] d\varepsilon d\xi d\eta \end{aligned} \tag{6.6}$$

where $f(\varepsilon)$, $g(\xi)$, and $h(\eta)$ are normal densities. The integration is performed numerically by using Gauss-Hermite quadrature (Abramowitz & Stegun, 1972: 890, 924). The joint marginal likelihood is then maximised to obtain the estimates of the unknown parameters.

The identification of the model parameters is ensured by the fact that the analysed events are repeated and the person-specific unobserved heterogeneity components are fixed over individuals' life-courses. According to Lillard et al. (1995), no additional identification conditions on exogenous covariates are necessary. To illustrate it, the authors estimated a multi-process hazard model with repeated events, with and without instruments; they found very little difference in the estimated effect of the endogenous covariate on the outcome of interest.

6.7 Empirical Findings

Our modelling strategy consisted of three steps. First, we estimated the single-process hazard models without accounting for the dependency across conception spells, non-employment spells, and employment spells in each equation. In other words, we did not control for women's unobserved characteristics. These empirical findings are presented in the first columns of all tables in this section as well as in the Appendix, Tables A.7, A.8, A.9, and A.10. In the second step, we took the unmeasured characteristics of women into account, but zero pair wise correlations between random effects were assumed. These estimation results are displayed in the second columns of the tables. Finally, we fitted the multi-process hazard model, which means that we allowed the unobserved heterogeneity terms to correlate. The findings are contained in the third columns of the presented tables. The estimation results of each of these three steps are compared. In this way, we demonstrate the change in the estimate of the impact of employment on fertility and vice versa after the unobserved characteristics of women are taken into account and the endogeneity bias caused by a failure to account for unobserved time-constant characteristics of women is accounted for.

We start our discussion by presenting the estimates of the standard deviations of the unobserved heterogeneity terms and their pair wise correlations (Section 6.7.1). This section provides a justification for the need to estimate the multi-process hazard models. Furthermore, it also answers the question on the type of selection bias and hence addresses the hypothesis on the selection into employment prior to birth as formulated in Section 6.3. In the following sections (6.7.2 and 6.7.3) we discuss the estimated impacts of employment on fertility and fertility on employment, respectively. Each time, we first present the results of single-process hazard model without and with controls for unobserved heterogeneity and later move to the estimates yielded by the multi-process hazard model.

6.7.1 Positive or Negative Selection?

The standard deviations of the person-specific residuals are significant in all our intensity regressions specified (Table 6.3). This outcome implies that there is a portion of woman-specific heterogeneity that is not accounted for by our covariates. It represents a woman-specific propensity to have children in the conception equations and a woman-specific propensity to work in the employment equations.

Furthermore, the person-specific unobserved heterogeneity terms are significantly correlated. This means that the hazards of conception are influenced not only by the unobserved woman-specific propensity to have children but also by the unobserved woman-specific propensity to work. Likewise, the transitions in and out of employment are determined by women's long-term fertility as well as employment intentions. The woman-specific unobserved propensity to conceive is positively correlated with the unobserved propensity to enter employment ($\rho_{\varepsilon\xi} > 0$) and negatively correlated with the unobserved propensity to exit employment ($\rho_{\varepsilon\eta} < 0$).

These findings point to a positive selection, which is consistent with our hypothesis. It implies that the majority of women tend to enter employment before they

Table 6.3 Unobserved propensity to have children and to enter/exit employment: standard deviations and correlations, Poland cohorts 1971–1981

Standard deviations of unobserved heterogeneity terms:		
Fertility	0.42	***
	(0.12)	
Employment entry	1.22	***
	(0.05)	
Employment exit	1.28	***
	(0.09)	
Correlations between unobserved heterogeneity terms:		
Fertility and employment entry	0.37	***
	(0.11)	
Fertility and employment exit	–0.25	**
	(0.13)	
Employment entry and exit	–0.51	***
	(0.06)	

Note: significance: * = 10%; ** = 5%; *** = 1%
Source: author's calculations on Employment, Family and Education Survey (2006)

have a child. They are more likely to conceive only after they have a job they can return to after birth. This employment-first strategy implies that the estimates of the mutual impacts of fertility and employment obtained from the single-process hazard models are biased. The direction and size of this bias are discussed in Sections 6.7.2 and 6.7.3.

6.7.2 *Effects of Employment on Fertility*

The single-process hazard models of conception yield positive effects of employment on first conception and no effects on subsequent conceptions (Table 6.4, columns 1–2). These findings change after we control for women's unobserved propensity to work (Table 6.4, column 3). Employment turns out to reduce childbearing risk. This effect is rather small and insignificant for women with no children – if employed they are 8 per cent less likely to give birth than similar women who are out of work. It intensifies at higher parity levels, however. Having a job reduces the risk of conceiving a second or higher-order child by 12 per cent.

Table 6.4 Mutual impacts of fertility and employment, relative risks. Poland, cohorts 1971–1981

Explanatory variables	Single-process, not controlling for unobserved heterogeneity (1)		Single-process, controlling for unobserved heterogeneity (2)		Multi-process (accounting for endogeneity) (3)	
Effects of employment on 1st conception						
Not employed	1		1		1	
Employed	1.10	*	1.09		0.92	
Effects of employment on 2nd or higher-order conception						
not employed	1		1		1	
employed	1.01		1.01		0.88	*
Effects of parity on employment entry						
No children	1		1		1	
One child	0.44	***	0.31	***	0.26	***
Two children	0.38	***	0.20	***	0.15	***
three or more children	0.32	***	0.14	***	0.09	***
Effects of parity on employment exit						
No children	1		1		1	
One child	2.98	***	4.55	***	4.95	***
Two children	2.35	***	4.67	***	5.78	***
Three or more children	3.48	***	7.29	***	10.31	***

Note: significance: *=10%; **=5%; ***=1%
Source: author's calculations on Employment, Family and Education Survey (2006)

These findings suggest that the single-process hazard models return estimates that are upward-biased. They consist of two counteracting components: the negative effect, reflecting the conflict between fertility and paid work, and the indirect and positive effect, caused by the unobserved propensity of women to enter employment (or to remain employed) before having a child. Positive selection to employment is observed not only with respect to women with no children but also with respect to mothers. The latter finding means that women decide to have another child only after they succeed in (re-)entering work after the previous birth.

6.7.3 Effects of Fertility on Employment

Our findings illustrate that children have a strong and clearly negative impact on women's employment (Table 6.4). Mothers are apparently less likely to take up a job and more likely to exit work than women who do not have children. These effects strengthen with an increase in parity.

These conclusions can be drawn on the basis of the estimates obtained from the single-process models as well as from the multi-process hazard model. It is clear, however, that the negative impact of parity on women's employment intensifies after we control for women's unobserved propensities to work and to have children. Again, we find evidence that a failure to account for woman-specific unmeasured characteristics leads to an underestimation of the conflict between fertility and paid work. This is due to positive selection. Women who plan to have a(nother) child tend to enter employment first. Conversely, those who leave employment do it for reasons other than increasing their family size. After accounting for positive selection, we found that the first child lowers the risk of employment entry four times and amplifies the risk of employment exit five times. These effects are twice as high for women with at least three children.

Apart from analysing the impact of parity on women's work transitions, we also investigated how women's employment patterns vary with the age of the youngest child. This variable was introduced in our employment equations as a conditional piecewise linear spline in interaction with parity status. The results are presented in Fig. 6.8a, b. They come from the multi-process hazard model.

It turns out that mothers face a lower risk of taking up a job and a higher risk of exiting work than women without children, irrespective of the age of their youngest child. The worst chances for entering and maintaining employment are observed among the pregnant and women with youngest children, up to 2–3 years old. Even 7 months before delivery, women expecting a baby are twice less likely to take up a job than the childless and non-pregnant. This effect is even more pronounced among women who already have at least one child. The intensity of entering paid work declines along the pregnancy to bottom out 4 months after birth. Depending on the parity, mothers at this point are six to fourteen times less likely to enter employment than the childless. From that moment on, however, the risk of taking up a job starts to increase. This upward trend continues for the following two and a half years and stops afterwards. Still, the intensity of taking up a job among mothers whose only

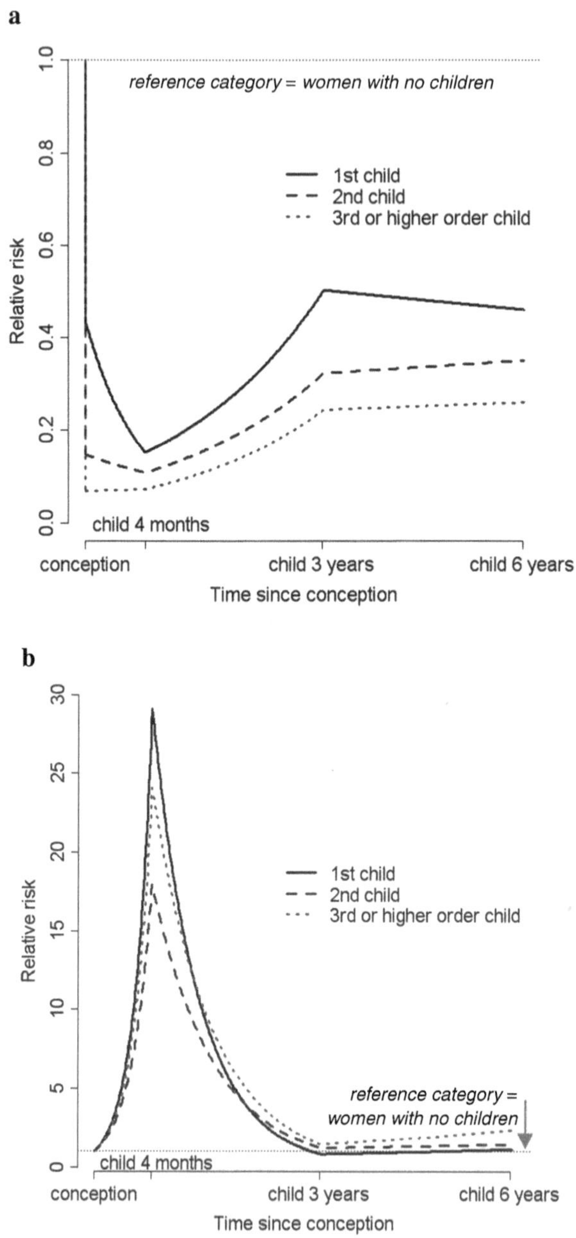

Fig. 6.8 (**a**) Effects of child's age on employment entry; (**b**) Effects of child's age on employment exit
Source: Author's calculations on Employment, Family and Education Survey (2006).

child is at least 3 years old is around twice as low as among the women with no children. For mothers with higher numbers of children, this gap is even larger.

Having a young child diminishes the chances of holding onto a job even more strongly than the chances of getting a job. The risk of employment exit increases gradually along the pregnancy and reaches the maximum for women with a 4-month-old child. The high intensity of leaving employment at that moment might be attributed to the fact that women decide to use their right to parental leave. As the child grows, the hazard of employment exit gradually declines and bottoms out when the child is 3 years old. At that point, clear differences emerge among mothers with respect to parity. Those with one child are as likely to exit employment as the childless. By contrast, mothers of at least two children among whom the youngest is three years old face a 30–50 per cent higher risk of leaving employment, depending on the parity. What is more, the risk of exiting paid work does not decline further with the age of the youngest child.

6.8 Discussion

In this Chapter we investigated interdependencies between fertility and women's work in post-socialist Poland. Compared to other CEE countries, the Polish context is particularly unfavourable to combining paid employment with childbearing and childrearing. Hence, although it is not representative of this region, the country provides a good illustration of women's decision-making in the situation when the two choice variables (employment and childbearing) are in a strong conflict, but at the same time women's earnings might be necessary for a decision to have a child.

Our study had two objectives. First, we aimed to take a closer look at the interrelationship between childbearing and women's employment. In particular, we tested a hypothesis presupposing that, under the new conditions of labour force participation, women postpone childbearing until they establish a position in the labour market. The hypothesis was addressed with reference to women with no children as well as to mothers. The rationale for formulating this hypothesis was the observed declining intensity of childbearing along with the growing uncertainty in the labour market, on the one hand, and the existing strong necessity to earn income in order to maintain the family, on the other hand. Second, we intended to show how one could eliminate the endogeneity bias in the estimates of mutual impacts of fertility and women's employment caused by the lack of data on women's needs and life goals. The statistical method used is the multi-process hazard model. This method allows for a correlation of the person-specific time-constant unobserved heterogeneity components, pertaining to each transition. In this way, women's unobserved time-constant propensities to work and have children are taken into account, and the potential endogeneity of each process with respect to all others is accounted for.

Our analysis revealed there is a conflict between fertility and women's employment in post-socialist Poland, estimated net of women's long-term plans regarding childbearing and paid work or any other person-specific, time-invariant unmeasured characteristics. The conflict is foremost reflected in markedly negative impacts of children on women's work. The first child lowers the intensity of employment entry four times and increases the intensity of employment exit five times. Births of higher order reduce the chances for women's involvement in the labour market to an even larger extent. The intensity of entering and holding onto a job depends on the age of the youngest child. It is lowest during the pregnancy and early phases of child's life. Although it increases thereafter, it does not reach the pre-birth level. The impact of employment on childbearing is less pronounced, but still it is negative. Working women are 8 per cent less likely to conceive their first child and 12 per cent less likely to have the second or higher-order child than non-employed women.

Such a strong conflict between fertility and women's employment could be expected given the strong institutional, structural, and cultural incompatibilities between the two activities, imposed by the macro-context. Its magnitude would be assessed as far weaker, however, if we based our conclusions on the estimates yielded by the single-process hazard models. This is because women seek to have a job before giving birth. This behaviour is observed with respect to women with no children as well as those who have at least one child. This means not only that women decide to enter motherhood after they find a job, but also that they return to work after birth before they choose to further increase their family size. These findings are consistent with the hypothesis pertaining to the first of our research objectives formulated in this chapter.

Our study has clearly shown that the existence of positive selection leads to an underestimation of the mutual negative impact of one variable on the other if women's time-constant preferences and plans regarding fertility and paid work are not accounted for. Referring to our second research objective, this capability of estimating the real conflict between childbearing and women's paid work demonstrates the superiority of the multi-process hazard model over the single-process hazard model. This approach is highly recommended if comprehensive data on women's needs are not available, which is most often the case.

Nevertheless, our method is far from a perfect one. First, it relies on an assumption that the person-specific unobserved heterogeneity term describing women's material and higher-order aspirations is constant over the life-course. This assumption is not very realistic; hence, attempts should be undertaken to eliminate it in the future. One possible solution is to estimate a random-slope model, in which the unobserved heterogeneity component is interacted with calendar time. Second, although the multi-process hazard model allowed us to estimate the conflict between fertility and women's work net of the income effect and any other aspirations of a woman that are time-invariant, we were not able to recognise the nature of woman's needs. It is thus not clear to us to what extent the selection to employment before birth is caused by financial necessities and to what extent it results from higher-order needs, like the desire for self-actualisation. Given the economic developments that occurred in Poland after 1989, reflected in a rising individual responsibility for securing living standards on the one hand, and increasing uncertainty in the labour market on the other, one can expect that women's labour supply has so far been primarily driven by material aspirations. This belief is further strengthened by other observations such as a strong social conviction that women should contribute to the household income, remarkable responsiveness of fertility intentions to the business cycle, as well as survey results that report financial aspects to be a key reason for women's work. Note, however, that the same data indicate also the self-actualisation needs to be the second important motive for women's economic activity. We expect the importance of these motives may increase in the future alongside the improvement in the economic situation of households and the strong increase in educational attainment of young Polish people. This issue requires more detailed data, but is certainly worth attention in future research.

Despite these shortcomings, we believe that the study presented in this chapter constitutes an important contribution to the research on the interdependencies between fertility and women's labour supply. It is also highly relevant from the policy-making perspective. First, it provides information on the magnitude of the conflict between fertility and women's work in post-socialist Poland. Second, it demonstrates that in spite of the strong incompatibilities between fertility and economic activity, the majority of women do not perceive employment as a barrier but rather as a pre-condition to childbearing. This employment-first strategy has its advantages as well as disadvantages. On the one hand, under unfavourable conditions of labour force participation, it obviously leads to fertility postponement. On the other hand, however, the employment-first strategy reflects women's interest in both economic activity as well as motherhood. It seems thus that measures directed at alleviating the conflict between childrearing and labour force participation as well as reducing the uncertainty in the labour market could moderate the tempo effect and lead to fertility increase. This is highly desirable from the perspective of alleviating the negative consequences of the changing age structure of the population.

This study was conducted only for Poland. In order to draw conclusions on fertility and labour market behaviours of women in the whole region, one should conduct similar analyses for other CEE countries. Nevertheless, given the information presented so far in this book, one could expect similar findings to be established. This outcome would imply that the estimates of the micro-level relationship between childbearing and women's employment obtained for this part of Europe by various researchers whose works were reviewed in Chapter 5 are upward-biased. In fact, women do experience a conflict while combining the two activities, but it is not directly observed since they condition the decision to conceive on having a job. Given the economic restructuring and globalisation processes of the times, finding and maintaining employment was not an easy task in the years following the collapse of state socialism. Altogether this situation would explain the co-existence of the moderate to high levels of women's labour supply with the lowest-low fertility in CEE. Further research on the issue is required to test the validity of our hypothesis.

Chapter 7
Conclusions

Our motivation to conduct this study was driven by inevitable and profound changes in the age structure of the population of Europe. These changes are reflected in a decline in the working age population along with an increase in the population of post-productive age and pose a serious threat to the sustainability of social security systems, economic growth, intergenerational relations, and social cohesion. A rise in fertility could undoubtedly help in counteracting the negative consequences of population ageing. One should take into account, however, that even if Europe succeeds in reaching this difficult goal, it will bring desired effects only after the newborns enter the labour force. Hence, policies aimed at facilitating childbearing are not sufficient to alleviate the consequences of demographic change. In this context, an increase in employment rates and a rise in the education level of the labour force seem to be particularly promising. Given that women are still relatively underrepresented in employment compared to men and are characterised by comparably high qualifications, attracting them to the labour force is strongly desired from the perspective of alleviating the consequences of changes in the population age structure. At that point a question emerges, however, whether and under what conditions it is possible to increase the labour force participation of women without negative repercussions on fertility. We addressed this question in this study.

Interdependencies between childbearing and female labour force participation have been already widely studied. Theoretical concepts were developed to explain the fertility and employment choices of women and empirical studies were conducted in large numbers to test the proposed theories under various contextual settings. The second objective of our study was thus to review the available empirical research on the topic conducted by the mid 2000s and to assess the extent to which it explains women's fertility and labour market decisions. Following our critical review of theories and empirical studies, we proposed a theoretical framework and an empirical approach that should bring us closer to the understanding of the complex interdependencies between childbearing and women's economic activity. In this Chapter we summarise our major findings and propose directions for future research.

A. Matysiak, *Interdependencies Between Fertility and Women's Labour Supply*, European Studies of Population 17, DOI 10.1007/978-94-007-1284-3_7,

7.1 Theoretical and Analytical Approach to Fertility and Employment Choices

One of the important contributions of the study is the critical evaluation of the microeconomic approach to fertility and women's employment choices, sometimes also called price-of-time model. This theoretical model has been predominantly adopted in research explaining interdependencies between fertility and women's labour supply. At the same time it has been widely criticised for its inability to account for the heterogeneity in women's preferences. The opponents of this model have argued that the proposed approach is simplistic since it tries to explain differences in fertility behaviours solely by differences in the contextual opportunities and constraints and this leads to a failure in predicting women's choices. Although we agree with this opinion, we did not reject the price-of-time model. Instead, we share the view that it constitutes a useful integrating framework for the interdisciplinary analysis of childbearing and labour force participation and opt for its extension with non-economic factors. For that purpose, we first followed the idea of Macunovich (1996) who suggested replacing the total household income, against which woman's utility is maximised, with the relative income, measured as a ratio of woman's material aspirations and the total income. This allows for explaining differences in behaviour, not only by differences in the household's financial resources but also by differences in material aspirations. Nevertheless, material aspirations constitute only one of several human needs. We thus allow for the heterogeneity of women's preferences, or heterogeneity of utility functions, by introducing the concept of family and work orientations to account for higher order needs. In our theoretical model, a woman evaluates the consequences of having a child, taking into account not only the foregone earnings, but also the contribution of these consequences to the fulfilment of her higher-order needs. As a result, the relationship between childbearing and women's work depends on three types of effects: price effect, income effect, and further selection effects caused by the heterogeneity in women's orientations towards family and work. For a better understanding of women's employment and fertility choices the study emphasises the need to disentangle the three effects from each other in empirical research as well as to investigate the nature of women's motives underlying their orientations towards work and family.

The overview of the empirical studies on the topic led us to the conclusion, however, that these effects have hardly been disentangled. The main underlying reason is the unavailability of appropriate data. As a result, the estimates of the micro-level relationship between fertility and women's labour supply (employment) do not reflect a real conflict but constitute a mix of a price effect and selection effects evoked by women's material aspirations and higher-order needs. This hinders substantially the comprehension of the mechanism underlying women's fertility and labour market decisions. Only a few researchers have undertaken an effort to control for the selection bias by implementing special statistical techniques. The very first attempts involved the use of the instrumental variables method. The difficulties with finding proper instruments led the researchers to the conclusion, however, that fertility and women's work should be analysed jointly.

In this study we proposed to account for selection bias by estimating a multi-process hazard model. This method allows for a correlation between the unobserved heterogeneity terms pertaining to fertility and employment processes. In this way, the unobserved propensity of women to conceive and to work is taken into account. As a result, the obtained estimate of the relationship between fertility and women's employment reflects the conflict between childbearing and women's labour supply. By estimating the single-process and the multi-process hazard models for Poland, we demonstrated that the former clearly underestimates the conflict between childbearing and paid employment. This is because the majority of Polish women are interested in combining motherhood with market work and for this reason select themselves into employment before having a child. The weakness of the multi-process hazard model is that it assumes the propensities of women to conceive and to work to be time-invariant. Further research and advancement in statistical techniques is desirable to relax this assumption.

Our data did not allow us to investigate the source of the positive selection and hence to recognise the motives underlying women's unobserved propensity to try to find a job before birth despite the strong unemployment pressure and unfavourable conditions to work and family reconciliation. In our opinion this motivation is largely driven by financial needs. Nevertheless, future studies should look more closely into the motives driving women's employment decisions in connection with fertility choices and investigate to which extent women choose to work for financial reasons, to which extent other factors come into play, what these factors are and how their role has been changing over time. This direction of research is particularly desirable in the context of post-socialist countries where women exhibit strong determination to participate in the labour force despite serious difficulties with combing paid work and care. Moving beyond a simple statement that some groups of women are strongly work-oriented could bring us closer to the understanding of the choices they make. It is notable at this point that realising this objective requires detailed data on women's motives as well as factors underlying these motives, most preferably in longitudinal form. Such data have not been available so far. Clearly, attempts should be undertaken to make up for this deficiency. Interdisciplinary research possibly with participation of psychologists could find the way towards a measurement of human motives. Indirect questioning and latent class and structural equation models supported by qualitative research are most likely a promising path to follow. The proposed questions are to be included into questionnaires, producing data first in cross-sectional and later in longitudinal form.

7.2 Macro-context and Incompatibilities Between Women's Employment and Childbearing

Apart from women's work and family orientations the macro-context held an important position in our study. We viewed it as a multi-dimensional structure that embodies information about opportunities and restrictions to the individuals.

This contrasts with the approach of many researchers who took a single dimension perspective and focused solely on the impact of family policies or gender norms on fertility and women's labour supply. Four dimensions of the macro-context were considered relevant to women's fertility and employment decisions: institutional (family policies), structural (labour market structures), cultural (gender norms), and economic (living standards). The first three influence the opportunity costs of childbearing, producing the so-called institutional, structural, and cultural incompatibilities between childbearing and market work. The intensity of these incompatibilities depends on the extent to which mothers' work is institutionally supported and socially accepted and the labour market is able to accomodate female labour. The fourth dimension of the context affects the magnitude of the income effect. We found it important for our study as we analysed countries that differ in wealth levels and living standards attained by their citizens and these differences may result in a variation in women's motives for entering paid employment, particularly in the childbearing and childrearing phase.

An important contribution of the study is the development of the indices for measuring the intensity of the institutional, structural, and cultural incompatibilities between work and care imposed by the macro-context. The indices were built on the basis of macro-level data measuring public support to working parents, barriers to labour market entry and opportunities of flexible organisation of working hours as well as social acceptance for mothers' involvement in paid employment. They were used for ranking the EU member states, Norway, and Switzerland with respect to the intensity of institutional, structural, and cultural incompatibilities between work and care imposed by the macro-context. A final ranking of countries that assesses the overall level of incompatibilities was also presented. As far as the Western European countries are concerned our ranking is largely consistent with what is already known in the literature on this topic: Nordic countries display the weakest incompatibilities between paid work and care, followed by Belgium, the United Kingdom, and France. The macro-context imposes the strongest tensions between childbearing and employment in Southern Europe. Not much has been known so far, however, on how the CEE countries compare to Western Europe in that respect. Our indices demonstrate that the conditions to work and family reconciliation in the new EU member states are rather poor, as poor as in Southern European countries, with Slovenia and Estonia doing the best and Poland the worst. A particular feature of CEE countries are rigid work arrangements and very traditional norms for gender roles (even though coupled with a belief that both spouses should contribute to household income). There is more variation with regard to family policies, with Estonia, Hungary, Slovenia, and Lithuania offering slightly better and Poland worse institutional support to working parents.

The general index of incompatibilities between work and care correlated negatively and quite strongly with Total Fertility Rate (TFR), Female Labour Force Participation Rate (LFPR) and Female Employment Rate (EMPR), suggesting that unfavourable conditions for work and family reconciliation might lead to lower fertility and lower women's economic activity and employment. In some countries, however, TFR or LFPR/EMPR deviated from the level that could be predicted on the basis of the incompatibilities between work and care. The higher labour force participation of women in Slovenia, Czech Republic Lithuania, Slovakia or Poland than in Western European countries characterised by similarly intense incongruities between women's employment and childbearing can be possibly atrributed to lower living standards in CEE which trigger women's participation in paid employment. Nonetheless, there might be also other reasons for these deviations as our method for measuring the conflict is far from perfect. On the one hand, the advantage of the adopted approach is undoubtedly that it allows us to measure the intensity of the conflict imposed by the macro-context in a quantitative manner and to rank the countries. On the other hand, the problem is that it assumes the three dimensions of the context that generate the incompatibilities to be equally important for fertility and labour supply decisions and it disregards interactions between policies, labour market structures, and social norms. Future research should attempt to relax this assumption. Improvements in the availability of comparative time series policy indicators should also allow to compute the proposed indices for several points in time and for studying the dynamics of the incompatibilities between work and care in connection with the dynamics in fertility and women's labour supply. We believe that further development of the proposed indices and improvement in the data necessary for the computation of the time series is a promising path to follow with the view of understanding women's fertility and employment choices. Not only would the indices allow for ranking and comparing the countries, but also for studying the impacts of the macro-context on individual behaviour directly, by feeding the empirical models with the quantitative information on the intensity of incompatibilities imposed by the context. In particular, estimating multi-level and multi-process hazard models, although computationally intensive, would give us the opportunity to assess the relative importance of the contextual dimensions for fertility and labour market decisions.

7.3 Explaining Fertility Levels and Women's Labour Supply Rates in Europe

7.3.1 Western Europe

Empirical studies depicting developments in fertility and women's labour supply in Western developed economies published in the early 2000s challenged the existing knowledge on the interdependencies between the two variables by showing that the cross-country correlation between Total Fertility Rate (TFR) and Female Labour Force Participation Rate (LFP) changed its sign from negative to positive. This phenomenon has been widely debated in the economic, sociological and demographic literature and it was shown to be caused by stronger declines in fertility in countries characterised by higher women's labour supply. This study contributes to this strand of research by showing that the emergence of the positive cross-country correlation between TFR and LFP in Western European countries was temporary and over the 2000s it has been approaching zero again. A closer look into the macro-level developments in the two variables reveals that the weakening in the macro-level correlation is due to continuing increases in women's economic activity in low- and medium-LFP countries accompanied by recent improvements in fertility which were substantial in some of them (Belgium, France, the United Kingdom) and very modest in the others (Austria, Germany, Spain).

The emergence of the positive cross-country correlation between TFR and LFP was widely explained in the literature by cross-country differences in the incompatibilities between motherhood and paid employment (Brewster & Rindfuss, 2000; Ahn & Mira, 2002; Castles, 2003; Engelhardt et al., 2004; Engelhardt & Prskawetz, 2004; Kögel, 2004; Rindfuss et al., 2004; Muszyńska, 2007). Does the weakening of the correlation imply that the conditions for work and family reconciliation do not matter for total fertility and women's labour supply? On the basis of our findings, we conclude that they do matter, but mainly for childbearing rates and less for women's labour supply. The latter has been rising in all Western European countries since the 1970s and over the last two decades the pace of this increase was usually stronger in countries displaying low women's labour supply than in countries where women's economic activity was high. As a result, the cross-country differences in female labour market participation started to narrow. The recent fertility improvements that occurred all over the Western Europe were definitely stronger in those countries where the incompatibilities between work and care are weaker, i.e. in Belgium, France, and the United Kingdom. By contrast, where fertility increased only slightly (Greece, Spain, Italy, Portugal) or stagnated at very low levels (Germany) incompatibilities between women's work and care are stronger. These findings suggest that women in Western Europe no longer give up economic activity for the sake of family and children. Instead, they lower their family size if paid employment cannot be combined with childbearing and childrearing.

Further research into the interrelationship between fertility and women's employment in Western Europe could address strategies women develop to reconcile work and care under various institutional, structural, and cultural settings, looking more deeply into spacing of births in connection with women's decisions on the duration of employment breaks. It is also desirable to investigate the role of partners, their labour market position as well as their participation in care for these decisions. Finally, a deeper insight is needed into the role of contextual factors for childbearing and employment choices in order to establish which of them are mainly responsible for generating incompatibilities between work and care. Realisation of these plans requires further improvements in data collection, in particular panel data that cover employment and childbearing histories of women and their partners and which could be merged with contextual indicators capturing the institutional, structural, and cultural incompatibilities between work and care.

7.3.2 Central and Eastern Europe

The developments in fertility and women's labour supply in the CEE countries have been hardly studied. Yet, they differ substantially from those observed in the

Western economies. Under state socialism, the CEE countries were characterised by relatively high female labour force participation and high birth rates. Although some decline in fertility in this part of Europe had started already in the 1970s, being visible particularly in Hungary and Slovenia, this process accelerated substantially after the onset of the economic transformation. At the same time, changes in the political and economic systems brought a considerable decline in the labour force participation (and employment) of both women and men. Interestingly the very recent improvements in fertility observed in that part of Europe turned out to be the strongest in those CEE countries that display higher labour force participation of women. These developments led to an emergence of the positive cross-country correlation between TFR and LFP this time in CEE. A more in-depth study conducted in this book shows that the post-socialist countries characterised by highest fertility and highest women's labour supply are characterised by weakest incompatibilities between work and care (e.g. Estonia and Slovenia). By contrast, where the economic activity of women and fertility are lower (e.g. Czech Republic, Slovakia, Poland) the conditions for work and family reconciliation are worse. Hungary constitutes a notable exception from this rule compared to other post-socialist countries since we found its macro-context to be fairly supportive of working parents, even though it displays the lowest women's labour supply in the CEE and one of the lowest fertility levels. Despite this exception tensions between paid work and care were found to be an important factor affecting fertility and women's labour supply also in the new EU member states.

Our study revealed also that the conditions for work and family reconciliation in post-socialist countries are worse than in the majority of Western European countries. In general public policies in the new EU member states are less supportive to working parents, working hours are more rigid and social norms for women's roles are more traditional. Consequently, the labour force participation rates of mothers of pre-school children in the East are lower than in the West. Despite the difficulties with combining work and care women in CEE countries, except for Hungary, are as often active in the labour market as women in the medium- and high-LFP countries of Western Europe. Furthermore, they are more frequently back in employment once a child reaches the school age and more frequently undertake full-time jobs than mothers in Western Europe. Empirical studies conducted at the micro-level show additionally that Hungarian, Czech, and Polish women are more likely to enter motherhood while employed than women in those Western European countries where work-family incongruities are strong. We interpret these behaviours of women in CEE as an indication of a strong determination to participate in the labour force. One reason for this determination we pointed at throughout the study are financial necessities of the households which are stronger in the East than in the West. The unmet material aspirations of Eastern Europeans and their desire to reach the Western living standards could have additionally coupled with pragmatic attitudes towards women's paid work developed during the period of forced women's labour force participation under state socialism. Altogether this might have led to the adoption of the dual earner / female double burden family model in that part of Europe. Women in CEE countries are perceived as main carers as well as supplementary income providers, expected to adjust their involvement in the labour market to family obligations. Under weak public support and rigid work arrangements they are not able to meet the competing demands and consequently postpone or even give up (further) childbearing. This might be one of the reasons explaining why even in high-LFP countries of CEE fertility is much lower than in the majority of Western European countries.

Further research is needed to look more deeply into the relationship between fertility and women's employment choices in post-socialist countries. In the first step, empirical studies are desirable that would assess the magnitude of the conflict between childrearing and paid employment and test for the presence of selection to employment prior to birth. Second, further investigation of motives driving women's strong determination to participate in the labour force is needed in order to establish whether it is triggered primarily by financial needs or any other higher-order needs come into play here. One might also look into how the relative importance of material aspirations and work orientations has been changing over time along the improvement in living conditions. Finally, an aspect which was not addressed in this study but is worth looking at is the intergenerational transmission of the picture of a working mother. It is possible that women in CEE countries are motivated to work as they treat economic activity as a natural part of their life course, remembering their mothers working for pay when they were young. The social internalisation of the picture of a working mother might be one of the reasons why women in CEE accepted to follow the dual earner / female double burden family model despite the change in the conditions for work and family reconciliation. Investigating women's motives for labour force participation in connection with childbearing seems to be a promising path to follow in order to understand women's fertility and employment choices in this part of Europe. One needs to keep in mind, however, that following this path requires access to individual data on women's behaviours, social background, economic situation as well as women's life goals and motives, preferably in longitudinal form. Such data are partly collected under the Generations and Gender Programme, but the data requirements formulated here should be taken into account in other data collection programmes.

7.4 Is it Possible to Increase Women's Labour Supply Without Negative Repercussions for Fertility?

Based on our findings, we conclude that it is certainly possible to increase women's labour supply without negative repercussions on fertility. What is more, the economic activity of women may rise at relatively high fertility levels or it may even be accompanied by increases in the birth rate. The incompatibilities between fertility and women's work need to be eased, however, for this scenario to be realised.

This conclusion implies that policies oriented at supporting the traditional male breadwinner, creating barriers or disincentives to women's employment, are very unlikely to bring satisfactory results. Instead, policy-makers should focus on facilitating the reconciliation between family and work and ensuring gender equality.

Note, however, that single policies directed at supporting employment of working mothers may be unsuccessful if the whole institutional, structural, and cultural setting continues to create serious barriers to the economic activity of mothers. What we need, in fact, is a more general welfare state reform, together covering social, labour market, and tax policies. Hence, apart from the wide access to low-cost childcare services of high quality, parents should also be given the opportunity to provide care on their own and to combine it with flexible working schemes. Parental leaves available to both parents and flexible work arrangements could serve this goal. Access to external care will not bring desired effects, however, unless mothers' employment is socially accepted, financial disincentives to women's work built in the tax or social security systems are eliminated, and the barriers to the labour market experienced by the young women are removed. Finally, the underlying idea of this reform should be not only an integration of mothers into the labour market but also an integration of fathers into housework and care duties. Public debate on reconciling work and care should not be confined to women only, but should recognise the role of men in childrearing. Institutional incentives are needed for fathers to withdraw temporarily from employment and stay at home with young children. Increased participation of fathers in childcare could help in minimising women's absenteeism from work, improving their position at work and reducing the burden childbearing places on their shoulders. Much progress has been made recently in that respect as statutory paternity rights have been introduced in many European countries (O'Brien, 2009; Moss, 2010). In order to bring satisfying results in terms of improvements in fertility this change at the legal level needs to be further accompanied by changes in behaviours.

At this point one might wonder what the future developments in fertility and women's labour supply would be like if the incompatibilities between fertility and women's employment were not alleviated but remained unchanged. On the basis of our study, we believe that in such a situation women's labour supply would continue to rise anyway, as the social and economic change in that respect is well advanced. The pace of this upward trend might be only slower. The delay in easing the tensions between work and care will have serious repercussions for fertility, however. The recent developments in fertility and women's labour supply demonstrate that fertility improvements are possible in countries with high levels of women's labour supply where incompatibilities between work and care are relatively weak. By contrast, in countries where mothers' economic activity is not supported the labour force participation rates continue to increase at low fertility levels.

Appendix

Table A.1 Short description of the surveys mentioned throughout the study

Employment, Family and Education Survey is a Polish retrospective survey conducted in October and November 2006 on a representative sample of 3,000 women born in 1966–1981 and their partners. The survey was prepared at the Institute of Statistics and Demography (Warsaw School of Economics) under the project 'Cultural and structural conditions of female labour force participation in Poland' financed by the Ministry of Science and Higher Education and coordinated by Professor Irena E. Kotowska. Instead of the traditional method of collecting retrospective data, a life history calendar method was applied. The dataset contains respondents' education, employment, partnership, fertility, and migration histories from the age of 15, recorded on a monthly basis.
European Labour Force Survey (ELFS) is conducted in the 27 EU member states, Norway and Switzerland. It is a large household survey providing quarterly data on labour force participation of people aged 15+. Persons carrying out obligatory military service are not covered. In each quarter the interviews are spread uniformly over all weeks. The institutions responsible for running the survey are the national statistical institutes. The survey started in 1983 in the Western European countries. The new EU member states joined the ELFS at the beginning of the 1990s, but the data for these countries is available in the ELFS harmonized micro-files since 1997.
European Social Survey (ESS) is designed to illustrate and explain 'the interaction between Europe's changing institutions and the attitudes, beliefs, and behaviour patterns of its diverse populations'. The survey aims also at developing a set of attitudinal social indicators that can be considered alongside existing economic and behavioural indicators. So far four rounds of the ESS were conducted, in 2002, 2004, 2006, and 2008. In the present study, we used data stemming from the third round. It covers 23 countries: Austria, Belgium, Bulgaria, Cyprus, Denmark, Estonia, Germany, Finland, France, Hungary, Ireland, Netherlands, Norway, Poland, Portugal, Russia, Sweden, Slovenia, Slovakia, Spain, Switzerland, Ukraine, and United Kingdom. The data are freely available online through the ESS website: http://www.europeansocialsurvey.org/.
European Values Study (EVS) is a cross-national survey that provides insight into the 'ideas, beliefs, preferences, attitudes, values, and opinions of citizens all over Europe'. It was initiated in 1981. Every nine years, the survey is repeated in an increasing number of countries. The fourth wave in 2008 covers 47 European countries. http://www.europeanvaluesstudy.eu

A. Matysiak, *Interdependencies Between Fertility and Women's Labour Supply*, European Studies of Population 17, DOI 10.1007/978-94-007-1284-3,

Table A.1 (continued)

International Population Policy Acceptance Study (IPPAS) was conducted in 14 European countries in the years 2000–2003 under the DIALOG project 'Population Policy Acceptance Study – The Viewpoint of Citizens and Policy Actors Regarding the Management of Population Related Change,' funded by the European Commission. The project was coordinated by the Federal Institute for Population Research in Wiesbaden, Germany. The database covers Austria, Belgium(Flanders), Cyprus, Estonia, Germany, Italy, Hungary, Finland, the Czech Republic, Lithuania, Netherlands, Poland, Romania, and Slovenia.

International Social Survey Programme (ISSP) is an annual programme of cross-national collaboration on surveys covering such topics as role of government, social networks, social inequality, religion, environment, citizenship, national identity, gender roles, etc. Currently the programme covers 43 nations. Opinions on gender roles were investigated in three waves of the ISSP: in 1988, 1994, and 2002. The 1988 ISSP wave covered Austria, Great Britain, Hungary, Ireland, Italy, Netherlands, the United States of America, and West Germany. In 1994, the country coverage was extended to Australia, Bulgaria, Canada, Czech Republic, East Germany, Ireland, Israel, Japan, New Zealand, Northern Ireland, Norway, Philippines, Poland, Russia, Slovenia, Spain, Sweden, the United States of America. The 2002 ISSP wave covered Australia, Austria, Brazil, Bulgaria, Chile, Cyprus, Czech Republic, Denmark, Finland, Belgium(Flanders), France, Germany, Great Britain, Hungary, Ireland, Israel, Japan, Latvia, Mexico, Netherlands, New Zealand, Northern Ireland, Norway, Philippines, Poland, Portugal, Russia, Slovakia, Slovenia, Spain, Sweden, Switzerland, Taiwan, United States of America. The data are freely available online through the Zentralarchiv für Empirische Sozialforschung in Cologne via the website: http://www.gesis.org/en/data_service/issp/index.htm.

Reconciliation of family and work was conducted in 2005 EU member states, Norway and Switzerland under the recommendation of Eurostat. The survey was carried out as a module of the European Labour Force Survey and covered persons aged 15–64. The Polish sample covered 37,849 individuals. The objectives of the survey were as follows: (1) to establish whether people participate in the labour force to the extent they wish to do and how this is related to their family responsibilities, (2) to collect information on the degree of flexibility at the workplace, (3) to assess the parental leave take-up rates as well as the frequency of absence from work due to care duties.

Reconciling work, family and education is a Polish survey designed to extend the standard 'Reconciliation of family and work' questionnaire. It was conducted in 2005 on the LFS sub-sample of individuals aged 18–64 ($N = 5,564$). The survey questionnaire was developed within the project 'Economic activity, education and family duties' financed by the Ministry of Labour and Social Policy and carried out at the Gdansk Institute of Market Economies, Institute of Statistics and Demography (Warsaw School of Economics) and Warsaw University.

Table A.2 Effects of motherhood on women's employment, EMPRs of women aged 25–40 by the number of children

	No children below age 15	One child	Two children	Three children	Effect of one child	Effect of two children	Effect of three children
	(1)	(2)	(3)	(4)	(1)–(2)	(1)–(3)	(1)–(4)
2004							
CEE							
Low-LFP	**80.9**	**61.4**	**60.4**	**28.8**	**19.5**	**20.5**	**52.1**
Hungary	80.9	61.4	60.4	28.8	19.5	20.5	52.1
Medium-LFP	**77.6**	**68.6**	**65.0**	**49.3**	**9.0**	**12.6**	**28.4**
Czech Republic	84.3	60.1	62.2	46	24.1	22.1	38.3
Estonia	77.8	78.3	60.9	51.3	–0.5	16.9	26.5
Poland	70.2	64.8	61.8	52.5	5.4	8.5	17.7
Latvia	78	75.3	74.4	53	2.7	3.6	25
Slovakia	77.8	64.5	65.8	43.5	13.3	12	34.3
High-LFP	**77.9**	**81.0**	**83.5**	**74.7**	**–3.1**	**–5.6**	**3.3**
Lithuania	74.8	75	78.6	67.9	–0.2	–3.8	6.9
Slovenia	80.9	86.9	88.3	81.4	–6	–7.3	–0.4
Western Europe							
Low-LFP	**76.2**	**62.2**	**52.2**	**41.2**	**14.0**	**24.0**	**35.0**
Greece	71.1	57.8	53.2	49	13.3	17.8	22
Ireland	88.7	70	57.2	42.6	18.7	31.5	46.1
Italy	70.4	60.3	47.4	33.3	10	23	37.1
Spain	74.6	60.5	51.1	39.9	14.1	23.5	34.7
Medium-LFP	**81.4**	**76.1**	**70.5**	**51.1**	**5.3**	**10.9**	**30.3**
Belgium	81.3	74.5	76.6	48.8	6.8	4.7	32.5
France	79.2	75	68.2	48.3	4.1	11	30.8
Portugal	80.4	81.1	74.7	62.9	–0.7	5.7	17.5
Austria	83.7	80.6	71.8	54.1	3.1	11.8	29.6
Germany	82.2	69.2	61	41.2	13.1	21.2	41
High-LFP	**84.5**	**76.1**	**75.8**	**61.6**	**8.4**	**8.7**	**22.9**
Denmark	80.6	79.7	83.3	65.6	1	–2.7	15.1
Finland	85.2	71.2	72.3	62.3	14	12.9	22.9
Netherlands	87.6	77.5	71.7	57	10.1	15.9	30.7
Sweden	na	na	na	na	na	na	na
1985							
CEE	na	na	na	na	na	na	na
Western Europe							
Low-LFP	**65.4**	**45.4**	**31.6**	**25.5**	**20.0**	**33.8**	**39.9**
Greece	63.7	46.3	39.7	38.4	17.3	24	25.2
Ireland	76.4	38.2	20.7	13.5	38.2	55.7	62.9
Italy	64.4	53.8	37.9	27.6	10.6	26.5	36.8
Spain	56.9	43.1	27.9	22.4	13.8	28.9	34.5
Medium-LFP	**75.2**	**60.2**	**51.9**	**34.8**	**15.1**	**23.4**	**40.4**
Belgium	73.4	64.2	54.6	34.2	9.2	18.7	39.2
France	79.9	74.5	62.8	34.5	5.5	17.1	45.4
Portugal	71.3	68.5	60.2	49.4	2.8	11.1	21.9
Austria	na	na	na	na	na	na	na

Table A.2 (continued)

	No children below age 15	One child	Two children	Three children	Effect of one child	Effect of two children	Effect of three children
	(1)	(2)	(3)	(4)	(1)–(2)	(1)–(3)	(1)–(4)
Germany	na	na	na	na	na	na	na
Netherlands	76.3	33.5	29.8	21.2	42.8	46.5	55.2
High-LFP	**80.2**	**78.5**	**81.4**	**69.8**	**1.7**	**–1.2**	**10.3**
Denmark	80.2	78.5	81.4	69.8	1.7	–1.2	10.3
Finland	na	na	na	na	na	na	na
Sweden	na	na	na	na	na	na	na

Source: Author's calculations on European Labour Force Survey

Table A.3 Effects of motherhood on women's employment, EMPRs of women aged 25–40 by age of the youngest child

	No children	Youngest child 0–5	Youngest child 5–10	Impact of children aged 0–5	Impact of children aged 5–10
	(1)	(2)	(3)	(1)–(2)	(1)–(3)
2004					
CEE					
low-LFP	**80.7**	**28.2**	**71.4**	**52.5**	**9.3**
Hungary	80.7	28.2	71.4	52.5	9.3
medium-LFP	**78.6**	**43.6**	**74.3**	**35.0**	**4.4**
Czech Republic	85.1	26.8	79.4	58.2	5.7
Estonia	79	45.8	77.8	33.2	1.2
Latvia	80	57.1	78	22.8	1.9
Poland	70.5	51	64.2	19.5	6.3
Slovakia	78.5	37.2	71.9	41.4	6.7
high-LFP	**79.5**	**78.4**	**83.5**	**1.1**	**–4.1**
Lithuania	77.3	71.1	80	6.2	–2.7
Slovenia	81.6	85.6	86.9	–4.1	–5.4
Western Europe					
low-LFP	**75.7**	**52.5**	**55.9**	**23.2**	**19.8**
Greece	70.3	50.9	56.4	19.4	13.8
Ireland	88.3	54	60.1	34.3	28.2
Italy	69.9	52.9	51.1	17.1	18.8
Spain	74.2	52.1	56.1	22.1	18.2
medium-LFP	**80.8**	**64.5**	**74.4**	**16.3**	**6.4**
Belgium	78.8	66.3	75.4	12.5	3.4
France	79.1	60.8	76.5	18.3	2.6
Portugal	80.4	77.5	77	2.9	3.5
Austria	83.6	64.9	77.2	18.7	6.4
Germany	82	53.1	65.8	28.9	16.1
high-LFP	**82.7**	**70.8**	**na**	**11.9**	**na**
Denmark	80.5	75.4	80.8	5.1	–0.3

Table A.3 (continued)

	No children	Youngest child 0–5	Youngest child 5–10	Impact of children aged 0–5	Impact of children aged 5–10
	(1)	(2)	(3)	(1)–(2)	(1)–(3)
Finland	85.7	59.4	83	26.3	2.6
Netherlands	87.1	71.2	72	16	15.2
Sweden	77.4	77.1	na	0.3	na
1985					
CEE	na	na	na	na	na
Western Europe					
low-LFP	**63.8**	**32.6**	**32.1**	**31.2**	**31.7**
Greece	61.1	39	40.1	22.1	21
Ireland	74.9	19.5	17.8	55.3	57.1
Italy	63.5	41.4	40.8	22.1	22.7
Spain	55.7	30.4	29.6	25.3	26
medium-LFP	**72.9**	**47.3**	**52.2**	**25.6**	**20.7**
Belgium	69.4	55	52.1	14.4	17.3
France	79	52.9	63.3	26.1	15.7
Portugal	69.1	58.7	64	10.4	5.1
Austria	na	na	na	na	na
Germany	na	na	na	na	na
Netherlands	74.2	22.7	29.5	51.5	44.6
high-LFP	**84.8**	**80.2**	**na**	**4.6**	**na**
Denmark	80.4	75.3	80.3	5.1	0.1
Finland	na	na	na	na	na
Sweden	89.4	83	na	6.4	na

Note: For Sweden, the age categories of children are different: 0–6 years and no child younger than 16, the data refer to women aged 25–44

Source: Author's calculations based on the European Labour Force Survey and for Sweden on the LFS aggregate data obtained from Statistics Sweden

Table A.4 Papers used in the meta-analysis

Employment entry

Bernardi, F. (2001). The employment behaviour of married women in Italy. In H.-P. Blossfeld & S. Drobnič (Eds.), *Careers of couples in contemporary societies* (pp. 121–145). Oxford: Oxford University Press.

Blossfeld, H.-P., Drobnič, S., & Rohwer, G. (2001). Spouses' employment careers in (West) Germany. In H.-P. Blossfeld & S. Drobnič (Eds.), *Careers of couples in contemporary societies* (pp. 53–76). Oxford: Oxford University Press.

Buchholz, S., & Grunow, D. (2006). Women's employment in West Germany. In H.-P. Blossfeld & H. Hofmeister (Eds.), *Globalisation, uncertainty and women's careers: An international comparison* (pp. 61–83). Cheltenham: Edward Elgar.

De Graaf, P., & Vermeulen, E. (1997). Female labour market participation in the Netherlands: Developments in the relationship between family cycle and employment. In H.-P. Blossfeld & C. Hakim (Eds.), *Between equalization and marginalization: Women working part-time in Europe and the United States of America* (pp. 191–209). Oxford: Oxford University Press.

Table A.4 (continued)

Drobnič, S. (2000). The effects of children on married and lone mothers' employment in the United States and (West) Germany. *European Sociological Review, 16*(2), 137–157.

Drobnič, S., Blossfeld, H.-P., & Rohwer, G. (1999). Dynamics of women's employment patterns over the family life course: A comparison of the United States and Germany. *Journal of Marriage and the Family, 61*(1), 133–146.

Giannelli, G. C. (1996). Women's transitions in the labour market: A competing risks analysis on German panel data. *Journal of Population Economics*, 9(3), 287–300.

Grimm, M., & Bonneuil, N. (2001). Labour market participation of French women over the life cycle, 1935–1990. *European Journal of Population, 17*(3), 235–260.

Grunow, D., & Leth-Sørensen, S. (2006). Danish women's unemployment, job mobility and non-employment, 1980s and 1990s: Marked by globalization? In H.-P. Blossfeld & H. Hofmeister (Eds.), *Globalisation, uncertainty and women's careers: An international comparison* (pp. 142–170). Cheltenham: Edward Elgar.

Grunow, D., Hofmeister, H., & Buchholz, S. (2006). Late 20th century persistence and decline of the female homemaker in Germany and the United States. *International Sociology, 21*(1), 101–132.

Hendrickx, J., Bernasco, W., & de Graaf, P. M. (2001). Couples' labour market participation in the Netherlands. In H.-P. Blossfeld & S. Drobnič (Eds.), *Careers of couples in contemporary societies* (pp. 77–98). Oxford: Oxford University Press.

Hunt, J. (2004). Convergence determinants of non-employment durations in Eastern and Western Germany. *Journal of Population Economics, 17*, 249–266.

Kalmijn, M., & Luijkx, R. (2006). Changes in women's employment and occupational mobility in the Netherlands: 1995 to 2000. In H.-P. Blossfeld, & H. Hofmeister (Eds.), *Globalisation, uncertainty and women's careers: An international comparison* (pp. 84–114). Cheltenham: Edward Elgar.

Leth-Sørensen, S., & Rohwer, G. (2001). Work careers of married women in Denmark. In H.-P. Blossfeld & S. Drobnič (Eds.), *Careers of couples in contemporary societies* (pp. 261–279). Oxford: Oxford University Press.

McCulloch, A., & Dex, S. (2001). Married women's employment patterns in Britain. In H.-P. Blossfeld, & S. Drobnič (Eds.), *Careers of couples in contemporary societies* (pp. 175–200). Oxford: Oxford University Press.

Ollikainen, V. (2006). Gender differences in transitions from unemployment: Micro evidence from Finland. *Labour, 20*(1), 159–198.

Transition to childbirth

Aassve, A., Burgess, S., Propper, C., & Dickson, M. (2006). Employment, family union and childbearing decisions in Great Britain. *Journal of the Royal Statistical Society, 169*(4), 781–804.

Baizán, P., Aassve, A., & Billari, F. C. (2003). Cohabitation, marriage, and first birth: The interrelationship of family formation events in Spain. *European Journal of Population, 19*, 147–169.

Baizán, P., Aassve, A., & Billari, F. C. (2004). The interrelations between cohabitation, marriage and first birth in Germany and Sweden. *Population and Environment, 25*(6), 531–561.

Berinde, D. (1999). Pathways to a third child in Sweden. *European Journal of Population, 15*, 349–378.

Bernardi, F., & Nanio, T. (2005). Globalization and the transition to adulthood in Italy. In H.-P. Blossfeld, E. Klijzing, M. Mills, & K. Kurz (Eds.), *Globalization, uncertainty and youth in society* (pp. 349–374). London: Routledge.

Bygren, M., Duvander, A.-Z., & Hultin, M. (2005). Elements of uncertainty in life courses: Transitions to adulthood in Sweden. In H. P. Blossfeld, E. Klijzing, M. Mills, & K. Kurz (Eds.), *Globalization, uncertainty and youth in society* (pp. 135–158). London: Routledge.

Table A.4 (continued)

Corijn, M. (2001). Transition to adulthood in Flanders (Belgium). In M. Corjin & E. Klijzing (Eds.), *Transition to adulthood in Europe* (pp. 103–130). Dordrecht: Kluwer.
De La Rica, S., & Iza, M. (2005). Career planning in Spain: Do fixed-term contracts delay marriage and parenthood? *Review of the Economics of the Households, 3*, 49–73.
Francesconi, M., & Golsch, K. (2005). The process of globalization and transition to adulthood. In H.-P. Blossfeld, E. Klijzing, M. Mills, & K. Kurz (Eds.), *Globalization, uncertainty and youth in society* (pp. 249–276). London: Routledge.
Garcia, T. M. (2006). *Women's education and fertility in Spain: The impact of educational attainment and the educational choice on first, second and third births*. Madrid: Centro de Estudios Avanzados en Ciencias Sociales, 56.
Kantorová, V. (2004). *Family life transitions of young women in a changing society: First union formation and birth of first child in the Czech Republic, 1970–1997*. Unpublished doctoral dissertation, Charles University Prague.
Kravdal, Ø. (1992). The emergence of a positive relation between education and third birth rates in Norway with supportive evidence from the United States. *Population Studies, 46*, 459–475.
Kravdal, Ø. (1994). The importance of economic activity, economic potential and economic resources for the timing of first births in Norway. *Population Studies, 48*, 249–267.
Kreyenfeld, M. (2001). *Employment and fertility: East Germany in the 1990s*. Unpublished doctoral dissertation, University of Rostock, Germany.
Kreyenfeld, M. (2004). Fertility decisions in the FRG and GDR: An analysis with data from the German Fertility and Family Survey. *Demographic Research,* Special Collection *3*, 275–318.
Kurz, K., Steinhage, N., & Golsch, K. (2005). Case study Germany: Global competition, uncertainty and the transition to adulthood. In H.-P. Blossfeld, E. Klijzing, M. Mills, & K. Kurz (Eds.), *Globalization, uncertainty and youth in society* (pp. 51–82). London: Routledge.
Liefbroer, A. C. (2005). Transition from youth to adulthood in The Netherlands. In H.-P. Blossfeld, E. Klijzing, M. Mills, & K. Kurz (Eds.), *Globalization, uncertainty and youth in society* (pp. 83–104). London: Routledge.
Liefbroer, A. C., & Corijn, M. (1999). Who, what, where, and when? Specifying the impact of educational attainment and labour force participation on family formation. *European Journal of Population, 15*, 45–75.
Meron, M., Widmer, I., & Shapiro, D. (2002). Unemployment leads women to postpone the birth of their first child. *Population, 57*(2), 301–330.
Olah, L. Sz. (2003). Gendering fertility: Second births in Sweden and Hungary. *Population Research and Policy Review, 22*, 171–200.
Pinnelli, A., & Di Giulio, P. (2003). Genere e determinanti della fecondità nei Paesi sviluppati. In A. Pinnelli, F. Racioppi, & R. Rettaroli (Eds.), *Genere e demografia* (pp. 281–310). Bologna: Il Mulino.
Róbert, P., & Bukodi, E. (2005). The effects of the globalization process on the transition to adulthood in Hungary. In H.-P. Blossfeld, E. Klijzing, M. Mills, & K. Kurz (Eds.), *Globalization, uncertainty and youth in society* (pp. 176–214). London: Routledge.
Santow, G., & Bracher, M. (2001). Deferment of the first birth and fluctuating fertility in Sweden. *European Journal of Population, 17*, 343–363.
Simó Noguera, C., Martin, T. C., & Soro Bonmatì, A. (2005). The Spanish case: The effects of the globalization process on the transition to adulthood. In H.-P. Blossfeld, E. Klijzing, M. Mills, & K. Kurz (Eds.), *Globalization, uncertainty and youth in society* (pp. 375–402). London: Routledge.
Vikat, A. (2004). Women's labor force attachment and childbearing in Finland. *Demographic Research,* Special Collection *3*, 175–212.

Table A.5 Effect of women's employment on fertility: meta-regression estimates after random exclusion of 10% of the sample, sensitivity analysis

Variable name	Variable categories	M2
Country	Norway	0.43 (0.31)
	Sweden	0.30* (0.17)
	Finland	1.12*** (0.28)
	Netherlands	0.38 (0.37)
	France	0.13 (0.18)
	Belgium	0.93** (0.40)
	United Kingdom	0.45 (0.65)
	Germany	0.61** (0.27)
	Spain	–0.37** (0.16)
	Italy	ref.
	post-socialist Hungary	2.70*** (0.73)
	post-socialist Czech Republic	0.64* (0.38)
Birth cohort	>=1960	–0.58*** (0.17)
	<1960	ref.
Method	Continuous time	0.66* (0.37)
	Discrete	ref.
Parity progression	Parity one	–0.01 (0.12)
	Parity two	*dropped*
	Parity three	–0.06 (0.16)
	All parities	ref.
Constant		0.27 (0.46)
adj-R^2		0.718
Number of studies		61

Note: *** <0.01, ** <0.05, * <0.1. Standard errors are reported in parentheses. The results are standardized for the construction of the variable describing the effect of employment on childbearing and the sample selected

Source: Author's calculations

Table A.6 Effect of young children on women's employment entry: meta-regression estimates after random exclusion of 10% of the sample, sensitivity analysis

Variable name	Variable categories	M2
Country	Denmark	2.49***
		(0.74)
	Finland	1.51*
		(0.73)
	France	0.77*
		(0.40)
	The Netherlands	1.70**
		(0.75)
	The United Kingdom	0.40
		(0.40)
	Germany	ref.
	Italy	–0.06
		(7.53)
Type of transition	From unemployment	0.05
		(0.18)
	from inactivity	0.58***
		(0.20)
	from non-employment	ref.
	to full-time job	–0.19
		(0.25)
	to part-time job	0.48**
		(0.22)
	to any job	ref.
Birth cohort	>=1960	–1.27**
		(0.51)
	<1960	ref.
Method	Continuous	1.36**
		(0.64)
	discrete	ref.
Constant		–1.19**
		(0.51)
adj-R^2		0.954
Number of studies		33

Note: *** <0.01, ** <0.05, * <0.1. Standard errors are reported in parentheses. The results are standardized for the construction of the variable describing the effect of children on mothers' employment entry
Source: Author's calculations

Table A.7 Parameter estimates for first conception hazard, Poland, cohorts 1971–1981

Explanatory variables	Single-process, not controlling for unobserved heterogeneity		Single-process, controlling for unobserved heterogeneity		Multi-process (accounting for endoegeneity)	
	(1)		(2)		(3)	
	Coeff. (st.error)	Sig.	Coeff. (st.error)	Sig.	Coeff. (st.error)	Sig.
Intercept	–5.56	***	–5.65	***	–5.69	***
	(0.20)		(0.21)		(0.21)	
Time since age 15						
15–20 years (slope)	0.54	***	0.55	***	0.57	***
	(0.05)		(0.05)		(0.05)	
20–24 years (slope)	0.14	***	0.16	***	0.18	***
	(0.03)		(0.03)		(0.03)	
24–28 years (slope)	0.03		0.06		0.07	
	(0.04)		(0.04)		(0.04)	
28–32 years (slope)	–0.06		–0.04		–0.04	
	(0.06)		(0.07)		(0.07)	
32–35 years (slope)	–0.31		–0.30		–0.30	
	(0.21)		(0.21)		(0.21)	
Time since 1986						
Slope	–0.03	***	–0.04	***	–0.04	***
	(0.01)		(0.01)		(0.01)	
Time since leaving education						
Tertiary-level education						
Shift for leaving education	0.26		0.23		0.29	*
	(0.17)		(0.17)		(0.17)	
0–4 years (slope)	0.13	**	0.13	**	0.14	**
	(0.07)		(0.07)		(0.07)	
>4 years (slope)	0.01		0.01		0.02	
	(0.09)		(0.09)		(0.09)	
Secondary-level education						
Shift for leaving education	1.09	***	1.09	***	1.12	***
	(0.12)		(0.12)		(0.12)	
0–3 years (slope)	–0.10	*	–0.10	*	–0.08	
	(0.05)		(0.06)		(0.06)	
>3 years (slope)	–0.05		–0.05		–0.05	
	(0.03)		(0.03)		(0.03)	
Vocational education						
Shift for leaving education	1.57	***	1.56	***	1.59	***
	(0.17)		(0.17)		(0.17)	
0–2 years (slope)	–0.13		–0.11		–0.10	
	(0.10)		(0.10)		(0.10)	
>2 years (slope)	–0.12	***	–0.11	***	–0.11	***
	(0.03)		(0.03)		(0.03)	

Table A.7 (continued)

Explanatory variables	Single-process, not controlling for unobserved heterogeneity		Single-process, controlling for unobserved heterogeneity		Multi-process (accounting for endoegeneity)	
	(1)		(2)		(3)	
	Coeff. (st.error)	Sig.	Coeff. (st.error)	Sig.	Coeff. (st.error)	Sig.
Primary education						
Shift for leaving education	1.62	***	1.59	***	1.56	***
	(0.49)		(0.50)		(0.50)	
0–2 years (slope)	0.07		0.11		0.14	
	(0.27)		(0.27)		(0.28	
>2 years (slope)	–0.17	***	–0.17	***	–0.17	***
	(0.04)		(0.04)		(0.04)	
Employed (ref=no)						
Yes	0.10	*	0.09		–0.08	
	(0.06)		(0.06)		(0.07)	
Place of residence (ref=rural)						
Urban	–0.02		–0.02		–0.02	
	(0.05)		(0.06)		(0.06)	
Mother's education (ref=high)						
Low	0.12	*	0.14	*	0.15	*
	(0.07)		(0.08)		(0.08)	
Father's education (ref=high)						
Low	0.19	**	0.21	**	0.21	***
	(0.08)		(0.08)		(0.08)	

Note: Significance: *=0.1; **=0.05; ***=0.01
Source: Author's calculations on Employment, Family and Education Survey (2006)

Table A.8 Parameter estimates for second or higher-order conception hazard, Poland, cohorts 1971–1981

Explanatory variables	Single-process, not controlling for unobserved heterogeneity		Single-process, controlling for unobserved heterogeneity		Multi-process (accounting for endoegeneity)	
	(1)		(2)		(3)	
	Coeff. (st.error)	Sig.	Coeff. (st.error)	Sig.	Coeff. (st.error)	Sig.
Intercept	–2.31 (0.23)	***	–2.44 (0.25)	***	–2.40 (0.25)	***
Age of youngest child						
0–1 years (slope)	1.67 (0.19)	***	1.72 (0.20)	***	1.70 (0.20)	***
1–3 years (slope)	–0.03 (0.05)		0.001 (0.05)		0.02 (0.05)	
>3 years (slope)	–0.12 (0.02)	***	–0.10 (0.02)	***	–0.09 (0.02)	***
Time since 1986						
slope	–0.05 (0.01)	***	–0.05 (0.01)	***	–0.06 (0.01)	***
Age at previous birth (ref=20–22)						
15–19	–0.001 (0.08)		–0.04 (0.09)		–0.07 (0.10)	
23–25	–0.20 (0.09)	**	–0.14 (0.10)		–0.12 (0.10)	
25–28	–0.29 (0.10)	***	–0.19 (0.13)		–0.14 (0.13)	
28+	–0.74 (0.16)	***	–0.57 (0.20)	***	–0.49 (0.21)	**
Number of children (ref=one)						
Two	–0.82 (0.08)	***	–0.97 (0.13)	***	–1.02 (0.13)	***
Three or more	–0.42 (0.13)	***	–0.76 (0.25)	***	–0.83 (0.25)	***
Employed (ref=no)						
Yes	0.01 (0.06)		0.01 (0.06)		–0.12 (0.07)	*
Education level (ref=vocational)						
Tertiary	–0.24 (0.14)	*	–0.32 (0.15)	**	–0.28 (0.15)	*
Secondary	–0.12 (0.07)	*	–0.16 (0.08)	*	–0.15 (0.08)	*
Primary	0.12 (0.10)		0.15 (0.11)		0.14 (0.11)	
Still in education	–0.67 (0.17)	***	–0.71 (0.17)	***	–0.74 (0.17)	***

Table A.8 (continued)

Explanatory variables	Single-process, not controlling for unobserved heterogeneity		Single-process, controlling for unobserved heterogeneity		Multi-process (accounting for endoegeneity)	
	(1)		(2)		(3)	
	Coeff. (st.error)	Sig.	Coeff. (st.error)	Sig.	Coeff. (st.error)	Sig.
Place of residence (ref=rural)						
Urban	–0.38	***	–0.41	***	–0.41	***
	(0.06)		(0.07)		(0.07)	
Mother's education (ref=high)						
Low	0.05		0.08		0.07	
	(0.09)		(0.10)		(0.10)	
Father's education (ref=high)	0.08		0.10		0.13	
Low	(0.10)		(0.10)		(0.11)	

Note: Significance: *=0.1; **=0.05; ***=0.01
Source: Author's calculations on Employment, Family and Education Survey (2006)

Table A.9 Parameter estimates for hazard of employment entry, Poland, cohorts 1971–1981

Explanatory variables	Single-process, not controlling for unobserved heterogeneity		Single-process, controlling for unobserved heterogeneity		Multi-process (accounting for endoegeneity)	
	(1)		(2)		(3)	
	Coeff. (st.error)	Sig.	Coeff. (st.error)	Sig.	Coeff. (st.error)	Sig.
Intercept	–1.5995	***	–2.50	***	–2.44	***
	(0.23)		(0.24)		(0.24)	
Time since age 15						
15–20 (slope)	0.3187	***	0.47	***	0.49	***
	(0.03)		(0.03)		(0.03)	
20–25 (slope)	–0.156	***	0.05	*	0.07	***
	(0.02)		(0.02)		(0.02)	
25–30 (slope)	–0.0598	***	0.10	***	0.12	***
	(0.02)		(0.03)		(0.03)	
30–35 (slope)	–0.006		0.07	*	0.07	**
	(0.03)		(0.04)		(0.04)	
Time since 1986						
<1994 (slope)	–0.1643	***	–0.17	***	–0.17	***
	(0.03)		(0.03)		(0.03)	
1995–98 (slope)	0.033	*	0.04	**	0.04	**
	(0.02)		(0.02)		(0.02)	

Table A.9 (continued)

Explanatory variables	Single-process, not controlling for unobserved heterogeneity		Single-process, controlling for unobserved heterogeneity		Multi-process (accounting for endoegeneity)	
	(1)		(2)		(3)	
	Coeff. (st.error)	Sig.	Coeff. (st.error)	Sig.	Coeff. (st.error)	Sig.
1999–2003 (slope)	–0.0458	**	–0.07	***	–0.08	***
	(0.02)		(0.02)		(0.02)	
2004–06 (slope)	0.0367	**	0.05	**	0.04	*
	(0.02)		(0.02)		(0.02)	
*Time since entering non-employment * Order of the non-employment spell*						
Second spell						
Shift for entering non-employment	–1.0455	***	–2.18	***	–2.00	***
	(0.21)		(0.23)		(0.23)	
0–0.5 year (slope)	2.655	***	3.24	***	3.23	***
	(0.4511)		(0.47)		(0.47)	
>0.5 year (slope)	–0.0233		–0.04	**	–0.04	**
	(0.02)		(0.02)		(0.02)	
Third or higher-order spell						
Shift for entering non-employment	–0.1413		–1.78	***	–1.45	***
	(0.24)		(0.26)		(0.27)	
0–0.5 year (slope)	2.3418	***	2.86	***	2.89	***
	(0.52)		(0.53)		(0.53)	
>0.5 year (slope)	–0.1077	***	–0.12	***	–0.11	***
	(0.03)		(0.04)		(0.04)	
Number of children (ref =no children)						
One	–0.83	***	–1.19	***	–1.35	***
	(0.05)		(0.07)		(0.07)	
Two	–0.98	***	–1.61	***	–1.90	***
	(0.07)		(0.10)		(0.11)	
Three or more	–1.14	***	–1.98	***	–2.41	***
	(0.13)		(0.17)		(0.18)	
Education level (ref=primary)						
Tertiary	1.65	***	1.82	***	1.70	***
	(0.10)		(0.15)		(0.16)	
Secondary	0.71	***	0.92	***	0.81	***
	(0.08)		(0.13)		(0.14)	
Vocational	0.45	***	0.83	***	0.71	***
	(0.08)		(0.13)		(0.14)	
Still in education	–1.30	***	–1.56	***	–1.68	***
	(0.09)		(0.13)		(0.14)	

Table A.9 (continued)

Explanatory variables	Single-process, not controlling for unobserved heterogeneity		Single-process, controlling for unobserved heterogeneity		Multi-process (accounting for endoegeneity)	
	(1)		(2)		(3)	
	Coeff. (st.error)	Sig.	Coeff. (st.error)	Sig.	Coeff. (st.error)	Sig.
Work experience (ref=0–3 years)						
3–6 years	0.08		–0.48	***	–0.62	***
	(0.07)		(0.10)		(0.10)	
>6 years	0.23	**	–0.90	***	–1.09	***
	(0.10)		(0.15)		(0.15)	
Place of residence (ref=rural)						
Urban	0.19	***	0.23	***	0.21	***
	(0.04)		(0.06)		(0.07)	
Mother's education (ref=high)						
Low	–0.06		0.03		0.03	
	(0.05)		(0.09)		(0.09)	
Father's education (ref=high)						
Low	0.11	**	0.23	**	0.25	**
	(0.05)		(0.09)		(0.09)	

Note: significance: *=0.1; **=0.05; ***=0.01
Source: Author's calculations on Employment, Family and Education Survey (2006)

Table A.10 Parameter estimates for hazard of employment exit, Poland, cohorts 1971–1981

Explanatory variables	Single-process, not controlling for unobserved heterogeneity		Single-process, controlling for unobserved heterogeneity		Multi-process (accounting for endoegeneity)	
	(1)		(2)		(3)	
	Coeff. (st.error)	Sig.	Coeff. (st.error)	Sig.	Coeff. (st.error)	Sig.
Intercept	–4.68	***	–6.05	***	–5.43	***
	(0.54)		(0.64)		(0.65)	
Work-experience						
0–0.5 years (slope)	1.85	***	2.72	***	2.61	***
	(0.41)		(0.45)		(0.45)	
0.5–3 years (slope)	–0.20	***	0.06		0.14	***
	(0.04)		(0.05)		(0.05)	
>3 years (slope)	–0.03	**	0.07	***	0.14	***
	(0.02)		(0.02)		(0.03)	

Table A.10 (continued)

Explanatory variables	Single-process, not controlling for unobserved heterogeneity		Single-process, controlling for unobserved heterogeneity		Multi-process (accounting for endoegeneity)	
	(1)		(2)		(3)	
	Coeff. (st.error)	Sig.	Coeff. (st.error)	Sig.	Coeff. (st.error)	Sig.
*Time since entering employment * Order of the employment spell*						
Second spell						
Shift for entering employment	–0.65	**	–1.70	***	–1.38	***
	(0.26)		(0.28)		(0.28)	
0–0.5 year (slope)	2.26	***	2.75	***	2.68	***
	(0.56)		(0.58)		(0.58)	
>0.5 year (slope)	–0.06	**	–0.04		–0.04	
	(0.03)		(0.03)		(0.03)	
Third or higher-order spell						
Shift for entering employment	1.11	***	–0.77	***	–0.24	
	(0.19)		(0.26)		(0.27)	
0–0.5 year (slope)	–0.84	*	–0.003		–0.08	
	(0.49)		(0.51)		(0.52)	
>0.5 year (slope)	–0.08		–0.07		–0.078	
	(0.06)		(0.06)		(0.06)	
Time since age 15						
15–20 (slope)	0.22	***	0.14		0.067	
	(0.07)		(0.08)		(0.09)	
20–25 (slope)	–0.12	***	–0.16	***	–0.27	***
	(0.02)		(0.03)		(0.03)	
25–30 (slope)	–0.08	***	–0.15	***	–0.24	***
	(0.02)		(0.03)		(0.03)	
30–35 (slope)	–0.08	**	–0.16	***	–0.23	***
	(0.04)		(0.04)		(0.04)	
Time since 1986						
<1994 (slope)	0.16	**	0.20	**	0.22	***
	(0.07)		(0.08)		(0.08)	
1995–98 (slope)	–0.04	*	–0.02		–0.01	
	(0.02)		(0.03)		(0.03)	
1999–2003 (slope)	0.04		0.06	**	0.07	**
	(0.02)		(0.03)		(0.03)	
2004–06 (slope)	0.03		0.05	*	0.06	**
	(0.02)		(0.03)		(0.03)	

Table A.10 (continued)

Explanatory variables	Single-process, not controlling for unobserved heterogeneity		Single-process, controlling for unobserved heterogeneity		Multi-process (accounting for endoegeneity)	
	(1)		(2)		(3)	
	Coeff. (st.error)	Sig.	Coeff. (st.error)	Sig.	Coeff. (st.error)	Sig.
Number of children (ref =no children)						
One	1.09	***	1.52	***	1.60	***
	(0.06)		(0.08)		(0.09)	
Two	0.85	***	1.54	***	1.75	***
	(0.09)		(0.13)		(0.15)	
Three or more	1.25	***	1.99	***	2.33	***
	(0.14)		(0.21)		(0.24)	
Education level (ref=primary)						
Tertiary	–0.75	***	–0.90	***	–0.97	***
	(0.13)		(0.20)		(0.21)	
Secondary	–0.48	***	–0.45	***	–0.56	***
	(0.10)		(0.17)		(0.18)	
Vocational	–0.26	***	–0.14		–0.31	*
	(0.10)		(0.17)		(0.17)	
Still in education	–0.45	***	–0.46	**	–0.50	***
	(0.12)		(0.18)		(0.19)	
Place of residence (ref=rural)						
Urban	–0.08		–0.04		–0.06	
	(0.05)		(0.08)		(0.08)	
Mother's education (ref=high)						
Low	–0.01		0.05		–0.01	
	(0.07)		(0.12)		(0.12)	
Father's education (ref=high)						
Low	0.09		0.12		0.04	
	(0.07)		(0.12)		(0.12)	
Type of employee (ref=employee)						
Helping family member	–1.62	***	–1.92	***	–1.93	***
	(0.29)		(0.35)		(0.35)	
Self-employed	–0.68	***	–0.76	***	–0.76	***
	(0.10)		(0.14)		(0.13)	
Type of employment contract (ref=permanent)						
Temporary	0.81	***	1.14	***	1.15	***
	(0.05)		(0.08)		(0.08)	
Sector (ref=private)						
Public sector	–0.14	**	–0.15	*	–0.15	*
	(0.06)		(0.08)		(0.08)	

Note: Significance: *=0.1; **=0.05; ***=0.01
Source: Author's calculations on Employment, Family and Education Survey (2006)

References

Aaberge, R., Colombino, U., Del Boca, D., Ermisch, J., Francesconi, M., Pasqua, S., et al. (2005). Labor supply and fertility in Europe and the U.S. In T. Boeri, D. Del Boca, & C. Pissarides (Eds.), *Women at work: An economic perspective* (pp. 125–153). Oxford: Oxford University Press.

Aassve, A., Burgess, S., Propper, C., & Dickson, M. (2006). Employment, family union and childbearing decisions in Great Britain. *Journal of the Royal Statistical Society, 169*(4), 781–804.

Abramowitz, M., & Stegun, I. A. (1972). *Handbook of mathematical functions*. New York: Dover Publications.

Abramowska, A., Balcerzak-Paradowska, B., Kotowska, I. E., Kowalska, I., Muszyńska, M., & Wróblewska, W. (2003). *Polityka ludnościowa – cele, rozwiązania, opinie* (Population Policy – objectives, measures, opinions). Research report prepared based on the Population Policy Acceptance Study. Warsaw: Institute of Statistics and Demography – Warsaw School of Economics.

Adserà, A. (2004). Changing fertility rates in developed countries: The impact of labor market institutions. *Journal of Population Economics, 17*, 17–43.

Adserà, A. (2005). Vanishing children: From high unemployment to low fertility in developed countries. *American Economic Review, 95*(2), 189–193.

Ahn, N., & Mira, P. (2002). A note on the changing relationship between fertility and female employment rates in developed countries. *Journal of Population Economics, 15*, 667–682.

Algan, Y., & Cahuc, P. (2006). *The roots of low European employment: Family culture?* Paper presented at the European Commission seminar 'Employment in Europe,' Occasional Seminars, Brussels, 13 December 2006. http://ec.europa.eu/employment_social/employment_analysis/docs/061213_algan_en.pdf

Amato, P. R., & Keith, B. (1991). Parental divorce and adult well-being: A meta-analysis. *Journal of Marriage and Family, 53*(1), 43–58.

Andersson, G. (1999). Childbearing trends in Sweden. *European Journal of Population, 15*, 1–24.

Andersson, G. (2000). The impact of labour-force participation on childbearing behaviour: Pro-cyclical fertility in Sweden during the 1980s and the 1990s. *European Journal of Population, 16*, 293–333.

Andersson, G. (2002). Fertility developments in Norway and Sweden since the early 1960s. *Demographic Research, 6*(4), 67–86.

Andersson, G., Duvander, A.-Z., & Hank, K. (2004). Do child-care characteristics influence continued childbearing in Sweden? An investigation of the quantity, quality, and price dimension. *Journal of European Social Policy, 14*, 407–418.

Andersson, G., Hoem, J. M., & Duvander, A.-Z. (2006). Social differentials in speed-premium effects in childbearing in Sweden. *Demographic Research, 14*, 51–70.

Angrist, J. D., & Evans, W. N. (1998). Children and their parents' labor supply: Evidence from exogenous variation in family size. *American Economic Review, 88*(3), 450–477.

Anttonen, A., & Sipilä, J. (1996). European social care services: Is it possible to identify models? *Journal of European Social Policy, 6*(2), 87–100.

Ariza, A., de la Rica, S., & Ugidos, A. (2005). The effect of flexibility in working hours on fertility: A comparative analysis of selected European countries. *Public Finance and Management, 5*(1), 110–151.

Bagozzi, R. P., & van Loo, M. F. (1980). Decision-making and fertility: A theory of exchange in the family. In T. K. Burch (Ed.), *Demographic behavior: Interdisciplinary perspectives on decision-making* (pp. 91–124). Boulder, CO: Westview Press.

Bagozzi, R. P., & van Loo, M. F. (1991). A purposeful behaviour theory of work and family size decisions. In J. J. Siegers, J. de Jong-Gierveld, & E. van Imhoff (Eds.), *Female labour market behaviour and fertility: A rational-choice approach* (pp. 101–129). Berlin: Springer.

Baizán, P. (2005). *Couples' careers and fertility: An event history analysis of the ECHP samples of Denmark, Italy, Spain, and United Kingdom.* Paper presented at the 25th IUSSP International Population Conference, Tours, France, 18–23 July 2005.

Baker M., & Milligan K. (2005). *How does job-protected maternity leave affect mothers' employment and infant health?* (National Bureau of Economic Research Cambridge, Massachusetts, Working Paper No. 11135).

Balcerzak-Paradowska, B. (1999). *Polityka rodzinn: Między dwoma modelami* [Family policy: In-between the two models]. Warsaw: Institute of Labour and Social Studies.

Balcerzak-Paradowska, B., Chłoń-Domińczak, A., Kotowska, I. E., Olejniczuk-Merta, A., Topińska, I., & Wóycicka, I. (2003). The gender dimensions of social security reform in Poland. In E. Fultz, M. Ruck, & S. Steinhilber (Eds.), *The gender dimensions of social security reform in Central and Eastern Europe: Case studies of the Czech Republic, Hungary and Poland* (pp. 187–313). Budapest: ILO Subregional Office for Central and Eastern Europe.

Beblo, M., & Wolf, E. (2000). *How much does a year off cost? Estimating the wage effects of employment breaks and part-time periods. ZEW Discussion Paper No 00-69.* Mannheim: Zentrum für Ökonomische Wirtschaftsforschung.

Beblo, M., & Wolf, E. (2002). *Wage penalties for career interruptions: An empirical analysis for West Germany. ZEW Discussion Paper No 02-45.* Mannheim: Zentrum für Ökonomische Wirtschaftsforschung.

Becker, G. S. (1965). A theory of the allocation of time. *Economic Journal, 75*, 493–517.

Becker, G. S. (1993). *A treatise on the family.* London: Harvard University Press.

Becker, G. S., & Lewis, H. G. (1973). On the interaction between the quantity and quality of children. *The Journal of Political Economy* (Part 2: New Economic Approaches to Fertility) *81*, 279–288.

Berger, L. M., & Waldfogel, J. (2004). Maternity leave and the employment of new mothers in the United States. *Journal of Population Economics, 17*, 331–349.

Berkowitz King, R. (2005). The case of the American women: Globalization and the transition to adulthood in an individualistic regime. In H.-P. Blossfeld, E. Klijzing, M. Mills, & K. Kurz (Eds.), *Globalization, uncertainty and youth in society* (pp. 305–326). London: Routledge.

Bernhardt, E. M. (1993). Fertility and employment. *European Sociological Review, 9*(1), 25–42.

Bettio, F., & Plantega, J. (2004). Comparing care regimes in Europe. *Feminist Economics, 10*, 85–113.

Biggerstaff, B. J., & Tweedie, R. L. (1997). Incorporating variability in estimates of heterogeneity in the random effects model in meta-analysis. *Statistics in Medicine, 16*, 753–768.

Bijak, J., Kupiszewska, D., Kupiszewski, M., Saczuk, K., & Kicinger, A. (2007). Population and labour force projections for 27 European countries, 2002–2052: Impact of international migration on population ageing. *European Journal of Population, 23*, 1–31.

Billingsley, S. (2010). Downward social mobility and fertility in Russia. *Stockholm Research Reports in Demography, 2010*, 1.

Blau, D. M., & Robins, P. K. (1989). Fertility, employment, and child-care costs. *Demography, 26*, 287–299.

Blossfeld, H-P. (1995). Changes in the process of family formation and women's growing economic independence: A comparison of nine countries. In H.-P. Blossfeld (Ed.), *The new role of women: Family formation in modern societies* (pp. 3–23). Boulder, CO: Westview Press.

Brandth, B., & Kvande, E. (2009). Gender or gender-neutral care politics for fathers? *The Annals of the American Academy of Political and Social Science, 624*(1), 177–189.

Brewster, K. L., & Rindfuss, R. R. (2000). Fertility and women's employment in industralised nations. *Annual Review of Sociology, 26*, 271–296.

Budig, M. J. (2003). Are women's fertility and employment histories interdependent? An examination of causal order using event history analysis. *Social Science Research, 32*, 376–401.

Burch, T. K. (1980). Decision-making theories in demography: An introduction. In T. K. Burch (Ed.), *Demographic behaviour: Interdisciplinary perspectives on decision-making* (pp. 1–22). Boulder, CO: Westview Press.

Carrasco, R. (2001). Binary choice with binary endogenous regressors in panel data: Fertility and female labour force participation. *Journal of Business and Economics Statistics, 19*(4), 385–394.

Castles, F. G. (2003). The world turned upside down: Below replacement fertility, changing preferences and family-friendly public policy in 21 OECD countries. *Journal of European Social Policy, 13*(3), 209–229.

Cochran, W. G. (1954). The combination of estimates from different experiments. *Biometrics, 10*, 101–129.

Coleman, J. S. (1990). *Foundations of social theory*. Cambridge: Belknap Press of Harvard University Press.

Colombino, U., & Di Tommaso, M. L. (1996). Is the preference for children so low, or is the price of time so high? A simultaneous model of fertility and participation in Italy with cohort effects. *Labour, 10*(3), 475–493.

Connelly, R. (1992). The effect of child care costs on married women's labor force participation. *Review of Economics and Statistics, 74*(1), 89–90.

Corijn, M. (2001). Transition to adulthood in Flanders (Belgium). In M. Corijn & E. Klijzing (Eds.), *Transition to adulthood in Europe* (pp. 103–130). Dordrecht: Kluwer.

Cramer, J. C. (1980). Fertility and female employment: Problems of causal direction. *American Sociological Review, 45*(2), 167–190.

Crompton, R., & Harris, F. (1998). Explaining women's employment patterns: 'orientations to work' revisited. *British Journal of Sociology, 49*(1), 118–136.

D'Addio, A. C., & M. M.d'Ercole. (2005). *Trends and determinants of fertility rates in OECD countries: The role of policies* (OECD Social, Employment and Migration Working Paper No. 27). Paris: OECD.

Duvander, A.-Z., Lappegard, T., & Andersson, G. (2006). Family policy and fertility: Fathers' and mothers' use of parental leave and continued childbearing in Norway and Sweden. *Journal of European Social Policy*, 20(1), 45–57.

De Bruijn, B. J. (1999). *Foundations of demographic theory: Choice, process, theory*. Amsterdam: Thela Thesis.

De Laat, J., & A. Sevilla Sanz. (2006). *Working women, men's home time and lowest-low fertility*. ISER Working Paper 2006–23. Essex: Institute for Social and Economic Research.

Del Boca, D. (2002). The effect of child care and part-time opportunities on participation and fertility decisions in Italy. *Journal of Population Economics, 15*, 549–573.

Del Boca, D., & Locatelli, M. (2006). *The determinants of motherhood and work status: A survey* (IZA Discussion Paper No. 2414). Bonn: Institute for the Study of Labour.

Del Boca, D., Pasqua, S., & Pronzato, C. (2005). Fertility and employment in Italy, France and the UK. *Labour, 19*, 51–77.

Del Boca, D., Pasqua, S., & Pronzato, C. (2009). Motherhood and market work decisions in institutional contexts. *Oxford Economic Papers, 61*, 147–171.

DerSimonian, R., & Laird, N. (1986). Meta-analysis in clinical trials. *Controlled Clinical Trials, 7*, 177–188.

Di Tommaso, M. L. (1999). A trivariate model of participation, fertility and wages: The Italian case. *Cambridge Journal of Economics, 23*, 623–640.

Drobnič, S. (1997). Part-time work in Central and Eastern European countries. In H.-P. Blossfeld & C. Hakim (Eds.), *Between equalization and marginalization* (pp. 71–89). Oxford: Oxford University Press.

Duclos, E., Lefebvre, P., & Merrigan, P. (2001). *A natural experiment on the economics of storks: Evidence on the impact of differential family policy on fertility rates in Canada.* Center for Research on Economic Fluctuations and Employment (Working paper No. 136). Université du Québec à Montréal.

Easterlin, R. (1976). The conflict between aspirations and resources. *Population and Development Review, 2*, 417–425.

Easterlin, R. A. (1980). Marriage and childbearing. In R. A. Easterlin (Ed.), *Birth and fortune: The impact of numbers on personal welfare* (pp. 37–59). New York: Basic Books.

Engelhardt, H. (2009). Zum Wandel der Korrelation von Fertilität und Frauenerwerbstätigkeit in Raum und Zeit: Eine empirische Analyse unter Berücksichtigung der Effekte ausgewählter sozialer Indikatoren. *Zeitschrift für Familienforschung, 21*(3), 246–263.

Engelhardt, H., Kögel, T., & Prskawetz, A. (2004). Fertility and women's employment reconsidered: A macro-level time-series analysis for developed countries, 1960–2000. *Population Studies, 58*(1), 109–120.

Engelhardt, H., & Prskawetz, A. (2004). On the changing correlation between fertility and female employment over space and time. *European Journal of Population, 20*, 35–62.

Ermisch, J. F. (1979). The relevance of the 'Easterlin hypothesis' and the 'New Home Economics' to fertility movements in Great Britain. *Population Studies, 33*, 39–58.

Ermisch, J. F. (1988). The econometric analysis of birth rate dynamics in Britain. *The Journal of Human Resources, 23*, 563–576.

Ermisch, J. F. (1991). Economic models of women's employment and fertility. In J. J. Siegers, J. de Jong-Gierveld, & E. van Imhoff (Eds.), *Female labour market behaviour and fertility: A rational-choice approach* (pp. 175–190). Berlin: Springer.

Ermisch, J. F. (2003). *An economic analysis of the family.* Princeton and Oxford: Princeton University Press.

Esping-Andersen, G. (1990). *The three worlds of welfare capitalism.* Cambridge: Polity Press.

Esping-Andersen, G. (1999). *Social foundations of postindustrial economies.* Oxford: Oxford University Press.

European Commission. (2005). *Confronting demographic change: A new solidarity between the generations.* Brussels: Communication from the Commission COM(2005) 94.

European Commission. (2006). *The demographic future of Europe – From challenge to opportunity.* Brussels: Green Paper, Commission Communication COM(2006) 571.

European Commission. (2007). *Europe's demographic future: Facts and figures.* Brussels: Commission Staff Working Document SEC(2007) 638.

Felmlee, D. (1993). The dynamic interdependence of women's employment and fertility. *Social Science Research, 22*, 333–360.

Fokkema, T., & Esveldt, I. (2008). *Child-Friendly Policies* (Comparative report on children and child-friendly policies). Wiesbaden: Bundesinstitut für Bevölkerungsforschung.

Fortin, B., Lacroix, G., & Rolet, S. (2004). Welfare benefits and the duration of welfare spells: evidence from a natural experiment in Canada. *Journal of Public Economics, 88*, 1495–1520.

Francesconi, M. (2002). A joint dynamic model of fertility and work of married women, *Journal of Labour Economics, 20*(2), 336–380.

Francesconi, M., & Golsch, K. (2005). The process of globalization and transition to adulthood. In H.-P. Blossfeld, E. Klijzing, M. Mills, & K. Kurz (Eds.), *Globalization, uncertainty and youth in society* (pp. 249–276). London and New York: Routledge.

Freedman, D., Thornton, A., Camburn, D., Alwin, D., & Young-DeMarco, L. (1988). The life history calendar: A technique for collecting retrospective data. *Sociological Methodology, 18*, 37–68.

Friedman, M. (1962). *Price theory. A provisional text.* Chicago: Aldine Publishing.

Gauthier, A. H. (1996). *The state and the family: A comparative analysis of family policies in industrialized countries.* Oxford: Clarendon Press.

Gauthier, A. H. (2007). The impact of family policies on fertility in industrialized countries: a review of the literature. *Population Research and Policy Review, 26*, 323–346.
Gauthier, A. H., & Hatzius, J. (1997). Family benefits and fertility: An econometric analysis. *Population Studies, 51*, 295–306.
Goldstein, J., Wolfgang, L., & Testa, M. R. (2003). The emergence of sub-replacement family size ideals in Europe. *Population Research and Policy Review, 22*, 479–496.
Góra, M. (1996). *The labour market in Poland: 1990–1995. Empirical and methodological studies.* Monografie i Opracowania, 421. Warsaw: Warsaw School of Economics Publishing.
Gornick, J. C., Meyers, M. K., & Ross, K. E. (1997). Supporting the employment of mothers: Policy variations across fourteen welfare states. *Journal of European Social Policy, 7*, 45–70.
Gornick, J. C., & Meyers, M. K. (2003). *Families that work: Policies for reconciling parenthood and employment*. New York: Russell Sage Foundation.
Gurgand, M., & Margolis, D. N. (2005). *Does work pay in France? Monetary incentives and the guaranteed minimum income* (IZA (Institute for the Study of Labor, Bonn) Discussion Paper No. 1467).
Gustafsson, S., & Stafford, F. (1992). Child care subsidies and labor supply in Sweden. *The Journal of Human Resources, 27*(Special Issue on Child Care), 204–230.
Haas, L., & Hwang, P. C. (1999). Parental leave in Sweden. In P. Moss & F. Deven (Eds.), *Parental leave: Progress or pitfall?* Research and Policy Issues in Europe (35). The Hague, The Netherlands, and Brussels: NIDI/CGBS Publications pp. 45–68.
Hakim, C. (2000). *Work-lifestyle choices in the 21st century: Preference theory*. Oxford: Oxford University Press.
Hank, K., & Kreyenfeld, M. (2003). A multilevel analysis of child care and women's fertility decisions in Western Germany. *Journal of Marriage and the Family, 65*, 584–596.
Higgins, J. P. T., & Thompson, S. G. (2004). Controlling the risk of spurious findings from meta-regression. *Statistics in Medicine, 23*, 1663–1682.
Higgins, J. P. T, Thompson, S. G., Deeks, J. J., & Altman, D. G. (2002). Measuring inconsistency in meta-analyses. *BMJ*, 327, 557–560.
Hoem, B. (2000). Entry into motherhood in Sweden: The influence of economic factors on the rise and fall in fertility, 1986–1997. *Demographic Research, 2*, Article 4.
Hoem, J. M. (1993). Public policy as the fuel of fertility: Effects of a policy reform on the pace of childbearing in Sweden in the 1980s. *Acta Sociologica, 36*(1), 19–31.
Hotz, V. J., & Miller, R. A. (1988). An empirical analysis of life cycle fertility and female labor supply. *Econometrica, 56*, 91–118.
Hoynes, H., & MaCurdy, T. (1994). Has the decline in benefits shortened welfare spells? *The American Economic Review, 84*(Papers and Proceedings of the Hundred and Sixth Annual Meeting of the American Economic Association), 43–48.
Huber, J. (1980). Will U.S. fertility decline towards zero? *Sociological Quarterly, 21*(4), 481–492.
Inglehart, R. (1977). *The silent revolution*. Princeton, NJ: Princeton University Press.
Inglehart, R. (1990). *Culture shift in advanced industrial societies*. Princeton, NJ: Princeton University Press.
Jaumotte, F. (2003). Labour force participation of women: Empirical evidence on the role of policy and other determinants in OECD Countries. *OECD Economic Studies, 37*, 52–108.
Joesch, J. M. (1994). Children and the timing of women's paid work after childbirth: A further specification of the relationship. *Journal of Marriage and the Family, 56*(2), 429–440.
Keck, W., Hessel, P., & Saraceno, C. (2009). *Database on intergenerational policy indicators*. Methodological Report. Multilinks Research Report.
Keiding, N. (1998). Selection effects and non-proportional hazards in survival models and models for repeated events. *Proceedings of the XIX International Biometric Conference, Cape Town, Invited Papers*.
Kimmel, J. (1995). The effectiveness of child-care subsidies in encouraging the welfare-to-work transition of low-income single mothers. *The American Economic Review, 85*, 271–275.

Klerman J. A., & Leibowitz, A. (1999). Job continuity among new mothers. *Demography, 36*, 145–155.

Klijzing, E., Siegers, J., Keilman, N., & Groot, L. (1988). Static versus dynamic analysis of the interaction between female labour force participation and fertility. *European Journal of Population, 4*, 97–116.

Knapp, G., & Hartung, J. (2003). Improved tests for a random effects meta-regression with a single covariate. *Statistics in Medicine*, 22, 2693–2710.

Kögel, T. (2004). Did the association between fertility and female employment within OECD countries really change its sign? *Journal of Population Economics, 17*(1), 45–65.

Konstantopoulos, S. (2006). *Fixed and mixed effects models in meta-analysis* (IZA Discussion Paper No. 2198). Bonn: The Institute for the Study of Labor.

Korpi, W. (2000). Faces of inequality: Gender, class, and patterns of inequalities in different types of Welfare States. *Social Politics, 7*, 127–191.

Kotowska, I. E. (1995). Discrimination against women in the labour market in Poland during the transition to a market economy. *Social Politics, 2*(1), 76–90.

Kotowska, I. E. (1999). Drugie przejście demograficzne i jego uwarunkowania (Second demographic transition and its circumstances). In I. E. Kotowska (Ed.), *Przemiany demograficzne w Polsce w latach 90. w świetle koncepcji drugiego przejścia demograficznego* [Demographic changes in Poland in the framework of the second demographic transition] (pp. 115–138). Warsaw: Warsaw School of Economics Publishing.

Kotowska, I. E. (2004). Zmiany demograficzne a przyszły rynek pracy [Demographic changes and the future labour market]. In S. Borkowska (Ed.), *Przyszłość rynku pracy w XXI wieku* [Future of the labour market in the 21st century] (pp. 115–138). Warsaw: Institute of Labour and Social Affairs and Central Statistical Office.

Kotowska, I. E. (2005). Europa wobec przeobrażeń rodziny. Czy potrzebna jest europejska stratega prorodzinna? [Europe towards family changes: Do we need a European family strategy?]. In J. M. Radlo (Ed.), *Polska wobec redefinicji Strategii Lizbońskiej* [Poland towards a redefinition of the Lisbon Strategy] (pp. 223–241). Warsaw and Gdańsk: Green Paper of the Polish Forum for Lisbon Strategy.

Kotowska, I. E., & Sztanderska, U. (2007). Zmiany demograficzne a zmiany na rynku pracy w Polsce (Population changes and labour market developments in Poland). In I. E. Kotowska, U. Sztanderska, & I. Wóycicka (Eds.), *Aktywność zawodowa i edukacyjna a obowiązki rodzinne w świetle badań empirycznych* (Economic and educational activity versus family obligations) (pp. 13–46). Warsaw: Scholar Publishing.

Kotowska, I. E., Jóźwiak, J., Matysiak, A., & Baranowska, A. (2008). Poland: Fertility decline – a response to profound societal change and transformations in the labour market? *Demographic Research, 19*(Article 22), 795–854.

Kowalska, I., & Wróblewska, W. (2008). Intergenerational changes in the value system in Europe. In C. Höhn, D. Avramov, & I. E. Kotowska (Eds.), *People, population change and policies: Lessons from the population policy acceptance study, Vol. 1: Family change* (pp. 181–202). Berlin: Springer.

Kravdal, Ø. (2002). The impact of individual and aggregate unemployment on fertility in Norway. *Demographic Research, 6*, 263–294.

Kreyenfeld, M. (2001). Work/family processes and socioeconomic outcomes. *Vierteljahrshefte zur Wirtschaftsforschung, 70*, 74–79.

Kreyenfeld, M. (2005). *Economic uncertainty and fertility postponement: Evidence from German panel data* (MPIDR Working Paper No 2005-034). Rostock: Max Planck Institute for Demographic Research.

Kurz, K., Steinhage, N., & Golsch, K. (2005). Case study Germany: Global competition, uncertainty and the transition to adulthood. In H.-P. Blossfeld, E. Klijzing, M. Mills, & K. Kurz (Eds.), *Globalization, uncertainty and youth in society* (pp. 51–82). London and New York: Routledge.

Lalive, R., & Zweimuller, J. (2005). *Does parental leave affect fertility and return-to-work? Evidence from a 'true natural experiment'* (IZA Discussion paper No. 1613). Bonn: Institute for the Study of Labor.

Lappegard, T. (2008). Changing the gender balance in caring: Fatherhood and the division of parental leave in Norway. *Population Research and Policy Review, 27*, 139–159.

Lehrer, E., & Nerlove, M. (1986). Female labour force behavior and fertility in the United States. *Annual Review of Sociology, 12*, 181–204.

Leibowitz, A., Klerman, J. A., & Waite, L. J. (1992). Employment of new mothers and childcare choice: Differences by children's age. *The Journal of Human Resources, 27*(Special Issue on Child Care), 112–133.

Lesthaeghe, R. (1992). Der zweite demographische Übergang in den westlichen Ländern: Eine Deutung [The second demographic transition in Western countries: An interpretation]. *Zeitschrift für Bevölkerungsforschung, 18*(3), 313–354.

Letablier, M.-T. (1998). Comparing family policies in Europe (Periodic Progress Report No. 1 of the thematic network 'Working and mothering: Social practices and social policies' TSER Programme of the European Commission, Area III: Research into Social Integration and Social Exclusion in Europe.

Lewis, J., & Ostner, I. (1995). Gender and the evolution of European social policies. In S. Leibfried & P. Pierson (Eds.), *European social policy: Between fragmentation and integration* (pp. 159–193). Washington, DC: Brookings Institution Press.

Liefbroer, A. C. (2005). Transition from youth to adulthood in the Netherlands. In H.-P. Blossfeld, E. Klijzing, M. Mills, & K. Kurz (Eds.), *Globalization, uncertainty and youth in society* (pp. 83–104). London and New York: Routledge.

Liefbroer, A. C., & Corijn, M. (1999). Who, what, where, and when? Specifying the impact of educational attainment and labour force participation on family formation. *European Journal of Population, 15*, 45–75.

Light, A., & Ureta, M. (1992). Panel estimates of male and female job turnover behavior: Can female nonquitters be identified? *Journal of Labor Economics, 10*, 156–181.

Lillard, L. A. (1993). Simultaneous equations for hazards: Marriage duration and fertility timing. *Journal of Econometrics, 56*, 189–217.

Lillard, L. A., & Panis, C. W. A. (1996). Marital status and mortality: The role of health. *Demography, 33*(3), 313–327.

Lillard, L. A., Brien, M. J., & Waite, L. J. (1995). Premarital cohabitation and subsequent marital dissolution: A matter of self-selection? *Demography, 32*(3), 437–457.

Lillard, L. A., & Waite, L. J. (1993). A joint model of marital childbearing and marital disruption. *Demography, 30*(4), 653–681.

Lück, D., & Hofäcker, D. (2003). *Rejection and acceptance of the male breadwinner model: Which preferences do women have under which circumstances?* (Globalife Working Paper No. 60). Germany: University of Bamberg.

Macunovich, D. (1996). Relative income and price of time: Exploring their effects on U.S. fertility and female labour force participation. *Population and Development Review, 22*(Supplement), 223–257.

Macura, M. (2000). *Fertility decline in the transition economies, 1989–1999: Economic and social factors revisited. Economic Survey of Europe 2000/1* (pp. 189–207). Geneva: Economic Commission for Europe, United Nations.

Maslow, A. H. (1943). A theory of human motivation. *Psychological Review, 50*, 370–396.

Maslow, A. H. (1954). *Motivation and personality*. New York: Harper and Row.

Mason, K. O., & Kuhlthau, K. (1992). The perceived impact of child care costs on women's labor supply and fertility. *Demography, 29*, 523–543.

Matysiak, A. (2006). Sharing professional and household duties within Polish couples: Preferences and actual choices. *Studia Demograficzne, 1/147*, 122–153.

Matysiak, A. (2007a). Organizacja czasu pracy i opieki [Combining work with care]. In I. E. Kotowska, U. Sztanderska, & I. Wóycicka (Eds.), *Aktywność zawodowa i edukacyjna a obowiązki rodzinne w świetle badań* empirycznych [Economic and educational activity versus family obligations] (pp. 345–380). Warsaw: Scholar Publishing.

Matysiak, A. (2007b). Indywidualne przesłanki zwiększenia aktywności ekonomicznej ludności [Individual prerequisities for increasing economic activity]. In I. E. Kotowska, U. Sztanderska, & I. Wóycicka (Eds.), *Aktywność zawodowa i edukacyjna a obowiązki rodzinne w świetle badań empirycznych* [Economic and educational activity versus family obligations] (pp. 383–403). Warsaw: Scholar Publishing.

Matysiak, A. (2009). Employment first, then childbearing: Women's strategy in post-socialist Poland. *Population Studies, 63*(3), 253–276.

Matysiak, A., & Steinmetz, S. (2008). Finding their way? Female employment patterns in West Germany, East Germany, and Poland. *European Sociological Review, 24*(3), 331–345.

Matysiak, A., & Vignoli, D. (2008). Fertility and women's employment: A meta-analysis. *European Journal of Population, 24*(4), 363–384.

McRae, S. (2003). Constraints and choices in mothers' employment careers: A consideration of Hakim's preference theory. *British Journal of Sociology, 54*(3), 317–338.

Meeker, B. F. (1980). Rational decision-making models in interpersonal behavior. In T. K. Burch (Ed.), *Demographic behaviour: Interdisciplinary perspectives on decision-making* (pp. 23–42). Boulder, CO: Westview Press.

Meulders, D., & S. O'Dorchai. (2008). The position of mothers in the comparative welfare state perspective. In D. Del Boca & C. Wetzels (Eds.), *Social policies, labour markets and motherhood: A comparative analysis of European countries* (pp. 1–27). Cambridge: Cambridge University Press.

Michalopoulos, C., Robins, P. K., & Garfinkel, I. (1992). A structural model of labor supply and child care demand. *The Journal of Human Resources, 27*(Special Issue on Child Care), 166–203.

Milligan, K. (2005). Subsidizing the stork: New evidence on tax incentives and fertility. *Review of Economics and Statistics, 83*, 539–555.

Mills, M., & Blossfeld, H.-P. (2005). Globalization, uncertainty and the early life course: A theoretical framework. In H.-P. Blossfeld, E. Klijzing, M. Mills, & K. Kurz (Eds.), *Globalization, uncertainty and youth in the society* (pp. 1–24). London and New York: Routledge Taylor and Francis.

Mincer, J. (1963). Market prices, opportunity costs and income effects. In C. F. Christ (Ed.), *Measurement in economics* (pp. 63–97). Palo Alto, CA: Stanford University Press.

Moffit, R. A. (1984). Profiles of fertility, labour supply and wages of married women: A complete life cycle model. *Review of Economic Studies, 51*, 263–278.

Muszyńska, M. (2004). *Family models in Europe in the context of women's status* (Working Papers on Population, Family and Welfare No 6). Budapest: Hungarian Central Statistical Office.

Muszyńska, M. (2007). *Structural and cultural determinants of fertility in Europe*. Warsaw: Warsaw School of Economics Publishing.

Neyer, G. (2003). *Family policies and low fertility in Western Europe* (MPIDR Working Paper WP 2003-021). Rostock: Max Planck Institute for Demographic Research.

Neyer, G. (2006). *Family policies and fertility in Europe: Fertility policies at the intersection of gender policies, employment policies and care policies* (MPIDR Working Paper 2006-010). Rostock: Max Planck Institute for Demographic Research.

Neyer, G., & Andersson, G. (2008). Consequences of family policies on childbearing behavior: Effects or artifacts? *Population and Development Review, 34*(4), 699–724.

Ni Bhrolchain, M. (1986a). Women's paid work and the timing of births: Longitudinal evidence. *European Journal of Population, 2*, 43–70.

Ni Bhrolchain, M. (1986b). The interpretation and role of work-associated accelerated childbearing in post-war Britain. *European Journal of Population, 2*, 135–154.

Ni Bhrolchain, M. (1993). How to answer the fertility employment question (and how not to). In M. Ni Bhrolchain (Ed.), *New perspectives on fertility in Britain. Studies on Medical and Population Subjects* (pp. 151–157). London: HMSO.

O'Brien, M. (2009). Fathers, parental leave policies, and infant quality of life: International perspectives and policy impact. *The Annals of the American Academy of Political and Social Science, 624*(1), 190–213.

OECD (2001). *Balancing work and family life: Helping parents into paid employment. OECD Employment Outlook* (pp. 129–166). Paris: OECD.

OECD (2003). *Making work pay – making work possible. Employment Outlook*. Paris: OECD.

OECD (2004a). *Benefits and wages. OECD Indicators*. Paris: OECD.

OECD (2004b). *Employment protection regulation and labour market performance. OECD Employment Outlook*. (pp. 61–125). Paris: OECD.

Olah, L. S. (2003). Gendering fertility: Second births in Sweden and Hungary. *Population Research and Policy Review, 22*, 171–200.

Orloff, A. S. (1993). Gender and the social rights of citizenship: The comparative analysis of gender relations and welfare states. *American Sociological Review, 58*, 303–328.

Pampel, F. C., & Peters, H. E. (1995). The Easterlin effect. *Annual Review of Sociology, 21*, 163–194.

Pascall, G., & Lewis, J. (2004). Emerging gender regimes and policies for gender equality in a wider Europe. *Journal of Social Policy, 33*, 373–394.

Pascall, G., & Manning, N. (2000). Gender and social policy: Comparing welfare states in Central and Eastern Europe and the former Soviet Union. J*ournal of European Social Policy, 10*, 240–266.

Pfau-Effinger, B. (1998). Gender culture and the gender arrangement: A theoretical framework for cross-national gender research. *Innovation, 11*, 147–166.

Philipov, D. (2008). Family-related gender attitudes. In C. Höhn, D. Avramov, & I. E. Kotowska (Eds.), *People, population change and policies: Lessons from the Population Policy Acceptance Study, Vol 2: Demographic knowledge – gender – ageing* (pp. 153–174). Berlin: Springer.

Pissarides, C., Garibaldi, P., Olivetti, C., Petrongolo, B., & Wasmer, E. (2005). Women's employment patterns: Some facts. In T. Boeri, D. Del Boca, & C. Pissarides (Eds.), *Women at work: An economic perspective* (pp. 12–24). Oxford: Oxford University Press.

Pollak, R. A., & Watkins, S. (1993). Cultural and economic approaches to fertility: Proper marriage or misalliance? *Population and Development Review, 19*, 467–496.

Pongracz, M., & Z. Spèder. (2008). Attitudes towards forms of partnership. In C. Höhn, D. Avramov, & I. E. Kotowska (Eds.), *People, population change and policies: Lessons from the population policy acceptance study* (pp. 105–205). Berlin: Springer.

Powell, L. M. (1998). Part-time versus full-time work and child care costs: Evidence for married mothers. *Applied Economics, 30*, 503–511.

Ribar, D. C. (1992). Child care and the labour supply of married women: Reduced form evidence. *The Journal of Human Resources, 27*(Special Issue on Child Care), 134–165.

Rindfuss, R. R., Guilkey, D. K., Morgan, S. P., & Kravdal, Ø. (2010). Child-care availability and fertility in Norway. *Population and Development Review, 36*(4), 725–748.

Rindfuss, R. R., Guzzo, K., & Morgan, S. P. (2003). The changing institutional context of low fertility. *Population Research and Policy Review, 22*, 411–438.

Róbert, P., & E. Bukodi E. (2005). The effects of the globalization process on the transition to adulthood in Hungary. In H.-P. Blossfeld, E. Klijzing, M. Mills, & K. Kurz (Eds.), *Globalization, uncertainty and youth in society* (pp. 176–214). London and New York: Routledge.

Robinson, W. C., & Harbison, S. F. (1980). Towards a unified theory of fertility. In T. K. Burch (Ed.), *Demographic behaviour: Interdisciplinary perspectives on decision-making*. (pp. 201–235). Boulder, CO: Westview Press.

Rønsen, M. (2004). Fertility and public policies: Evidence from Norway and Finland. *Demographic Research, 10*, 143–170.

Rønsen, M., & Sundström, M. (2002). Family policy and after-birth employment among new mothers: A comparison of Finland, Norway and Sweden. *European Journal of Population, 18*, 121–152.

Rosenzweig, M. R., & Schultz, T. P. (1985). The demand for and supply of births: Fertility and its life-cycle consequences. *American Economic Review, 75*(5), 992–1015.

Rosenzweig M. R., & Wolpin, K. I. (1980). Life-cycle labour supply and fertility: Causal inferences from household models. *Journal of Political Economy, 88*(2), 328–348.

Rostgaard, T. (2004). *Family support policies in Central and Eastern Europe – A Decade and a half transition*. Budapest: UNESCO.

Rychtarikova, J. (1999). Is Eastern Europe experiencing a second demographic transition? *Acta Universitatis Carolinae Geographica, 1*, 19–44.

Rychtarikova, J. (2000). Demographic transition or demographic shock in recent population development in the Czech Republic? *Acta Universitatis Carolinae Geographica, 1*, 89–102.

Saraceno, C., & Keck, W. (2008). *The institutional framework of intergenerational family obligations in Europe: A conceptual and methodological overview*. Multilinks Research Report.

Schmitt, C. (2005). *Gender-specific effects of unemployment on family formation: Evidence from a cross-national view*. Paper presented at the 25th IUSSP International Population Conference, Tours, France, 18–23 July 2005.

Schneider, H., & Uhlendorf, A. (2004). *The transition from welfare to work and the role of potential labor income* (IZA Discussion Paper No. 1420). Bonn: Institute for the Study of Labor.

Schröder, J. (2005). *Der Zusammenhang zwischen Erwerbstätigkeit und Fertilität: Ein Überblick über den Forschungsstand* (MZES Working Paper No. 89). Mannheim: Mannheim Centre for Social Research.

Shadish, W. R., Cook, T. D., & Campbell, D. T. (2002). *Experimental and quasi-experimental designs for generalized causal inference*. Boston: Houghton Mifflin.

Shaw, K. (1994). The persistence of female labour supply: Empirical evidence and implications. *The Journal of Human Resources, 29*(2), 348–378.

Siegers, J. J. (1991). Towards a better understanding of the relationship between female labour market behaviour and fertility. In J. J. Siegers, J. de Jong-Gierveld, & E. van Imhoff (Eds.), *Female labour market behaviour and fertility: A rational-choice approach* (pp. 265–274). Berlin: Springer.

Siegers J. J., de Jong-Gierveld, J., & van Imhoff, E. (1991). Editors' introduction. In J. J. Siegers, J. de Jong-Gierveld, & E. van Imhoff (Eds.), *Female labour market behaviour and fertility: A rational-choice approach* (pp. 1–7). Berlin: Springer.

Siemieńska, R. (1997). Wartości i postawy warunkujące obecność kobiet na rynku pracy [Values and attitudes determining women's labour supply]. In R. Siemieńska (Ed.), *Wokół problemów zawodowego równouprawnienia kobiet i mężczyzn* [On gender equality in the labour market]. Warsaw: Institute of Philosophy and Sociology, Polish Academy of Sciences, pp. 61–84.

Sigle-Rushton, W. (2008). England and Wales: Stable fertility and pronounced social status differences. *Demographic Research, 19*(Special Collection Volume on Childbearing Trends and Policies in Europe), Article 15, 455–502.

Simó Noguera, C., Castro Martin, T., & Soro Bonmatì, A. (2005). The Spanish case: The effects of the globalization process on the transition to adulthood. In H.-P. Blossfeld, E. Klijzing, M. Mills, & K. Kurz (Eds.), *Globalization, uncertainty and youth in society* (pp. 375–402). London and New York: Routledge.

Sjöberg, O. (2004). The role of family policy institutions in explaining gender role attitudes: a comparative multilevel analysis of thirteen industralised countries. *Journal of European Social Policy, 14*, 107–123.

Smith, N., Dex, S., Vlasblom, J. D., & Callan, T. (2003). The effects of taxation on married women's labour supply across four countries. *Oxford Economic Papers, 55*, 417–439.

Smith-Lovin, L., & Tickamyer, A. R. (1978). Nonrecursive models of labor force participation, fertility behavior, and sex role attitudes. *American Sociological Review, 43*, 541–557.

Sobotka, T. (2004). *Postponement of childbearing and low fertility in Europe*. Amsterdam: Dutch University Press.

Sobotka, T., Wolfagang, L., & D. Philipov. (2005). *'Missing births': Decomposing the declining number of births in Europe into tempo, quantum and age structure effects* (European Demographic Research Papers No. 2). Vienna: Vienna Institute of Demography.

Soja, E. (2005). *Hipoteza Easterlina w świetle zachowań prokreacyjnych generacji urodzonych w latach 1942–1966 w Polsce* [The Easterlin Hypothesis and the fertility behaviours of

cohorts born 1942–1966 in Poland]. Warsaw: Fundacja Promocji i Akredytacji Kierunków Ekonomicznych i Polskie Towarzystwo Ekonomiczne.
Spitze, G. (1988). Women's employment and family relations: A review. *Journal of Marriage and the Family, 50*(3), 595–618.
Stankunienie, V., & Mauslauskaite, A. (2008). Family transformations in the post-communist countries: attitudes towards changes. In C. Höhn, D. Avramov, & I. E. Kotowska (Eds.), *People, population change and policies: Lessons from the population policy acceptance study* (pp. 127–157). Berlin: Springer.
Stanley, T. D. (2001). Wheat from chaff: Meta-analysis as quantitative literature review. *The Journal of Economic Perspectives, 15*(3), 131–150.
Stolzenberg, R. M., & Waite, L. J. (1984). Local labor markets, children and labor force participation of wives. *Demography, 21*, 157–170.
Stuck, A. E., Walthert, J. M., Nikolaus, T., Büla, C. J., Hohmann, C., & Beck, J. C. (1999). Risk factors for functional status decline in community-living elderly people: A systematic literature review. *Social Science & Medicine, 48*, 445–469.
Sundström, M., & Duvander, A.-Z. (2002). Gender division of childcare and the sharing of parental leave among new parents in Sweden. *European Sociological Review, 18*(4), 433–447.
Sztanderska, U. (2005). Aktywność zawodowa kobiet w Polsce. Jakie szanse? Jakie rezultaty? [Labour force participation of women in Poland? What opportunties? What outcomes?] In *Szanse na wzrost dzietności – jaka polityka rodzinna?* [Possibilities of increasing fertility: Which family policies?] (pp. 43–63). Blue paper of the Polish Forum for Lisbon Strategy. Warsaw-Gdansk: Gdansk Institute on Market Economics.
Sztanderska, U., & Grotkowska, G. (2007). Zatrudnienie i bezrobocie kobiet i mężczyzn [Employment and unemployment of women and men]. In I. E. Kotowska, U. Sztanderska, & I. Wóycicka (Eds.), *Aktywność zawodowa i edukacyjna a obowiązki rodzinne w świetle badań empirycznych* [Economic and educational activity versus family obligations] (pp. 170–218). Warsaw: Scholar Publishing.
Taniguchi, H., & Rosenfeld, R. A. (2002). Women's employment exit and re-entry: Differences among whites, blacks and Hispanics. *Social Science Research, 31*, 432–471.
Testa, M. R. (2006a). *Childbearing preferences and family issues in Europe.* Research Report from the Special Eurobarometer 253/Wave 65.1, European Commission, October 2006.
Testa, M. R. (2006b). Childbearing preferences and family issues in Europe: Evidence from the Eurobarometer 2006 Survey. *Vienna Yearbook of Population Research*, 2007, 357–379.
Thevenon, O. (2010). *Macro-level database on fertility and policies supporting families with children in European and OECD countries.* Deliverable within the REPRO project.
Treas, J., & Widmer, E. D. (2000). Married women's employment over the life course: Attitudes in cross-national perspective. *Social Forces, 78*, 1409–1436.
Trifiletti, R. (1999). Southern European welfare regimes and the worsening position of women. *Journal of European Social Policy, 9*, 49–64.
Turchi, B. A. (1991). How economics, psychology and sociology might produce a unified theory of fertility and labour market participation. In J. J. Siegers, J. de Jong-Gierveld, & E. van Imhoff (Eds.), *Female labour market behaviour and fertility. A rational-choice approach* (pp. 237–262). Berlin: Springer.
Tymicki, K. (2008). *Przemiany wzorca dzietności w Polsce w latach 1989–2007. Analiza i opracowanie danych z rejestracji urodzeń* [Changes in fertility patterns in Poland in the years 1989–2007: Analyses based on register data]. Research report prepared at the Institute of Statistics and Demography. Warsaw: Warsaw School of Economics.
Udehn, L. (2002). The changing face of methodological individualism. *Annual Review of Sociology, 28*, 479–507.
UN (1983). *Report of the meeting on population. Sofia, 6–12 October 1983* (Document No. ECE/AC.9/2). Geneva: United Nations.
Van de Kaa, D. J. (1987). Europe's second demographic transition. *Population Bulletin, 42*(1). Washington, DC: Population Reference Bureau.

Van de Kaa, D. J. (1988). *The second demographic transition revisited: Theories and expectations.* Paper presented at the Conference on Population and European Society by the Commission of the European Economic Community and the European University Institute, Florence, Italy, 7–9 December 1988.

Van Peer, C., & Rabušic, R. (2008). Will we witness an upturn in European fertility in the near future? In C. Höhn, D. Avramov, & I. E. Kotowska (Eds.), *People, population change and policies: Lessons from the population policy acceptance study* (pp. 215–241). European Studies of Population 16/1. The Hague: Springer.

Vemer, E. C., Marilyn, G., Lowrence, H., & Cooper, H. (1989). Marital satisfaction in remarriage: A meta-analysis. *Journal of Marriage and Family, 51*(3), 713–725.

Vikat, A. (2004). Women's labor force attachment and childbearing in Finland. *Demographic Research, 3*(Article 8), 175–212.

Vikat, A., Spéder, Z., Beets, G., Billari, F. C., Bühler, C., Désesquelles, A., et al. (2007). Generations and gender survey (GGS): Towards a better understanding of relationships and processes in the life course. *Demographic Research, 17*(Article 14), 389–440.

Vitali, A., Billari F. C., Prskawetz, A., & Testa, M. R. (2009). Preference Theory and low fertility: A comparative perspective. *European Journal of Population, 25*, 413–438.

Wagner, M., & Weiss, B. (2006). On the variation of divorce risks in Europe: Findings from a meta-analysis of European longitudinal studies. *European Sociological Review, 22*(5), 483–500.

Waite, L. J., & Stolzenberg, R. M. (1976). Intended childbearing and labor force participation of young women: Insights from nonrecursive models. *American Sociological Review, 41*, 235–252.

Waldfogel, J., Higuchi, Y., & Abe, M. (1999). Family leave policies and women's retention after childbirth: Evidence from the United States, Britain, and Japan. *Journal of Population Economics, 12*, 523–545.

Waldorf, B., & Byrun, P. (2005). Meta-analysis of the impact of age structure on fertility. *Journal of Population Economics, 18*, 15–40.

Weichselbaumer, D., & Winter-Ebmer, R. (2005). A meta-analysis of the international gender gap. *Journal of Economics Survey, 19*(3), 479–511.

Weller, R. H. (1977). Wife's employment and cumulative family size in the United States, 1970 and 1960. *Demography, 14*(1), 43–65.

Westoff, C. F. (1978). Marriage and fertility in the developed countries. *Scientific American, 239*(6), 51–57.

Willekens, F. J. (1991). Understanding the interdependence between parallel careers. In J. J. Siegers, J. de Jong-Gierveld, & E. van Imhoff (Eds.), *Female labour market behaviour and fertility: A rational-choice approach* (pp. 11–31). Berlin: Springer.

Willekens, F. J. (1999). The life-course approach: Models and analysis. In L. J. G. Van Wissen, & P. A. Dykstra (Eds.), *Population issues. An interdisciplinary focus* (pp. 23–51). Dordrecht: Kluwer.

Willis, R. J. (1973). A new approach to the economic theory of fertility behavior. *Journal of Political Economy, 81*(Part 2: New Economic Approaches to Fertility), 14–64.

Zhang, J., Quan, J., & Van Meerbergen, P. (1994). The effect of tax-transfer policies on fertility in Canada, 1921–1988. *The Journal of Human Resources, 29*, 181–201.

Zhang, J., & Yu, K. F. (1998). What's the relative risk? *Journal of the American Medical Association, 280*(19), 1690–1691.

Index

Kolibri 360 GmbH
Ferdinand-Jühlke-Straße 7
99095 Erfurt, Deutschland
produktsicherheit@kolibri360.de